Storm Warning

The Coming Persecution
of Christians and Traditionalists
in America

D0377675

All Scripture quotations are from the King James Version of the Holy Bible.

Printed in the United States of America

ISBN 1-57558-48-9

Storm Warning

The Coming Persecution of Christians and Traditionalists in America

Don McAlvany

Table of Contents

Introduction

The 1990s, especially the latter half of the decade, found American Christians, conservatives, and those who believe in traditional, constitutional, biblical, and family values under the greatest attack in America's three hundred-year history. Such attacks against the followers of Jesus Christ and the biblical principles which the God of the Bible long ago laid down in Scripture are not new.

Since the crucifixion of Jesus Christ, there have been periodic waves of persecution directed against the followers of Christ and those who would espouse and defend righteousness in their day. In the first three hundred years of the Christian era, a titanic effort was made by the Roman Empire to exterminate Christianity.

Most of the original apostles were martyred for their faith in Jesus Christ, along with tens of thousands of Christians who were tortured, burned alive at Nero's garden parties, sewn in sacks with vipers, fed to lions, boiled in oil, placed on red-hot iron beds, crucified upside down, etc.

But in the end (i.e., A.D. 476) it was the Roman Empire which collapsed, and Christianity which survived. As one of the most eminent historians of the twentieth century, Will Durant, wrote in his multi–volume history of the world: "There was no greater drama on human record. . . . Caesar and Christ had met in the arena, and Christ had won."

Jesus Christ and His followers came under tremendous attack in the Middle Ages. Hundreds of thousands of Christians were persecuted, jailed, or executed for their faith in Jesus Christ—sometimes by the official church. This was true of the Waldensians, the Hussites, the Lutherans, the Calvinists, and the Anabaptists. It was true of the Church of England's persecution of the Pilgrims and Puritans. Many evangelical Christians as well as Orthodox Jews fell victim to the Spanish Inquisition. People who believed in, translated, or taught the Scriptures were burned at the stake for their faith by the Inquisition, which banned the Bible and forbade the people to read the Scriptures. And in England, many evangelical Christians were beheaded or burned at the stake for heresy by the Church of England or the Crown.

A classic book, *Foxe's Book of Martyrs,* was written in the sixteenth century and described a number of the Christian persecutions under the Roman Empire and well into the Middle Ages. But as John Foxe wrote: "And yet, notwithstanding all these continued persecutions and horrible punishments, the church daily increased, deeply rooted in the doctrine of the apostles and of men apostolical, and watered plenteously with the blood of the saints."

As Tertullian, one of the early church fathers, said: "All your ingenious cruelties can accomplish nothing; they are only a lure to this sect. **Our number increases the more you destroy us. The blood of the Christians is their seed.**"

The greatest attacks and persecutions against Christians, however, were not during the Roman Empire or the Middle Ages, but have been during the twentieth century. Millions of Christians have been persecuted and martyred by history's greatest-ever enemy of Christianity—communism. Millions of Christians have been killed by the followers of Marx and Lenin in Russia, the former East bloc countries, Red China, Cuba, and the Marxist-dominated countries of central and southern Africa.

Today, millions of Christians are being persecuted, imprisoned, or martyred in communist China while 2.1 million Christians have been martyred in southern Sudan by the followers of Islam in the 1990s alone. Over a million Christians have been martyred in Burundi, the central African republic, and in the Marxist frontline states of southern Africa in recent years. About one thousand Christians *a day* are being martyred somewhere in the world today—the greatest number since the beginning of the Christian church.

And in the "former" communist bloc countries of Eastern Europe, in the "former" Russian republics, and in Russia, Christians who have emerged from the persecuted, underground church in the "former" Soviet Union are preparing to go back underground as a "born again" communism/nationalism reasserts itself. Members of the persecuted and underground church in the "former" communist countries believe that the window of opportunity for the Gospel to enter that region has begun to close, that the now rapidly growing Christian church in that region may again be forced underground, and that the persecution of Christians in the "new communist federation" may recommence, just as it is presently doing—in high gear—in the Peoples Republic of China.

But persecution of Christians and those who follow biblical, righteous principles is not just going to be manifested in China, Africa, the Moslem countries, or the "former" Soviet Union. It is now emerging in many Western countries, and especially in the United States in the midst of what Francis Schaeffer referred to as "the post-Christian era." There are some unique parallels today between the rise of anti-Semitism in the 1930s in Nazi Germany and the anti-Christian/anti-traditionalist sentiment which is building in America today.

Christians from the underground church in "formerly" communist Romania and Russia, and communist China today (such as Richard Wurmbrand, the late Dumitru Duduman, Harry Wu, and many others) see in America today **the same** seeds of anti-Christian sentiment being sown; **the same** spiritual, moral, and cultural sea change; **the same** winds of coming persecution of Christians blowing that they saw in Russia, China, Cuba, and other communist countries **shortly before** the Marxist-Leninists took over. These survivors of communist persecution believe that similar persecutions, like a huge black cloud, are moving ominously toward America's shores.

Meanwhile, even as the anti-Christian, anti-traditionalist sentiment builds in America, the average American, including a great number of evangelical/fundamental/born-again Christians (and pastors) basks in a comfort zone—spoiled and softened by over fifty years of uninterrupted prosperity since the end of World War II and convinced that the good life will go on forever.

As the black clouds of persecution grow ever closer, a small remnant see it (and are preparing for it), but the vast majority of Americans (and American Christians) remain in a deep sleep—as if they were blinded by some spirit of deception, confusion, or delusion.

The Political Left Has Declared War on Christians
and Traditionalists in America

Evangelical Christians and people espousing traditional values have never been popular among the political left in America—including the liberals, secular humanists, socialists, communists, the homosexuals, the abortionists, the New World Order crowd, the atheists, and the radical environmentalists. Satanists, many New Agers, and people who are into witchcraft or other forms of the occult also hate evangelical Christians and other traditionalists.

Unfortunately, the levers of power in America today are dominated by activists from these groups who operate in the government, the judiciary, the media, the educational system, the arts, the entertainment industry, etc. And they have dictated an agenda over the past few decades (but especially since 1990) that has taken prayer and any mention of God out of the public schools and out of public life; that has totally denigrated Christians and traditionalists on television, in movies, in popular books, and in the print media; and which is now beginning to portray Christians and traditionalists as a dangerous threat to the nation.

In the wake of the Clinton Administration's attack on, and massacre of over eighty men, women, children, and babies at the Branch Davidian compound in Waco, Texas, in the spring of 1993, Bill Clinton and Janet Reno warned that "Waco should be a warning to other dangerous religious cults, that the same thing can happen to them."

And the major mainline press began to describe how you could recognize a dangerous religious cult: they're radical Christians who are hung up on Bible prophecy; preoccupied with what they see as the imminent second coming of Jesus Christ; who see world events in relationship to the Armageddon scenario; many of whom are home schoolers; who believe in guns, in survival food, etc.; most are child abusers because they "beat" their children under the dictum of "spare the rod, spoil the child"; in the past their "dangerous" beliefs contributed to the Cold War and the arms race; and at present those beliefs are contributing to poverty, crime, gang warfare, divisiveness, homophobia, overpopulation of the planet, pollution of "Mother Earth," etc.

A growing number of liberal books are attacking Christian conservatives (traditionalists) **who dare** to get involved in the political process; **who dare** to oppose the murder of the unborn; **who dare** to support the Constitution; **who dare** to support the return to traditional values; and **who dare** to take a stand against the globalist, society-wrecking agenda of the political left.

One such book, *When Time Shall Be Nore More—Prophecy Belief in Modern American Culture* by liberal historian Paul Boyer, was widely quoted in the mainline press in the aftermath of the Branch Davidian massacre in Waco in 1993. *USA Today* (4/21/93) in an article entitled "Experts Weighing How to Deal With Cults in the Future" (published two days after the Waco tragedy) wrote:

> Today these [cult] groups tend to believe the Bible predicts the end of the world is near. "In the past couple of decades, we've had a sharp upsurge in interest in Bible prophecy," said historian Paul Boyer, author of a study called *When Time Shall Be No More.*
>
> Boyer said such seemingly unrelated events as the Israelis gaining control of Jersualem in 1967, the threat of nuclear war and shifts in the global economy are among the "signs" **cultists** see—as prophesied in the Bible—that the end is near and Jesus Christ will return.

The doctrine of the imminent second coming of Christ has been taught and believed by Christians since the early days of the church. But today, if you believe in the last-days scenario and the imminent return of Jesus Christ, the political left has defined you as a "cultist." And in Waco, Texas, in April 1993, "religious cultists" were shot, gassed, and burned.

In recent years, the Clinton Administration and the liberal leadership of the Democratic Party have launched a broadside attack against Christians and Christian conservatives via an effort to outlaw the mention of God in the work place (on pain of fines, business closure, or jail) and against Christian traditionalists in the Republican Party.

A broadside attack from the Democratic leadership and the liberal media against the "dangerous religious right" has been launched. It is a very transparent effort to divide and conquer the Republicans by changing the subject from Bill Clinton's debauchery and socialism to the "dangers of a right-wing religious coup in the GOP and in America."

Unprecedented in U.S. political history are the growing attacks on Christians and traditionalists being orchestrated by the Clintons and their comrades, by the leftist leadership of the Democratic Party, by the liberal media, and by the liberal Establishment that controls them all. 0

Former Surgeon General Joycelyn Elders (alias the "Arkansas condom queen"), addressing a lesbian and gay health conference, mocked the conservative Christians' faith, and accused them of "selling out our children" because the conservative Christians don't want their children subjected to AIDS and safe sex education from kindergarten on up. She went on: "We've got to be strong and take on. those people who are selling our children in the name of religion."

The Wall Street Journal (6/9/94), in an op-ed piece entitled "The Religious Right Is a GOP Albatross," accused the Republican Party of being dominated by "religious right activists—a thundercloud hanging over the bright political hopes for this year and beyond." It described how "the Democratic Congressional Campaign Committee has a special task force to expose the agenda of the Christian right."

Vic Fazio (D-CA), former chairman of the Democratic Congressional Campaign Committee, for a number of years led the charge against Christian conservatives, along with Bill Clinton and former governor Ann Richards (D-TX) who has portrayed Christians as a "trojan horse in the midst of the GOP. . . . They have created a tremendous danger for all of us." She has called Christian traditionalists "the radical juggernaut swallowing the Republican Party before going on to conquer the country, a major threat to the Republic." The leftist People for the American Way produced a propaganda film a few years ago attacking the Christian right; and the networks have devoted much prime time coverage to airing attacks on the Christian traditionalists—equating them to dangerous "cultists" and even "terrorists."

The 193 -page book released in 1994 by B'nai B'rith's Anti–Defamation League entitled *The Religious Right: The Assault on Tolerance and Pluralism in America,* says: "The religious right brings to the debate over social and moral issues a rhetoric of fear, suspicion, and even hatred that strains the democratic process." Larry Witham wrote in the *Washington*

Times: "The ADL charges members of the religious right with anti–Semitism, Christian 'triumphalism,' Nazi sympathies, and denials of the Holocaust."

As Pat Buchanan has written:

> Are you now, or have you ever been a Christian? The way things are going, congressional committees are likely to be asking that question in a few years. The grandchildren of the men and women who came here to make America "God's Country" now hear their Christian faith equated with bigotry, and themselves declared unfit for participation by virtue of their religious beliefs. . . .
>
> What's the Christian-bashing all about? Simple. A struggle for the soul of America is underway, a struggle to determine whose views, values, beliefs, and standards will serve as the basis of law, and who will determine what is right and wrong in America. And the intensifying assault on the "Christian right" should be taken as a sign that these folks are gaining ground and winning hearts. . . .
>
> They simply want America to again become the good country she once was. They want the popular culture to reflect the values of patriotism, loyalty, bravery, and decency it used to reflect. They want magazines, movies, and TV shows depolluted of raw sex, violence, and filthy language. . . .
>
> They want the schools for which they pay taxes to teach the values in which they believe; they want their kids to have the same right to pray that they had; and yes, they do want chastity taught as a moral norm, and traditional marriage taught as "God ordained, natural, and normal." Is that so wicked and sinister an agenda?

Yes, these are dangerous goals, at least as far as the political left is concerned. And why are these dangerous goals? Because the Clintons, the Gores, the Renos, the Shalalas, the Elders, the Kennedys, the Ted Turners, the Jane Fondas, the Vic Fazios, the Ann Richards, the Madelyn Murray O'Hairs, and the legions of the political left stand for exactly the opposite values. And look at what their values and agenda have done to destroy America.

Attacking the Pro-Lifers

Pro-lifers are presently the foremost target of the government's onslaught to attack Christians and traditionalists. They have been the most outspoken and active of all Christian/traditionalist groups, and so they are to be made a target and example of by the Clintonites, the abortionists, and the political left. Attorney General Janet Reno has suggested that the pro-life movement is one giant terrorist conspiracy (equating the tens of thousands of Christians, including ministers, laymen, priests, and nuns who peacefully stand or kneel to pray in front of abortion clinics as criminal terrorists). Someone should remind the Clinton attorney general that she ordered the destruction in cold blood of eighty-six men, women, children, and babies in Waco. Some observers would call that terrorism—especially the victims!

Janet Reno has ordered U.S. marshals to protect the abortionists and to arrest the pro-life demonstrators for the new federal crime of praying in front of abortion clinics. Does something seem wrong here? The people praying outside are called the "criminals" and can be jailed, fined, and have their property seized under new racketeering statutes and other laws, while the people doing the killing of babies inside are called the "honest, law-abiding citizens" and are protected by federal marshals. Shades of Nazi Germany! And most Americans can't even see anything wrong with this! As **Isaiah 5:20** says: "Woe unto them that call evil good, and good evil; that put darkness for light, and light for darkness; that put bitter for sweet, and sweet for bitter!" . . . woe to those who acquit the guilty for a bribe, but deny justice to the innocent.

The present attacks on the Christian right by the political left in America did not just begin in the past year or so. They "officially" started in 1993 with the government massacre of the Branch Davidians and the concurrent media propaganda blitz against "dangerous religious cults" and the "dangerous religious right." The current political left's preoccupation with attacking and trashing the "Christian right" is not just a passing fancy. A long-term war of attrition—a war to the death—has been declared by the political left and the global socialists (i.e.,the globalists who are pushing for a world government) against religious traditionalists.

The communists in Russia, China, Cuba, and Eastern Europe, and the Nazis in Germany did the same thing. The present government attacks against the pro-life movement; the EEOC regulations attempting to restrain religious free speech; the U.N. Convention on the Rights of the Child; the present blitz of books, newspaper and magazine articles, movies, and television programs attacking the "Christian right" are part of a long-term campaign to silence (or "terminate with extreme prejudice") their opposition.

They are the beginning of real statist persecution of the Christian church in America—a phenomenon which is also occurring at present in China, in Africa, in the Moslem countries, and in many of the supposedly "former" communist countries. Hundreds of thousand of Christians are now being martyred each year in various parts of the world.

The accelerating attacks against Christian traditionalists (which have only just begun) have a supernatural, occultic, satanic dynamic behind them. Just as the Nazi Third Reich was led by occultists and satanists and had an evil supernatural dynamic behind it, so the present thrust of the political left in America today is similarly energized as the political left (in the 1993 inaugural words of Bill Clinton) tries to "force the spring" on America. As **Ephesians 6:12** says: "For we wrestle not against flesh and blood, but against principalities, against powers, against the rulers of the darkness of this world, against spiritual wickedness in high places."

This book will attempt to analyze the growing onslaught (which could shortly move to full-blown persecution) against the Christian right, conservatives, and traditionalists, by the political left in America and the global socialists. It will examine the emerging world government (exemplified by the European Union, the new European currency [the Euro], NAFTA, GATT, WTO, etc.) which a growing number of students of world history and Bible prophecy believe could be the rising kingdom of the Antichrist.

This book will explore why and how the God of the Bible may be about to judge America; America's plunge toward a totalitarian, socialist police state; the growing surveillance of all Americans which could culminate in a national I.D. card and even a government-enforced number or "mark" on every citizen; and the myriad of laws, rules, and regulations emanating from Washington, from the United Nations, and from other governments around the world designed to control every aspect of people's lives from the cradle to the grave.

This book will analyze the ominous and growing parallels between Nazi Germany in the 1930s and the United States in the 1990s with the same stereotyping, marginalizing, and ostracizing of Christian traditionalists today as was directed against the Jews in Germany in the early to mid 1930s. It will look back in history at past persecutions, at present persecutions of Christians in communist and Moslem countries, and at what could eventuate here in America in the not-too-distant future if a great awakening and turning back to the faith and foundations of our Founding Fathers does not occur.

And finally, this book will try to provide practical suggestions for preparing spiritually for the coming persecution—from believers who have suffered persecution, imprisonment, and torture for their faith—such as Richard Wurmbrand, Brother Andrew, Corrie ten Boom, Dimitru Duduman, etc. We will discuss how the underground church is functioning today in communist countries and how it may function in the anti-Christian/socialist/globalist dispensation now emerging in America and all over the world.

Matthew 16:18 assures us that the gates of hell shall not prevail against God's church. And the entire Bible gives testimony to God's victory over Satan and the forces of evil—a victory which was accomplished at the cross. But the Bible does not say that Christians and those who would live godly lives would not suffer for the cause of Christ. In **Second Timothy 3:12–13** Paul writes: "Yea, and all that will live godly in Christ Jesus shall suffer persecution. But evil men and seducers shall wax worse and worse, deceiving, and being deceived." Persecution of Christians is presently accelerating all over the world, and in this writer's strong opinion, Christians and traditionalists in America will not be immune to it. The signs of the coming persecution are multiplying all around us for those who have "eyes to see."

Jesus wrote of a future time of great persecution of His followers in **Matthew 24:9–13:**

Then shall they deliver you up to be afflicted, and shall kill you: and ye shall be hated of all nations for my name's sake. And then shall many be offended, and shall betray one another, and shall hate one another. And many false prophets shall rise, and shall deceive many. And because iniquity shall abound, the love of many shall wax cold. But he that shall endure unto the end, the same shall be saved.

The great majority of Americans (including the great majority of evangelical Christians) would never read or believe this book or its message of warning. This book is not written to that great majority. It is written to the remnant of believers, of righteous people (found in every declining country and civilization) who do love God and hate evil, who do understand the times, and who will try to the best of their ability to "stand in the gap," for God and country, and against the evil of our day.

This remnant, though a small minority, is found scattered all over the world—in Russia, China, South Africa, Sudan, Europe, America, and wherever people still seek and follow God and His principles, while the majority have turned away from Him. In many parts of the world (such as China and Sudan) the remnant is already underground and under severe persecution. Elsewhere, persecution is emerging and the remnant may soon be forced underground.

This book and its message is dedicated to that remnant and the suffering persecuted church of our day around the world, which has not bent its knee to the gods of our day—but only to the true God of the Bible and His Son, Jesus Christ. Danger is approaching and the great majority of Americans and people around the world are almost totally oblivious to it. As **Proverbs 27:12** says, "A prudent man foreseeth the evil, and hideth himself; but the simple pass on, and are punished." The God of the Bible is our ultimate refuge and will watch over and help His remnant. It is to those "prudent ones" that this book has been written.

[Note: This is a controversial, politically incorrect book which will anger many Christians as well as those on the political left. Readers are encouraged to pray over the material as they read the book and ask the Lord to reveal to them the accuracy or inaccuracy of the information, conclusion, and recommendations. It is this writer's prayer that the Lord will give readers a sense of urgency in their spirits to be about their Father's business and to spiritually prepare for what could be one of the most challenging periods in world history.]

Part One

As America Loses Its Freedom:
The Prelude to Persecution

In every country (in the ancient world, in Russia or the former Iron Curtain countries, Nazi Germany, Red China, Cuba, or present-day Sudan or other Islamic countries) where persecution has broken out (of Christians, Jews, traditionalists, the politically incorrect, or critics of the government of the day) the people have first lost their freedom before the persecution began.

Totalitarian governments persecute those groups whom they fear threaten their political power base or who are convenient scapegoats to cover their nefarious activities. Nero, an evil Roman emperor and dictator, used the Christians as scapegoats when he burned Rome; Hitler used the Jews as scapegoats for most of Germany's problems during the ill-fated Weimar Republic. The Romans feared the Christians would undermine their power base, as did the communists in Russia, Romania, China, Cuba, and other communist countries—and hence the widespread persecution of the Christian church in those countries.

There is also a supernatural (satanic) dynamic behind these persecutions. Satan and his minions wish to damage and destroy the Christian church and also to destroy the Jewish people—as became perfectly clear under Hitler's anti-Semitic reign of terror. There was definitely a supernatural/satanic/occultic dynamic which energized the Nazis and their Third Reich, just as this writer believes that there is behind the present momentum toward world government.

Part I of this book will analyze the momentum in the United States toward socialism and massive people control initiatives; the growing surveillance society in America; the drive for a cashless society and a national ID card; and the potential for a freedom-strangling "State of National Emergency" and martial law during some economic, political, or terrorist crisis.

It should be remembered that when people lose their freedom, one of the first elements of that freedom to go is feedom of religion—and specifically freedom to worship and spread the Gospel of Jesus Christ. The thrust for people-control, socialism, and world government is setting the stage for widespread persecution of Christians and traditionalists in America and around the world in the not-too-distant future—which will be discussed in Part II.

Chapter 1

Storm Warnings: Is God's Judgment Descending Upon America?

And I will utter my judgments against them touching all their wickedness, who have forsaken me. . . .

—Jeremiah 1:16

For by fire and by his sword will the Lord plead with all flesh: and the
slain of the Lord shall be many.

—Isaiah 66:16

For God shall bring every work into judgment, with every secret thing,
whether it be good, or whether it be evil.

—Ecclesiastes 12:14

The Lord standeth up to plead, and standeth to judge the people. The
Lord will enter into judgment with the ancients of his people. . . .

—Isaiah 3:13–14

For the time is come that judgment must begin at the house of God. . . .

—1 Peter 4:17

The decline of America should be obvious to any thinking American.
The explosion of crime, gang warfare, and drive-by shootings in our
cities; the disintegration of the American family, with proliferating divorce, infidelity, child abuse, single parent families, and teenage rebellion; the explosion of drug usage (the highest in the world); the killing of
40 million babies in their mother's wombs over a twenty-six–year period; the rampant spread of promiscuity, pornography, homosexuality,

and sexually transmitted diseases; the dumbing down of American children in the public school system; high taxation; the ignoring of our Constitution; exploding governmental controls over every aspect of the American peoples' lives; and gross immorality and corruption at the highest levels of the U.S. government, are all irrefutable evidence of a country whose culture, morality, traditions, and spiritual life are in a free fall.

Other great nations and empires have risen and fallen throughout history (i.e., the Roman Empire; Israel before the Babylonian invasion and captivity in about 600 B.C.; Babylon; Assyria; the Persian Empire; the British Empire; czarist Russia; pre-World War I Germany; and more recently South Africa), and America may be next. In almost all of these cases, wicked men had risen to power; morality had plunged; traditional values had been ignored; the culture had disintegrated; and the people had forgotten God.

In examining the reasons for America's present decline, the most obvious is the ascendancy of socialism, secular humanism, and liberalism to power in America over the past forty years—collectivist ideologies which have helped to destroy our traditions, values, heritage, and the character and freedom of our people. These ideologies now dominate virtually all levels of power and influence in America (i.e., the government, the courts, the media, the entertainment industry, the school system, and most of the mainline religious denominations).

When Alexander Solzhenitsyn was asked on BBC television almost two decades ago why the Russian people had lost their freedom under communism, he replied: "It was because we forgot God." With over five decades of uninterrupted, unprecedented prosperity and affluence in America since the end of World War II, and the pervasive influence of liberalism for most of that period, it appears to this writer that Americans (by-and-large) have also forgotten God. It appears that God has now removed His hand of blessing and protection from America, is instead letting His judgment fall upon this once great nation, and is allowing evil to proliferate with no restraint.

This judgment appears to be coming in the form of massive earthquakes, storms, floods, and fires (i.e., accelerating physical disasters); the removal of our financial prosperity; the proliferation of deadly diseases and plagues (i.e., consider AIDS, Hanta virus, the flesh-eating virus or bacteria, or the Gulf War syndrome); increasing oppression of the people and their freedoms by an all-powerful, collectivist government; the ascendancy of wicked, evil leaders who reject our traditional values, morality, history, and culture; and eventually via attack by foreign powers (whether a new world [U.N.] army, a "reborn" Russian and world communist movement [including China], radical Islam, or some combination of these groups).

This chapter will analyze God's warnings to America in the larger context of an America which is in massive decline (or freefall); which has forgotten God and His rules as laid out in the Bible; and which could be coming under God's judgment as evil now begins to proliferate almost completely unrestrained.

Though many readers of this book will be Christians, with some Jewish, some agnostic, and a few even Buddhist, Moslem, or atheist, the implications of the unfolding events which are destabilizing America (and the entire world) will affect us all. God has set up principles of life and conduct which work for believers and nonbelievers alike. But when they are ignored or violated, nations, families, and individuals go into decline and suffer for it.

Since the mid-1980s, America has suffered one awesome disaster after another. There have always been disasters, but now they are happening regularly and with increasing intensity. Consider what has happened to America since the mid-1980s. The West (especially California) and Midwest suffered the worst drought in history, destroying huge amounts of crops. The drought was then followed by record rains in both sections, followed by severe flooding. In 1989 Hurricane Hugo struck Charleston, South Carolina, with fierce winds causing great damage. Soon after Hugo hit, a powerful earthquake rocked San Francisco causing great damage.

In the year 1992, a number of incredible events occurred. Four powerful earthquakes hit California. Those quakes were all in remote areas so the damage was not severe. In fact, ten of the most powerful quakes in the world in 1992 were centered in California, including the most powerful earthquake in the world that year at a magnitude of 7.6. That quake was centered near the major faults of Southern California. Hurricane Andrew, one of the most powerful and destructive ever, hit southern Florida. That hurricane was one of the most expensive natural disasters in American history. The worst rioting since the Civil War took place in Los Angeles. A record number of tornadoes swept across America. Record forest fires raged throughout the West, but especially in California.

The year 1993 saw record storms slam the East Coast, causing severe damage and flooding. The worst terrorist attack in American history struck New York City at the World Trade Center. This was soon followed by the worst fiasco in federal law enforcement history as four agents were killed and sixteen were wounded at Waco, Texas, during an unprecedented, unconstitutional government attack (an attack that eventually led to the deaths of eighty-six men, women, children, and babies). The worst flooding ever ravaged the Midwest. California was again hit with record wildfires. Mass killings and serial killings which were rare in America thirty years ago now seem to be a regular occurrence in the 1990s.

These incredible disasters continued into 1994. The coldest temperatures ever recorded since records have been kept in the 1890s covered the Midwest and East. The cold was so intense that the wind chill hit near ninety below zero in some states. Record cold temperatures were set in hundreds of locations. The cold and snow paralyzed entire states. Pennsylvania was hit by the most powerful earthquake ever recorded in the state. The quake was mild by California standards, registering only 4.6, but Pennsylvania is not an earthquake zone. The quake was centered in Reading, Pennsylvania. It buckled roads, and was felt as far away as Philadelphia and New York City. Two days later a powerful earthquake measuring 6.6 struck Los Angeles causing tremendous damage. This earthquake, maybe America's most costly natural disaster, even surpassed the destruction of Hurricane Andrew. First the East Coast was rocked by an earthquake, then the West Coast two days later.

These disasters have cost tens of billions of dollars and have weakened many institutions, like the insurance industry. Tens of thousands of people have been left homeless, and thousands of businesses have been destroyed. By 1994 entire states were being affected by these disasters. America went from being the world's largest creditor nation in the 1980s to the world's largest debtor nation in the 1990s. The years 1991–92 saw the most severe recession since the Great Depression of the 1930s, and Orange County, California, for the first time since the Depression, went bankrupt. Many other states are today in their worst financial condition since the Great Depression. From 1990 through 1998, nine million Americans went bankrupt, with 1.44 million personal bankruptcies in 1998 alone—a record since the peak of the Great Depression.

Is it possible that these events are not just happening by coincidence, but are warnings from God? Americans are now either practicing or tolerating lifestyles which the Bible clearly states will remove God's blessings and bring the wrath of God. God has warned in the Bible that He will destroy any nation which openly practices fornication, adultery, homosexuality, sexual perversion, and the shedding of the blood of innocent children—including abortion and partial-birth abortion. Concerning abortion, the Bible makes no difference between children in the womb and a newly born child. The following Bible verses show God's attitude toward a nation that practices open disobedience to His standards:

> Moreover thou shalt not lie carnally with thy neighbour's wife, to defile thyself with her. And thou shalt not let any of thy seed pass through the fire to Molech, neither shalt thou profane the name of thy God: I am the LORD. Thou shalt not lie with mankind, as with womankind: it is abomination. Neither shalt thou lie with any beast to defile thyself therewith: neither shall any woman stand before a beast to lie down thereto: it is confusion. Defile not ye yourselves in any of these things: for in all these the nations are defiled which I cast out before you: And the land is defiled: therefore I do visit the iniquity thereof upon it, and the land itself vomiteth out her inhabitants.
>
> **—Leviticus 18:20–25**

> He turneth rivers into a wilderness, and the watersprings into dry ground; A fruitful land into barrenness, for the wickedness of them that dwell therein.
>
> **—Psalm 107:33–34**

Since the mid-1980s, America has been severely warned by God that as a nation we are on a collision course with Him. The Bible records the total destruction of the cities of Sodom and Gomorrah as an example of what happens to a nation that practices open sexual immorality, but especially homosexuality. "Even as Sodom and Gomorrha, and the cities about them in like manner, giving themselves over to fornication, and going after strange flesh, are set forth for an example, suffering the vengeance of eternal fire" (**Jude 7**).

God is extremely merciful and longsuffering. He will warn and warn before judgment, but if a nation will not turn from open homosexuality and the shedding of the blood of innocent children, He promises that He will judge that nation.

A careful study of the events surrounding many of these disasters reveals that they occurred in connection with abortion and/or homosexual-related events. It appears to this writer that the Lord has given America many clear warnings. The following examples strongly suggest that America has already been clearly warned by God about shedding the blood of innocent children in the womb and about practicing open homosexuality. These warnings show that America is on a collision course with the God of the Bible and awesome judgment may be immediately ahead.

America: A Nation That Has Rejected God

On June 17, 1963, the United States Supreme Court issued the final decision that forbade Bible reading and prayer in the public schools. Bible reading and prayer had been a part of America's schools since the beginning of the country. The prayer the court objected to follows: "Almighty God, we acknowledge our dependence upon Thee, and we beg Thy blessings upon us, our parents, our teachers, and our country."

God had honored prayer by giving America, up to 1963, the finest educational system in the world. The Scholastic Aptitude Test (SAT) scores were the highest ever. America prior to 1963 had a violent crime rate below the national population growth rate. The divorce rate was dropping steadily from the 1940s, and the teenage premarital sex rate was unchanged. By the 1990s, the bogus "separation of church and state" was fully established and everything to do with God had been removed from the public schools and most governmental institutions.

When the Supreme Court rejected God and His Word, immediate judgment did not appear to fall. It appeared nothing happened and the country continued on. At first the consequences of rejecting God were not felt or seen, but thirty-six years later it is clear that in 1963 the blessings of God were removed from America. Looking back to 1963, it is clear that awesome judgment began to fall on America. The year 1963 literally became the transition year between God's blessings and judgment. For the nation that honors God, the Bible states: "Blessed is the nation whose God is the LORD; and the people whom he hath chosen for his own inheritance" (**Psalm 33:12**). For the nation that rejects God, the Bible states: "The wicked shall be turned into hell, and all the nations that forget God" (**Psalm 9:17**).

In 1963 the three greatest problems in school were talking, gum chewing, and noise. By the 1990s the three greatest problems in the public schools were rape, robbery, and assault. The SAT scores have literally plummeted since the very year of 1963. Prior to1963 serial killers and mass murders were almost unheard of. Today they both occur with frightening regularity, and America is becoming an increasingly violent nation. America's cities have become like those of a third world nation. Sexual diseases have skyrocketed along with premarital sexual relations among our teenagers.

Since 1963 every statistic showing a social problem has risen dramatically, while the statistics for things that are good have dropped. America is literally being turned into hell as the Bible states would happen to all the nations that reject God. More police will not prevent crime. More money will not improve the school system. More taxes will not solve the nation's problems. America needs national repentance for rejecting God and allowing such acts as abortion, adultery, drugs, promiscuity, homosexuality, and pornography to become the order of the day. The nation needs to turn to the Lord Jesus Christ, repent, and be healed.

America: "The Voice of Thy Children's Blood Crieth Unto Me From the Ground"

On January 22, 1973, the U.S. Supreme Court overturned all state laws that protected children in the womb, and then legalized the killing of children throughout the entire pregnancy. The aborting of babies was actually made a constitutional right by the court. Today in America there are "doctors" who specialize in killing full-term babies in the womb. America aborts a reported 1.6 million babies a year. After the ruling in 1973, more than 40 million children have been killed in the womb.

Many abortions are not reported, so the real figure is probably higher. However, the figure is so large that it has become meaningless. Abortion is so ingrained in America that politicians, including the president, actually run for office proclaiming their pro-abortion position, and the people still elect them.

Although America has turned its back on defending children in the womb, each child killed was special to God: "Lo, children are an heritage of the LORD: and the fruit of the womb is his reward" (Ps. 127:3). God sends children as a blessing, but Americans literally throw His children by the millions in the garbage (or, like the Nazis, use the bodies of these innocent victims for medical experimentation). The Lord has clearly warned in the Bible that His judgment will fall on any nation that kills its children.

The Bible says that the killing of babies angers the Lord, who in turn judges (or punishes) such a nation. "And the land is defiled: therefore I do visit the iniquity thereof upon it . . ." (**Lev. 18:25**). "Wherefore I poured my fury upon them for the blood that they had shed upon the land . . ." (**Ezek. 36:18**). God literally hates the shedding of innocent blood: "These six things doth the LORD hate . . . hands that shed innocent blood" (**Prov. 6:16–17**). The shed blood of the innocent cries out to God: "And he said, What hast thou done? the voice of thy brother's blood crieth unto me from the ground" (**Gen. 4:10**).

On January 22, 1973, when killing babies in the womb was legalized, judgment from God did not appear immediately. There was no apparent reaction from the Lord, just as after the decision to ban prayer in schools the country continued on. However, looking back to 1973, things began to deteriorate rapidly in America. The judgment that began in 1963 for rejecting God was intensified in 1973: "The wicked shall be turned into hell, and all the nations that forget God" (**Ps. 9:17**).

The blessings of God that began to be removed in 1963 were fully removed in 1973. From 1960 until 1973 the people living in poverty in America dramatically fell from 40 million to 22 million. The year with the lowest number of people in poverty was 1973. After 1973 the poverty rate has increased to the point that now over 34 million Americans are in poverty. The year 1973 was literally the dividing line between decreasing poverty and increasing poverty. It is clear that something happened in 1973.

The Index of Social Health uses sixteen criteria for tracing the social condition of America. These criteria include: child abuse, teen suicide, health insurance coverage, weekly earnings, high school dropout rate, drug abuse, homicides, infant mortality (not including abortion), and others. The highest rating which indicates a healthy social condition was 79.4 in 1972. The rating started dropping in 1973 and continued to drop every year until 1990 when it fell to 42. The very year that America legalized killing of babies in the womb was when the terrible social deterioration started that is now at crisis levels in the 1990s.

The current social condition of America can be traced directly back to 1973 when the Lord's anger fell on America. The nation was immediately judged in 1973. It just took some years for the judgment to become apparent. Federal government statistics disclose that since 1973 almost 40 million Americans have been injured by acts of crime.

Since 1982 violent crime has increased twenty-four percent. America is being consumed by violence. The violence against the innocent unborn in the womb has now spread throughout the entire society. As a society we have a preoccupation with violence and death. The popular movies of our day certainly reflect it. Any form of bloodshed always leads to more bloodshed. Note how we are now moving from abortion to euthanasia. In the 1930s Germany saw a similar escalation in its culture of death, until life became so cheap that the horror of the death camps became a reality.

The Bible refers to this as bloodshed touching bloodshed. It almost seems every aborted baby (i.e., over 40 million) is matched by one American falling victim to a violent crime. The current violence level in America may well be judgment from God on the nation for the violence in the womb. The Bible very clearly states that for killing children God will give that nation what it deserves: "Therefore I do visit the iniquity thereof upon it . . ." (**Lev. 18:25**). The violence in the womb appears to be matched by violence in the streets and cities. America is getting what it deserves.

The violence in America is the just reward for the violence in the womb. How can Americans expect God to bless the nation with peace, when legally His children are slaughtered in the womb with the sanction of the government and the people? An attitude of disrespect and violence against all life has now gripped America, just as it did in the 1930s in Nazi Germany. The violence in Germany first started in the womb via abortion. [*Note:* And now pro-life demonstrators are being imprisoned and having their property seized by the government for the new federal crime of praying in front of an abortion clinic while the government protects the doctors who are dismembering the babies inside. **Isaiah 5:20** says: "Woe unto them that call evil good, and good evil. . . ."

Examples of the Warning Judgments
[*Note:* The information in this chapter on the physical disasters hitting America and their possible connection with various abortion and gay rights activities comes from an excellent book by John McTernan (co-founder of **Cops for Christ**) entitled *God's Final Warning to America*. To order the book, call Southwest Radio Church at 1-800-652-1144 or 405-789-1222 or FAX 405-789-2589. Cost: $18.00 including S&H.]

1. **October 17, 1989:** A 7.1 magnitude earthquake, the fifth most powerful this century to hit America, struck near San Francisco. This quake struck during a World Series game and was broadcast live to the nation. Millions watched as the earthquake shook San Francisco. Although the earthquake was extremely strong, miraculously, very few people died. Just two days before this earthquake, on October 15, 1989, a huge pro-abortion rally took place in San Francisco. The newspapers reported the crowd reached up to fifty thousand people. The center of the rally was City Hall where many pro-abortion politicians addressed the crowd.

   Two days later, the awesome earthquake struck and shook the

city to its foundation. Ironically, the newspapers reported that City Hall (which was the center of the pro-abortion rally) was shaken so terribly that people fled the building screaming in terror. *Could this have been a powerful warning that the killing of children in the womb has America on a collision course with God?*

2. **April 25, 1992:** During a fierce counterprotest in Buffalo against Operation Rescue, a 6.9 magnitude earthquake, the sixth most powerful in this century, struck northern California. Operation Rescue is a nonviolent Christian organization that uses peaceful means to block abortion centers. The counterprotest was led by homosexuals and lesbians who chanted such phrases as, "God is a lesbian, God is a dyke." Also during the ten days of Operation Rescue, the jury in California was deliberating the verdict of the police officers for beating Rodney King.

The Operation Rescue protest ended on April 29, 1992, with fierce opposition from pro-abortionists and homosexuals. That very same day, the jury made its decision and Los Angeles went up in flames. The sixth and eleventh greatest earthquakes this century, plus the worst rioting since the Civil War, took place during this ten-day protest to save the lives of the innocent unborn. Was the Lord again sending a series of warnings?

3. **June 28, 1992:** Hundreds of thousands of homosexuals and their supporters attended national gay pride parades across America. The last Sunday in June has been designated as "Gay Pride Day." Almost all the major cities hold parades celebrating homosexuality. Hundreds of thousands turn out to march and support the homosexuals.

On the morning of Gay Pride Day, the fourth and ninth most powerful earthquakes this century hit Southern California. These quakes were so powerful that their effects were felt as far away as Idaho. The *Los Angeles Times* actually reported that the marchers had to brave the earthquakes to get to the Gay Pride Day parade.

The fourth most powerful quake was 7.6 magnitude and was called the Landers quake because it occurred near Landers, California. The Landers quake was the most powerful earthquake in the world during 1992. The second quake was 6.5 magnitude. Both of the earthquakes were in remote areas, so California was spared from great loss of life and extensive damage. These quakes were dangerously close to the San Andreas fault line. If an earthquake occurred on this fault, it could devastate California.

Scientists studying the Landers quake were astonished by its impact on the entire western region of the nation. The March 1993 issue of *Earth Magazine* contained an article titled "Lessons from Landers." This article documented how bizarre and powerful this earthquake really was. One geologist said in the article, "I think the Landers event will go down in history as one of the most important earthquakes from a scientific standpoint." The scientists found that the Landers quake was bizarre. They reported: "Landers was not only powerful—it was bizarre. In most earthquakes, the land tears along a single fault. But not this quake—the rupture hopscotched from fault to fault, growing more powerful with each successive jump."

The scientists reported the strange phenomenon that immediately followed the Landers quake—a swarm of smaller quakes jolted the entire West. The Landers quake triggered smaller quakes in northern California, Idaho, Utah, Nevada, and even 750 miles away in Yellowstone National Park. Small earthquakes were detected, minutes after the Landers quake, under Lassen Peak and Mount Shasta, both in northern California. Both of these mountains are volcanoes. A magnitude 5.5 quake struck in southern Nevada. The scientists reported that "in the past most scientists would have scoffed at suggestions that one quake could trigger activity at such great distances."

One scientist stated: "So many areas became active—as if someone had flicked on a switch. Tremors started in regions hundreds of miles away from Southern California mere seconds after the Landers quake." This was the first time scientists ever detected that an earthquake set off other quakes hundreds of miles away! The scientists had no explanation for the distant earthquake-triggering phenomenon of the Landers quake. The Landers quake was unique. This is why the Landers quake was said to go down in history as the most important ever, from a scientific standpoint.

What a powerfully clear warning from God! During the very morning of Gay Pride Day two powerful earthquakes literally shook the entire West Coast of America. Ironically the very next day, the Supreme Court handed down the *Planned Parenthood v. Casey* decision which failed to overturn the legalization of abortion. Is it possible that one earthquake was for Gay Pride Day and the second was for the Supreme Court decision? Was the Lord again sending us warnings?

A major earthquake hit Southern California on April 23, 1992, the day the Supreme Court heard the *Planned Parenthood v. Casey* case. Just two months later, the very day before the decision, the fourth and ninth most powerful earthquakes this century hit Southern California. Could there be a clear spiritual connection between these quakes and the Supreme Court's involvement in this abortion case?

It is extremely noteworthy that scientists who study earthquakes believe the earthquakes on April 23 and June 28, 1992, were connected. The *Los Angeles Times* reported this connection in a January 20, 1994, article titled "Scientists Ponder Northward Concentration of Quakes." In this article scientists were quoted as saying: "Frequent aftershocks following the magnitude 6.3 Joshua Tree quake of April 23, 1992, migrated in a northwestern direction and appeared to some scientists to have triggered the much larger 7.6 Landers quake of June 28, 1992." The earthquakes appear connected, and the earthquake on April 23 actually set up the powerful quake on June 28. Could all this be a coincidence?

These earthquakes were both physically connected. Could they have been spiritually connected as well? They were linked together and occurred almost the very same day the Supreme Court heard arguments and then failed to overturn legalized abortion. The timing and connection of these earthquakes could be a warning judgment from God! God's mercy is shown in the Landers quake. It occurred in an isolated area with very little damage and loss of life.

An earthquake of this power in a heavily populated area would have caused tremendous damage. This earthquake seemed to showcase the Lord's awesome power and timing. The quake was on the very morning of Gay Pride Day, and the Bible states God will shake nations that practice open homosexuality.

America could have been seriously crippled on the morning of June 28, 1992, with the Landers quake. This quake could have triggered the San Andreas fault and destroyed California. Those quakes that were triggered hundreds of miles away could have been 7.0 in power and destroyed huge sections of the West. More powerful quakes might have triggered the volcanoes to erupt. The entire western section of the nation could have been decimated on the very morning of Gay Pride Day.

Think of all the roads and bridges that would have been destroyed; the water aqueducts; the electric grids; the gas and oil pipelines; the railways; the food production; and industry. How would the injured be helped? The destruction would have thrown the nation into a tailspin. The Lord in His mercy sent a warning. The Landers earthquake by itself was enough of a warning from God that awesome judgment is ahead. America has been warned!

4. **Gay Pride Day 1993** brought monumental judgment from God. During the entire spring of 1993, heavy rains fell on the Midwest. As Gay Pride Day approached, June 27, 1993, the rains increased until the newspapers reported that on June 27, 1993, the Mississippi and Missouri Rivers overflowed their banks like a bathtub full of water. The Great Flood of 1993, the worst in American history, started on Gay Pride Day.

5. **January 17, 1994:** The Los Angeles area was rocked by a powerful 6.6 magnitude earthquake. The quake was centered in Northridge, about twenty-five miles from downtown Los Angeles. This powerful quake caused an estimated $30 billion to $50 billion in damage and caused widespread destruction. God was again very merciful because the loss of life was very low. This quake occurred one day after Sanctity of Life Sunday and five days before the twenty-first anniversary of *Roe v. Wade,* the Supreme Court decision which le-

galized abortion. Sanctity of Life Sunday was started in 1984 and occurs the Sunday before the anniversary of *Roe v. Wade*. On January 16, 1994, over fifty thousand churches in America were praying to end abortion.

More than 310,000 babies are aborted every year in California; however, the majority are aborted in Southern California, making this area one of the abortion centers of the nation. The epicenter of the quake was Northridge, which is also the pornography center of America. Over eighty percent of all video pornography is made in Northridge. The earthquake severely damaged the pornography industry, as the entire pornography center was within five miles of the epicenter. One day after Sanctity of Life Sunday and five days before the anniversary to legalize abortion, the pornography and abortion centers of America were rocked by a powerful earthquake! *Are the warnings escalating?*

[*Note:* To put these disasters into perspective, six of the top eleven earthquakes to hit America this century have occurred on or very near to major abortion and/or homosexual related events. Five of the earthquakes have been since April 1992! The Lord has been very merciful, because most of the quakes were centered in remote areas, or if the quake hit a populated area, few lives were lost. Nevertheless, they serve as awesome warnings!]

6. **March 1994:** In March, several hundred members of Operation Rescue attempted to save babies from being aborted in Birmingham, Alabama. The event, called "Holy Week Passion for Life," took place between March 25 and April 3. This event was totally nonviolent; however, approximately two hundred demonstrators were arrested for praying on the sidewalk in front of the abortion centers. No arrests were made for violence. The militant pro-abortion supporters, including homosexuals and lesbians, were present as "clinic defenders" to insure the abortion centers stayed open. They wanted to insure that the babies would continue to be killed. The lesbians and homosexuals made up a large percent of the clinic defenders.

The homosexuals and lesbians, while they were guarding the doors to the abortion centers, made profane statements against theLord.

A group of ministers from various religious backgrounds and denominations even held a news conference to voice their support for the "Emergency Coalition for Choice." This coalition was organized to insure the abortion centers were kept open during the protest. On March 27, two days after Holy Week Passion for Life began, a series of violent and destructive thunderstorms and powerful tornadoes roared across Alabama and then the South, causing death and awesome destruction.

The storms spread to Georgia and North and South Carolina, killing dozens of people. A spokesman for the National Weather Service in Birmingham described the tornadoes as "some of the worst ones I've seen, some of the worst ones this century." The tornadoes were characterized as F4, which means the winds were between 207 and 260 miles per hour. These are awesome tornadoes. It is interesting to note that the tornadoes destroyed three churches. *USA Today* printed a map of the areas hit by the storm with the heading "Route of Killer Storm." The map illustrated the tornadoes first touched down in north central Alabama, the Birmingham area, and then spread to the other states. That some of the worst tornadoes this century touched down near Birmingham during an attempt to save the lives of innocent babies in the womb, while pro-abortion and gay rights activists were screaming obscenities against God and the pro-life protestors, and the government agents were keeping the abortuaries open, appears to have been much more than just a coincidence.

7. **August–October 1995:** The year turned out to be a record for the most hurricanes and tropical storms. The 1995 hurricane season was the second busiest in 125 years of recordkeeping. There were nineteen named storms for that year. Although there were nineteen storms, only two hit the United States. Hurricane Erin hit the Florida panhandle on August 3, and Hurricane Opal also hit the Florida panhandle on October 4.

The timing of these two hurricanes hitting the country appears to have been closely connected to abortion-related issues. In late July and early August pro-life congressmen tried to prevent Planned

Parenthood from receiving $193 million dollars in federal funds. Planned Parenthood is the largest abortion organization in the United States. It has abortion centers throughout the United States, and these centers are responsible for killing more than 120,000 babies every year. The battle to block the funding obtained national significance and was reported by the national media.

On August 2 the battle was lost and the funding for Planned Parenthood was approved. On this same day Tropical Storm Erin tore through central Florida and entered into the Gulf of Mexico. The storm gained strength over the gulf and developed into a hurricane. Hurricane Erin turned north, and on August 3 it slammed into the Florida panhandle.

On Saturday, September 30, 1995, Hurricane Opal entered the Gulf of Mexico and headed in a very slow easterly direction. Opal was classified as a Category 3 in power. The course of this hurricane was parallel to the United States, but headed directly toward Mexico. On October 2, around 11:00 a.m. (EST) the hurricane suddenly changed direction. The storm made a sharp ninety degree turn, began to strengthen in intensity, accelerated in speed, and headed directly for the Florida panhandle. It was as if an unseen force pulled this powerful hurricane off course toward the U.S. Hurricane Opal hit on October 5, very near the same location as Erin.

What is truly amazing is that on October 2 the Supreme Court of the United States made a pro-abortion ruling. The court refused to hear a challenge to the Freedom of Access to Clinic Entrances Act (FACE) law. The FACE law was created to limit pro-life protests at the abortion centers and has become a powerful tool against peaceful pro-life protesters. The law was challenged as being unconstitutional. The court refused to hear the challenge and let the law stay intact. This became a major pro-abortion victory.

Although Hurricane Opal hit the United States three days after the Supreme Court's decision, the hurricane actually changed course about the time of the decision, accelerated, and headed directly for the United States. Opal was a large, powerful storm that pounded 120 miles of the Florida coast. It hit with winds of 140 miles per hour and caused $3 billion in damage. Opal became the third most destructive hurricane to hit the United States.

8. **March 1997:** On February 25, 1997, the Senate passed legislation to release $385 million overseas into one hundred countries for "family planning." Pro-life forces in the Senate tried to stop the release of the funds because some of the money would be used for abortion. The Clinton Administration backed this release of funds and pushed the date of release of the funds to March 1.

On March 1, 1997, President Clinton signed the legislation into law, and the money was released. On the very next day, March 2, powerful tornadoes roared across Texas, into Arkansas, Mississippi, Tennessee, and Kentucky. The storm stalled over Ohio, and torrential rains fell over Ohio, causing record flooding on the Ohio River. The tornadoes were so powerful, they were compared to the Palm Sunday storms of March 27–28, 1994. This storm in 1994 also hit directly during an abortion-related event. The storm that hit Arkansas was so powerful that Governor Huckabee described the damage as of "apocalyptic proportions." The tornadoes actually destroyed the small town of Arkadelphia, Arkansas. Police chief Bob Johnson said one tornado was ten blocks wide. Arkansas Emergency Services reported: "These types of casualty figures are pretty much unprecedented here. It's a major disaster."

The storm caused record flooding along the Ohio River. The town of Falmouth, Kentucky, was nearly totally destroyed by the flooding. The flooding along the Ohio lasted for several weeks, causing extensive damage. This storm was identified as one which occurs every five hundred years.

What is truly ironic is that President Clinton signed the legislation on March 1 which released the "family planning" money overseas. The very next day he signed disaster declaration legislation for nine counties in his own home state!

9. **June 1998:** The first weekend in June has become Gay Days at Disney World in Orlando, Florida. Starting in 1991, tens of thousands of homosexuals gather the first weekend in June at Disney World. The 1998 event started June 3 and ran through June 7. The month

of June has also been designated as Gay Awareness Month. The last Sunday of June has become Gay Pride Day.

The president of the United States sent a letter of congratulations for the 1998 Gay and Lesbian Pride Celebration at Disney World. In the letter the president stated:

> Our ideals and our history hold that the rights guaranteed us as Americans are inalienable. They are embedded in our Constitution and amplified over time by our courts and legislature, and I am bound by oath of office and the burden of history to reaffirm them. . . . And we stand to lose when any person is denied or forced out of a job because of sexual orientation.

The president was saying that homosexuality was a constitutional right! A review of the Gay Days '98 schedule of events was amazing! On June 3 from 9:00 p.m. to 3:00 a.m. was an event titled "Who's Your Daddy?" The description of the event follows: "A Leather, Latex, and Bondage Party . . . Featuring live flogging and spanking, dominatrix, masters and slaves . . . plus live piercing. Sponsored by Absolute Leather, B.D/S.M. Group of Florida." There were two events called "Seductive Dancing." There were male strippers and female impersonators. Gay Days ended on June 7 with a Sunday "Gospel Brunch" from 10:15 a.m. until 3:30 p.m. and an event titled "S.I.N. Tonight, Repent Tomorrow"! The president of the United States sent a letter of congratulations for events like this!

On May 30, 1998, Operation Rescue began a week-long prayer vigil and intercession in Orlando. They prayed in front of the city's abortion centers; they exposed child pornography being sold at Barnes and Noble Bookstores; and they prayed in front of Disney World as the homosexuals entered. The city of Orlando flew the homosexual flag (the rainbow) on the flag poles around City Hall.The flags remained up for the entire month of June. Christians went to City Hall and warned that the month-long flying of the homosexual flag would offend and anger God. They were ignored. In fact, Operation Rescue received very little support from the churches in Florida.

Operation Rescue ended the prayer vigil on June 6 at approximately 2:30 p.m.

At approximately 2:30 p.m. on June 6, fires erupted northeast, east, and southeast of Orlando and burned eastward, away from the city. There had been wildfires burning since May 25. These fires had been controlled and didn't receive national attention. At the very time Operation Rescue closed in prayer on June 6, the fires began to burn out of control and did so for the rest of Florida's Gay Month. For the rest of June, fires burned all over Florida, but especially northeast of Orlando. In total, there were over 2,100 fires and 500,000 acres burned. With all the fires, only 300 houses were destroyed with no loss of life. The fires and draught caused over $1 billion damage in crop loss.

Gay Days ended at Disney World on June 7 with a "Gospel Brunch." On June 7 Florida governor Lawton Chiles declared a state of emergency because of the fires and mobilized the National Guard. The fires were burning totally out of control. President Clinton issued a letter of congratulations to the homosexuals for Gay Days and then just twelve days after it ended, he declared Florida a disaster area for the release of federal assistance. What irony!

The fires closed 130 miles of I-95, and 40,000 people were forced to evacuate their homes. A draught settled over Florida and huge amounts of crops were lost. The danger from the fires was so real that the governor even requested the citizens pray and ask God for rain. At the very height of the danger, when the fires could have merged into an unstoppable wall of fire miles long, the rains came. The state was spared and on July 7 the people were allowed to go back home.

On June 30 the federal district court in Miami halted the enforcement of the state law banning the partial-birth abortion technique. This was at the height of the fire. This federal injunction occurred in conjunction with the worst fires in the state's history.

What an awesome warning to the state of Florida and the entire nation. Operation Rescue warned Orlando and Disney World of the dangers of open homosexuality and killing babies in the womb. They were rejected by Orlando. They were ignored by the entire state, but they warned of the possible judgment to come. Operation Rescue closed in prayer, and thus began the worst fires in the state's history. People that were too busy or did not care about the 100,000 homosexuals gathering in Orlando and the city flying the gay flag were now, a few days later, pleading with God for rain. They were fleeing their homes in panic as the fires threatened entire cities. This all occurred during Gay Month and while the homosexual flag was flying over one of the state's largest cities.

From this disaster, it could be concluded that America is moving very close to dramatic judgment from God. God's warning judgments are coming to an end. The fires exploding right after Operation Rescue's warnings appear to have been no coincidence. The fires seem to have been a strong warning to Florida and the nation of the coming judgment for open and bold homosexuality and the killing of children in the womb.

10. **January 1999:** Late on January 21 and into the early morning of January 22, a series of powerful tornadoes roared across Arkansas and then into Tennessee. This was a powerful storm that did over $1 billion in damage. This was a record-setting storm. The previous record for most tornadoes in one day in a state in January was 20; however, 38 hit Arkansas in less than 24 hours. The record for total tornadoes nationwide in January had been 52, but January 1999 witnessed 163. The majority fell in Arkansas and Tennessee. The center of the storm was Little Rock, Arkansas, where tremendous damage occurred. The governor's mansion was in the direct path of the storm. Although the mansion was not damaged, several trees on the grounds were destroyed.

On January 21, ex-Senator Dale Bumpers of Arkansas spoke on behalf of President Clinton before the United States Senate. Senator Bumpers made a passionate speech to have the Senate dismiss the impeachment charges against the president. What was disturbing about Bumpers' speech was that he actually used the name of Jesus Christ on the floor of the Senate in a joke! Senator Bumpers told a story about an evangelist at a revival meeting. The evangelist asked a question: "Who has ever known anybody who even comes close to the perfection of our Lord and Savior, Jesus Christ?" This question then led into a joke. The purpose of this joke was to show that no one is perfect—including Bill Clinton.

This use of the Lord's name was made by a man who twice supported the president's veto of the partial-birth abortion ban. He made the statement in front of the Senate which twice failed to overturn the president's veto of the partial-birth abortion ban. In addition, Bumpers had a nearly one hundred percent pro-abortion voting record while he was a senator.

Soon after Bumpers' speech, this powerful storm tore into his home state and zeroed in on Little Rock. Meteorologists reported that it was one of the most unusual storms ever seen in January because it was strong and volatile. The storm triggered a phenomenon called "training" in which one tornado follows another like a freight train. The tornadoes came out of the sky in waves—one after another. This storm generated 292 warnings during the twelve-hour period beginning at four p.m. (EST). This was a record amount of warnings in the state for one storm. This was the second major storm to generate tornadoes in Arkansas in a week. This was the first time since records were started in 1878 that there were two storms in January that generated tornadoes. In many ways this was a record breaking storm.

January 22 was the twenty-sixth anniversary of *Roe v. Wade,* the Supreme Court decision which legalized abortion on demand. On this day, Hillary Clinton addressed the National Abortion Rights Action League (NARAL). She said that the president was going to seek $4.5 million dollars from Congress to protect abortion centers. While Mrs. Clinton was making this speech, her home state was being declared a disaster area by the Federal Emergency Management Agency. The tornadoes that hit Little Rock literally tore down a tree on the governor's grounds which was called Chelsea's Tree. Chelsea is Clinton's daughter, and when the president was the governor of Arkansas, he had a tree house built for her. The tree which held her tree house was destroyed by these violent tornadoes. The

destruction of Chelsea's tree received national attention. The head-line of the Associated Press stated, "Twisters Rip South, Wreck Chelsea's Old Tree House."

From the time ex-Senator Bumpers ended his speech defending the president until Hillary Clinton ended her pro-abortion speech, 48 tornadoes fell on America, 38 of which fell on Bumpers' and Clinton's home state. After hitting Arkansas, the tornadoes then hit Tennessee. The storm destroyed thousands of homes, left 100,000 homes without power, and did $1 billion in damage. The states of the most pro-abortion president and vice-president in U.S. history were devastated on the anniversary of *Roe v. Wade.*

Apparently joking about Jesus Christ as our Lord and Savior on the floor of the Senate is something that should not be taken lightly; especially by a senator who has done everything possible to promote abortion. The people of Arkansas elected both Bumpers and Clinton.

America: My People Know Not the Judgment of the Lord

God always warns a nation before judgment. God is extremely merciful and very slow to anger, but there is a point when He will move to punish. The punishment could mean the total destruction of a nation or empire. The Bible records the destruction of God's ancient Jewish people, and their removal from the land of Israel in 586 B.C. God sent prophet after prophet for two centuries before the destruction to warn Israel of the coming disaster. The people for the most part refused to turn from their wicked ways. The result was that multitudes died as the country was destroyed and the survivors were taken captive to Babylon.

The prophet Jeremiah was alive when Israel was destroyed. He warned of the coming destruction and pleaded with Israel to turn from sin to God. The people would not listen to his warning. Jeremiah wept over his people, and to this day he is known as the weeping prophet. When the people failed to recognize that the calamities coming on them were warn-ings from God of impending destruction, Jeremiah said, ". . . my people know not the judgment of the LORD" (**Jer. 8:7**).

Modern America is very similar to ancient Israel. Both nations were founded for the glory of God and had a godly heritage. Both nations turned from God and went into gross sexual immorality while yet still appearing to remain religious. Both nations practiced child killing, and tolerated, if not encouraged open homosexuality. Just before destruction, both nations were consumed with violence. And both nations were clearly warned by God of the coming destruction.

When the Supreme Court in 1963 banned prayer and Bible reading in the public schools and then in 1973 legalized the killing of innocent children in the womb, the country was destabilized. It now seems very clear that judgment from God began in 1963 and was intensified in 1973. Since 1963 the education system, once the best in the world, is now second rate. The family unit through adultery, divorce, and violence is disintegrating. The cities are now drug infested war zones. Our children are abused and sexually molested.

Homosexuals parade openly in the streets, and vile pornographers degrade women and children while making millions of dollars. One such pornographer is even a friend and ally of the president of the United States—who came to Clinton's aid during his Senate impeachment trial. Sexual immorality (which is now rampant from Main Street America to the White House) has brought with it the deadliest disease known to mankind—AIDS.

America cannot continue in this direction and remain a great nation. "Righteousness exalteth a nation: but sin is a reproach to any people" (**Prov. 14:34**). Remember that the Index of Social Health has pinpointed 1973 as the very year the deterioration of America began.

The Bible states, "If the foundations be destroyed, what can the righteous do?" (**Ps. 11:3**). The foundations of America have been destroyed. The husband-and-wife family unit, which is ordained by God, is being replaced with the term "domestic partners," and homosexuals are being allowed to adopt children. America is coming unglued! The nation is full of violence as innocent blood is being shed from coast to coast. It seems every week a mass murderer kills several people. This was unheard of before 1963. It seems that regularly a serial killer is caught, and these killings are more and more bizarre. This was virtually unheard of before 1963. The violence that started against children in the womb has now spread like a cancer throughout the entire society. It is truly ironic that America has developed the technology to allow men to walk safely in space, yet in most of our cities it is unsafe to walk in the streets.

Conclusion

God's judgment is not a popular topic among most people, even many Christians. The church in America today shares in the responsibility for the decline in this once great land. Americans have become fat, dumb, lazy, apathetic, and complacent, in part due to being spoiled by fifty years of nearly uninterrupted prosperity since the end of World War II. Many can no longer discern the difference between good and evil, nor do they in any way take a stand against evil. Jesus said in **Matthew 5:13:** "Ye are the salt of the earth: but if the salt have lost his savour, wherewith shall it be salted? it is thenceforth good for nothing, but to be cast out, and to be trodden under foot of men."

God's judgment against America may have already begun. This judgment may indeed include the Christian church. The great tragedy is that there seems to be a growing blindness over the eyes of so many Americans, even American Christians. This is often accompanied by an escapist mentality that says we will be raptured before anything bad happens. This could be (in fact, let us hope so), but that belief did not help millions of Chinese Christians who were taught the Rapture over fifty years ago. Mao TseTung and his successors have still made life a living hell for the Chinese since then. We can have similar persecution and horrors in America in coming years—*before* the return of the Lord Jesus Christ.

God's judgment can take many forms, such as natural disasters and economic woes, as well as wicked, evil political leadership. God sometimes gives a country the political leaders it deserves and judges a country with them (i.e., like Ahab and Jezebel, and perhaps the Clinton Administration). Oppressive governments will take the people's freedoms away, including those of Christians. Could the socialist police state and New World Order emerging in America and globally be part of God's judgment against a disobedient, decadent generation, including the Christian church?

[*Note:* For readers who are skeptical that the God in heaven can still get angry or judge men, the following example may be instructive. About fifteen years ago, Samora Machel, the ruthless communist dictator of Mozambique, gave a speech in which he shouted that there was no God, that he was god; and as he shook his fist at the God he said *wasn't* there, he screamed at the God who *was* there, "If you are God, kill me!" Twenty minutes later he boarded a Russian Tupolov transport plane with twenty Soviet advisors. It took off in a thunderstorm, was hit by lightning, and all on board, including Machel, were killed instantly in the crash that followed. God heard his challenge and answered "the man who would be god."]

Chapter 2

Toward a Socialist America:
To Control the People

> Their aim [the global socialists who are pushing for world government] is nothing less than to create a world system of financial control in private hands, able to dominate the political system of each country and the economy of the world as a whole.
>
> —Carol Quigley (friend and teacher of
> Bill Clinton) in *Tragedy and Hope*

America and most of the countries in the western world, the third world, and the "former" communist countries, are dominated today by global socialists—people who espouse a global government and socialistic control over every aspect of peoples lives. The goal of this elitist group of socialists (many of whom are extremely wealthy and include the corporate and financial leaders of the various nations) is **to control the people, resources, and wealth of the world, and to amass great power and wealth for themselves.**

A world government which they rule (variously called the New World Order, the New Civilization, or the New International World Order) is their goal over the next five to ten years. This world government will have many common characteristics with the Nazi Third Reich, with the communism of the "former" Soviet Union and present-day communist China, and especially with the fascism of Italy under Mussolini—with its marriage of big business and big government.

The communists of Russia, who are still very much alive and well, who are still running the country from behind the scenes, and who are emerging in the open as the leadership in Russia as this book goes to press, are major players in the thrust for world government. Former Soviet dictator Mikhail Gorbachev remains one of the most powerful leaders in the globalist movement today.

There are dozens of internationalist organizations pushing for world government, including the U.S.-based Council on Foreign Relations and Trilateral Commission, the European-based Bilderbergers, Club of Rome, Socialist International, the Fabian Socialists, and Russian and Chinese-based communism. Their major vehicle for moving the world to global socialism and world government is the United Nations; dozens of U.N. subagencies and organizations (i.e., like UNICEF and UNESCO); and the United Nations' (New World) Army (which is currently growing rapidly in size, strength, and influence).

There is an occultic/satanic dynamic behind the present thrust for world government, just as there was behind the Nazi Third Reich, with many of the top globalist leaders in this movement up to their eyeballs in the occult, witchcraft, or Satanism. A growing number of Christian prophecy/conservative/traditionalist observers believe that the rapidly emerging New (International) World Order (or New Civilization) is actually the rising kingdom of the Antichrist, and is setting the stage for the Armageddon scenario and the second coming of Jesus Christ. This was discussed in some detail in this writer's book *Toward the New World Order: The Countdown to Armageddon.*

Meanwhile, there are a number of obstacles standing in the way of the global socialists and their goals for world government: America and its vast economic industrial strength (which must be reduced to communist bloc or third world status in order to merge it into a world system); the U.S. Constitution, which is a major obstacle to the socialists' agenda; almost 300 million firearms in the hands of over 100 million Americans; and several million Christian/conservative/traditionalist activists who hate and oppose the New World Order and the evil its global socialist agenda represents. These obstacles must be removed or neutralized before the global socialists' agenda can be implemented. Hence the coming persecution of Christians, conservatives, and traditionalists in America and elsewhere around the world.

The Clinton Administration, and before it that of George Bush and

Jimmy Carter, have played major roles in moving America toward global socialism by implementing the agenda of the Liberal Eastern Establishment. It is important to note that even though the Carters, Bushs, and Clintons are faithful implementors of the global socialist agenda, they are *not* calling the shots, they are *not* ultimately in charge (though while in office they do exert great power) and they *are* totally expendable. The situation in the Russian leadership (whether a Yeltsen, Gorbachev, Primikov, Lebed, etc.) is similar.

It should also be understood that the globalist establishment also controls the hierarchy of the Republican Party (as well as the Democratic Party) and its leaders such as former House Speaker Newt Gingrich, former Senate Majority Leader Bob Dole, etc. There is no real difference in the two parties at the leadership level—both will faithfully implement the global socialist agenda—with, by and large, only their rhetoric differing.

Bill Clinton's first term gave the global socialists a quantum leap forward in their agenda for controlling the American people and globalizing America, and his second term is proving to be even more fruitful for the Establishment. And, Al Gore, a global socialist with even more impressive Establishment credentials, is standing in the wings to pick up where Clinton leaves off.

The four major thrusts of the Clintons and the Establishment which directs and controls them include:

1. Implementation of NAFTA as a major stepping stone to the New World Order (accomplished in Clinton's first term);
2. Passage and implementation of the socialized medicine program which will not only give it control of eighteen percent of the U.S. economy, but will enable it to impose socialist controls on the entire U.S. population never heretofore dreamed of in America;
3. Imposition of a national identification card (a computerized smartcard) for every American, as a way of electronically monitoring, tracking, and controlling the entire U.S. population; and
4. Total gun control—which will include the national licensing of all firearms owners, the registration of all U.S. firearms, and ultimately

the confiscation of all U.S. firearms (except for those carried by the military, local police, government agents, and the national police force).

Additional elements of the Clinton Liberal Establishment agenda are:

5. Passage of a series of people-control initiatives under the banner of "crime control," "counterterrorism," and "hate crimes," and installation of an American national police force;
6. The total eradication of the pro-life movement—which will open the floodgates to even more abortions, partial-birth abortions, and to euthanasia of the elderly;
7. Mandatory inoculation of all U.S. children, including computerization and tracking of same;
8. Restrictions on cash withdrawals from banks (i.e., cash rationing) and foreign exchange controls;
9. Vastly expanded environmental laws, rules, and regulations, as well as enforcement; and
10. Socialization of the entire U.S. economy under the innocuous label of "economic democracy," which encompasses government control of housing, energy, insurance, health, the banks, government confiscation of wealth and private property, and a sharp increase in progressive taxes.

Part of this socialist agenda was realized in Clinton's first term, and Draconian efforts are underway to implement the balance in his second term.

To Control the People

America is beginning to look more and more like Nazi Germany of the early 1930s or the Soviet Union from the 1920s through the 1980s. True criminals (murderers, rapists, burglars, robbers, etc.) are given light (or negligible) jail sentences, while the government is now reclassifying honest, law-abiding Americans as criminals and giving them severe jail sentences, or confiscating their assets or property via Draconian Nazi/Marxist/Leninist-style seizure laws.

The legal system and government now allows the "have nots" to plunder the assets of the "haves," and a gargantuan U.S. government passes tens of thousands of new regulations each year to control every aspect of Americans' lives.

As the U.S. is moved toward a socialist America and the New World Order, the strategy of Antonio Gramsci, founder of the Italian Communist Party, is being utilized. Gramsci believed the communists could not seize political power until they first seized cultural power. Gramsci said that the social revolution would be brought about by the transformation of a society's culture and values, not through political or military power. The establishment of radical socialism would come via the undermining and transformation of traditional western values.

The strategy of the socialists is to change the way society thinks about problems—to gain control over the minds of the population. Gramsci strategized a "convergence" of religion and socialism (with religion stripped of all spiritual content) and a takeover of the entire field where culture is manifest (i.e., schools, universities, the media, Hollywood, etc.). Following Gramsci's strategy, the socialists of our day (in America, Europe, South Africa, and throughout the West) have developed a superstructure reflecting a socialist culture—replete with socialist literature, films, plays, poetry, and various forms of art and music.

People-control is essential to any totalitarian state, whether Nazi Germany, the former Soviet Union, Cuba, the socialist America of the 1990s, or the emerging global government.

First consider the explosion of government regulations: Congress passes almost twenty-five hundred new laws each year. Most of these new laws carry both criminal and civil penalties for violations. To implement these new laws, tens of thousands of new regulations are written each year by several hundred thousand government bureaucrats who are part of dozens of huge government agencies (i.e., IRS, FBI, SEC, ATF, DEA, FDA, EPA, OSHA, HUD, etc.).

These new regulations (many of which carry criminal penalties) fill over 85,000 pages of *The Federal Register* (in fine print) each year. You are responsible for following every one of those regulations on pain of fines, asset forfeiture, or imprisonment for violation. Ignorance of the law in America is no excuse. You have been "legally" advised via *The Federal Register* and are assumed to have read it. Incredibly, the government has created a situation in which you are almost certain to be a criminal. You are breaking one or more of these regulations right now and don't even know it.

Let's consider one category of regulations—environmental regulations. The Clean Water Act, Clean Air Act, and a host of other environmental laws and regulations passed in recent years give the government Draconian dictatorial controls over virtually every business and person, over every piece of private property, every car, and every action of every American in the U.S. Environmental laws and regulations (both domestic and international) will be a primary vehicle for moving us into socialism and global government.

Seventy percent of private property in America is already considered by the government to be "wetlands" (whether there is surface water on it or not) and therefore under their control. Environmentalists are pushing to make that one hundred percent. Thousands of U.S. citizens (or businesses) each year are being fined, having their property seized, or jailed for "wetlands" or other environmental "violations."

One Hungarian refugee living in Pennsylvania was fined, had his property seized, and was jailed for not getting prior permission from the EPA to place fill dirt on his own property. A Taiwanese farmer living in central California was fined, jailed, and had his property seized after he accidentally ran over five kangaroo rats while plowing on his tractor. The rats were on the government's endangered species list. These are just two of thousands of such examples which happen in America each year.

The socialists believe in crisis management to solve crises (real or manufactured) in order to greatly expand their power and control over the people. The war on drugs, the environmental crisis, the war on crime, discrimination against minorities, "hate crimes," firearms violations, terrorism, child abuse, etc., are all "crises" which supposedly justify the passage and enforcement of new laws and regulations, expansion of bureaucratic agencies, and the installation of police state power over the people.

Bill Clinton and Al Gore in their book *Putting People First* called for a national police force of 100,000 officers (made up of former retired military personnel, other government employees, etc.) to fight the crime war and America's other crises. President Clinton is now deploying 100,000 new police via the Crime Control Act of 1994.

Former CIA director Robert Gates has called for the CIA to be given the power to spy on American businesses and individuals and to help support the Justice Department and other federal agencies in enforcing the myriad of new governmental laws and regulations. If criminal enforcement agents of the DEA, FBI, CIA, BATF, EPA, FDA, IRS, and various other government agencies and departments are included, the U.S. could soon have a national police force of 200,000 to 300,000 people spying on the public and enforcing regulations. Shades of the Gestapo in Nazi Germany or the KGB in Russia!

The global socialists are also talking about an **international police force** made up of U.N. troops from member countries to control *internal crises,* environmental abuses, and eventually opponents of the New World Order. The New World Army (U.N.) police force will soon reach 250,000 and could grow to 500,000 or more over the next five years. An undisclosed number of U.N. troops (estimated to be between 10,000 and 30,000) are now training on U.S. soil, and could be used in America in some future state of national emergency, civil unrest such as the Los Angeles riots, or other upheaval. As we have seen in Haiti, Somalia, and Bosnia, U.S. military forces are being moved under the U.N. command.

Police State Tactics

U.S. military and National Guard personnel have been undergoing training and exercises for several years for house-to-house searches (presumably for drugs or guns), for crowd control, and for domestic counterterrorism measures. Roadblocks are being randomly set up on highways around America by local, state, and federal officials to conduct drivers license checks, or warrantless spot checks of cars or their occupants for drugs, liquor, or firearms. A law, passed by Congress in 1996 and signed into law, facilitates police roadblocks within a half mile of any school to check cars for firearms.

Local, state, or military helicopters are, with greatly increased frequency, overflying cities, towns, neighborhoods, and individual houses, at low levels looking for drugs, for surveillance, or for intimidation purposes. Many of these helicopters are black and unmarked.

Over the past few years, as training and enforcement exercises have increased, SWAT teams in black ninja suits, and other government marshals and enforcement teams, have had an increasing number of shootouts with innocent victims who are characterized by the government as "religious fundamentalists," "cultists," "white supremacists," "left- or right-wing extremists," "tax protestors," "gun law violators," etc. (i.e., Randy Weaver, Donald Scott, the Branch Davidian cult in Waco, etc.). The general tactic (whether used by local or federal police officials) is to overwhelm and intimidate the "suspected" money launderer, environmental or financial "criminal," gun law violator, etc. by invading his home or business with a SWAT team and/or federal marshals or other government agents numbering ten to twenty to thirty (i.e., one hundred in "Operation Waco"). Guns are often drawn, and if the victim of the attack makes any move, he is often shot.

Toward American Gun Control

1935 will go down in history! For the first time, a civilized nation has full gun registration! Our streets will be safer, our police more efficient and the world will follow our lead into the future!

—Adolph Hitler

Laws that forbid ownership of arms disarm only those who are neither inclined, nor determined to commit crimes. Such laws make things worse for the assaulted and better for the assailants. They serve rather to encourage than to prevent homicides, for an unarmed man may be attacked with greater confidence than an armed man.

—Thomas Jefferson

As part of this whole trend, Draconian gun control laws are being passed, turning hundreds of thousands (or millions) of honest, freedom-loving U.S. gun owners who refuse to comply into instant criminals.

Disarming the American people via Nazi-style gun control laws is an essential part of moving America toward a socialist police state and into the New World Order. With over 100 million Americans (about half of the American electorate) owning up to 300 million firearms, the armed resistance to the occupation of America by New World Order, U.N., Russian, or other foreign troops would be too great. The American people must be disarmed via the present gun control express.

The anti-gun propaganda is running high in the U.S. media, with a barrage of articles describing the dangers of firearms and the need for stringent gun control. *USA Today, The Wall Street Journal,* and other Establishment publications are keeping up a steady drumbeat. Handgun Control, Inc., seeks to ban all private ownership of guns in America.

The political left has proposed that anyone who owns twenty or more guns or one thousand or more rounds of ammunition should be forced to acquire a three-year, $300 "federal arsenal" license. Arsenal licensees would be subject to unannounced warrantless BATF inspections (or searches) of their homes up to three times a year. Why are even more gun control measures being proposed? Congress and the media claim that America is engulfed in a "violent crime crisis" caused by easy access to guns.

The *Washington Times* has written: "The Clinton Administration has agreed to participate in a discussion of ways for the United Nations to control the manufacture of guns and their sales to civilians. This represents the first U.N. effort to foster regulations of the multibillion-dollar trade in small arms."

A U.N. working paper on global gun control declares: "The arms permitted for civilian use . . . should be subject to control at all points in the chain, from production and/or acquisition up to the time they are sold to an individual. From then on, they should remain subject to monitoring and control." The U.N. also called for "harmonization" of national gun control laws, which means *the total gun bans found in England, Japan, Australia and Mexico would become U.S. law.* Virtually all guns have been banned and confiscated in England and Australia.

Chapter 3

The End of Privacy:
Toward a Total Surveillance Society

> Ever feel you're being watched? You will! There won't be anything you do that won't be collected and analyzed by the government. This national information infrastructure is a better surveillance mechanism than Orwell or the government could have imagined. This (blank, blank) thing is so pervasive, and the propensity to connect it is so great that it is unstoppable.
>
> —William Murray, an information security consultant
> to Deloitte and Touche, writing in *Digital Media*.

> We're under constant observation; everything goes on a permanent record; much of what we say, do, and feel may be recorded by others we don't know.
>
> —Gary Marx, speaking at the recent conference on "Privacy and
> New Information Technologies" at the University of Colorado

In George Orwell's classic (and prophetic) novel *1984,* Big Brother, the all-powerful socialist dictator of America, enslaves the people. His primary tool for the destruction of the peoples' freedom was the abolition of all forms of privacy. Big Brother watched the people twenty-four hours a day in a total surveillance society. **Privacy is a major element of freedom and its elimination is a major element of slavery.**

Today, in an electronic, computerized, high-tech age that even Orwell did not envision, it is possible to track, watch, or listen to Americans from the cradle to the grave. If Hitler, Lenin, Stalin, or Mao had had the high-tech people-tracking devices now available to governments around the world, their tyrannical, people-controlling dictatorships might have lasted much longer.

Today, using your Social Security number, each adult American has comprehensive files in a dozen or more federal government databases—with information ranging from tax, medical, police, educational, and military records, to financial, bank, credit card, securities, and other investment records. Through the Financial Crimes Enforcement Network (Fin-CEN), these records are assembled (via computers) from your various government files. Profiles (very accurate, computerized profiles) on each adult American can be assembled—showing your likes, dislikes, political and religious preference, spending habits, etc.—**and whether you are politically correct or incorrect** (i.e., liberal, conservative, Christian, patriotic, etc.).

Public surveillance devices are now in use wherein you are being videotaped in government and public office buildings; grocery, liquor, drug, and other retail stores; on a growing number of city streets and highways; in airports, train stations, subways; in parking garages; and very shortly, in virtually all public places. Overhead satellites photograph and catalog each square inch of the earth (several times a day), with accuracy that can spot and identify by brand a package of cigarettes lying on your driveway.

All passports and drivers licenses are now computerized. When passing through customs or at a routine traffic stop, the government or law enforcement officer can instantly pull up on his computer screen hundreds or thousands of items of information about you from databases in Washington, D.C. This instant information on you is now being established in **international** databases.

Your hand may soon become your passport. Experiments for the past five years (at the Newark, JFK, and Toronto airports) have demonstrated the feasibility of using a biometric hand measurement. A three-dimensional reading of the hand's shape is encoded on an INPASS card. To pass immigration, card holders approach a special kiosk and swipe the card through an apparatus, much the way it is done at some ATMs. The computer prompts the traveler to place one hand on a flat plate, and then it compares that hand with the details recorded on the card to test the identity of the cardholder. Next, the name is automatically checked against a federal database to ensure that the traveler isn't a known drug lord or other undesirable [*Note:* i.e., perhaps politically incorrect or someone guilty of a hate crime.] The traveler keys in the flight arrival number and receives a printout confirming passage through immigration. A gate clicks open ahead, ushering the cardholder through to customs.

A January 1995 article in *World Travel Magazine* entitled "Your Hand Is Your Passport: Technology Cuts the Time Spent in Line" reported:

> The eyes may be the window to the soul, but at a few airports, the hand is the door to the future. . . . The ultimate goal, according to Jake Achterberg, an INS assistant chief inspector, is to get such a system into major U.S. ports of entry for use by *all* travelers. Eventually the system would be compatible with those of other countries. The cards could hold all kinds of passport, visa, and other data, and could even be used to identify passengers boarding planes in the coming age of ticketless travel.

[*Note:* **The ultimate goal is to have computerized control of all people movement—inside and outside your business, public office buildings, your city, airports, train stations, crossing borders, etc.** It will be the high-tech equivalent of "show me your papers" in the former communist countries, in Nazi Germany, or in Red China, Cuba, or North Korea today—only with instant, accurate, and comprehensive computerized background checks. Fingerprints, faces, and retina scans are also being used in the same way.]

The IRS has been closely scrutinizing most Americans for the past five years by checking their various government databases against returns. As the *Los Angeles Times* (2/15/98) reported in an article entitled "Online IRS Checks Databases Against Returns":

> If you have a back tax bill with the Internal Revenue Service, watch out. In the midst of a program called "Economic Reality," the federal tax agency is going online, searching for signs of noncompliance as well as electronic records of cars, credit, and real estate it can seize from delinquent taxpayers.

A cadre of IRS agents with computers and modems now will be searching records filed with the Department of Motor Vehicles, county tax assessor's offices, credit-reporting companies, and the U.S. Bureau of the Census in an effort to find people who are underreporting their business sales, overestimating their deductions, or trying to hide assets—or themselves—from federal tax collectors, IRS officials say.

Automatic ID News (12/94) described how the U.S. military, under directives from President Clinton, developed and tested on 50,000 Cuban and Haitian refugees a Deployable Mass Population Identification and Tracking System (DMPITS). It involves a **nonremovable** wrist or ankle band which can be used to electronically track a refugee, immigrant, or alien. Similar devices are used on U.S. prisoners on work release programs or under house arrest or detention. **Hitler would have found such devices far more efficient than the yellow arm bands he placed on all his Jewish victims.**

In like manner, biochips (in wide use for a decade in pets and farm animals) are now being experimented with on children, military personnel, and prison inmates. In another government people-tracking development, the *Orange County Register* (10/12/98) reported in an article entitled "DNA Database Raises Fears of Big Brother" how the **FBI (ostensibly to fight crime) has gone online with a new national database of DNA samples of millions of citizens.** It is presently being proposed in England by the government that such DNA database tracking of people is now to be expanded from just sex offenders **to all British citizens.** As the *Orange County Register* reported: "The U.S. government could consider connecting the FBI's new DNA database with the other national databases now being set up for new employees, medical patients, and drivers license holders."

The National ID Card: "Show Me Your Papers"
Over the sixty-three years since the Social Security system was introduced in 1935, we have seen the gradual evolution of a national ID card. Today more than forty government agencies already depend on the Social Security number as their universal identifier, **even though the gov-**

ernment promised they would never use the number for that purpose. Since the Clintons came to power, there has been a strong push for a national ID card—actually several ID cards: a medical ID card; an INS ID card; and a general purpose national ID smartcard.

The National Medical ID Card

In the summer of 1998, the Clintons began pushing hard for a medical identification number and card for every American. As the *New York Times* (7/20/98) reported in an article entitled "Administration Preparing to Issue Medical ID to Every American":

> The Clinton Administration is quietly laying plans to assign every American a "unique health identifier": **a computer code that could be used to create a national database that would track every citizen's medical history from the cradle to the grave.** The electronic code would be the first national identity system since the Social Security number was introduced in 1935. **With this new national health ID card and database, sensitive health information might be linked to financial data, tax records, criminal records, etc., compromising already tenuous privacy protections.**

If the federal government is allowed to create a medical dossier on every American, the information (which should be highly private) will be exchanged between various government agencies (like our financial, tax, and other personal data is), people will be hurt, and your freedom of privacy destroyed.

The Kennedy-Kassebaum law (the Health Insurance Portability and Accountability Act) calling for **"unique health care identifiers,"** so that **the government can electronically tag, track, and monitor every citizen's personal medical records,** was passed by Congress in 1996.

A National ID Drivers License

On June 17, 1998, the U.S. Department of Transportation published in the *Federal Register* the proposed "National Identification Document

Guidelines," which would lay the groundwork for establishing a national ID card, by compelling states to adopt and comply with these Draconian rules by October 1, 2000. This backdoor approach seems innocuous on the surface; but those states that do not comply will find that their citizens will not be allowed to participate in routine, essential business transactions after the imposed federal deadline of October 1, 2000.

The state-issued driver's licenses will be the initial vehicle for the national ID card, and must include virtually every bit of personal data about you, including your Social Security number. Non–conforming licenses will not be accepted for identification by any federal government agency. The proposal includes (but is not limited to) plans to deny access to the following: (1) jobs under the new hires database guidelines, (2) boarding commercial airliners, (3) opening a bank account or cashing a check, (4) health insurance benefits under your employer–provided, or individual insurance plans, (5) Medicare or Medicaid, (6) obtaining a passport, (7) marriage licenses or other privilege licenses—and many, many more services that only a resourceful bureaucrat could imagine. **The state-issued drivers license is the vehicle the Clintons have chosen as the path of least resistance.**

In 1996 the Congress, led by a Republican majority, passed the "Illegal Immigration Reform and Immigrant Responsibility Act of 1996." Buried in the immigration reform act was Section 656(6) titled "State-Issued Drivers Licenses and Comparable Identification Documents" which forbade the use of state drivers licenses after October 1, 2000. The Free Congress Foundation wrote in a press release about the new national drivers licenses: "The effect of the law and the proposed Department of Transportation regulations will be to create a national ID card that will allow the government to monitor your movements and track your medical and financial transactions."

The National ID card will be necessary for opening a bank or securities account, or using your bank account, getting a loan, buying a gun, flying on an airplane, securing medical care, etc., and with the Social Security number attached, will feed every transaction, activity, and move you make back into the government's centralized databases.

The Free Congress Foundation went on to say that

the Clinton Department of Transportation wants to see incorporated into the ID card: digitized biometric features, including, but not limited to fingerprints, retina scans, voice prints, and DNA prints. This personal biometric data would be electronically stored via a magnetic strip on the back of the card as part of the mandated securities features of the card. [A large memory capacity chip or integrated circuit is also likely to be incorporated into the"smartcard"—similar to the MARC card presently used by the Department of Defense to track and control military personnel around the world.]

Did you get that??? **A national ID card which will require every citizen to be fingerprinted, DNA tested, have their eye retina scanned, or submit to other intrusions of privacy is being planned for us.** The August 1998 issue of *Monetary and Economic Review* reported in an article entitled "Citizen Suspects and the National ID Card":

> In what ways will the new National ID card affect you? **Obviously, the flagrant abuses of your privacy—scanning parts of your body, DNA sampling, fingerprinting, etc.—relegates the individual to the status of a criminal being watched by the state—in other words, a "citizen suspect."** If this act is allowed to be implemented, you will, on a daily basis, be disallowed from privately performing routine activities common to all of us.
>
> For example, without the national ID card you will not be able to use your bank. The FBI's Financial Crimes Enforcement Center (FinCEN) requires banks to identify new account holders and non-account holders cashing checks by "appropriate" ID.
>
> If you are a recipient of Social Security, Medicare, Medicaid, or any other government assistance, you will not be allowed those services and payments without the national ID card. You cannot get a new job without the national ID card. It would seem that the **federal government has designed a national "new hires database" that requires all employers to use the national ID card to make a federal record of their employees through this new database.**
>
> You will be required to have the card to purchase a gun. This, in

conjunction with the already unconstitutional Brady Bill waiting period, will stop the purchase of weapons by those who are currently protected from such intrusion by the Second Amendment. This will make federal tracking and confiscation of weapons incredibly easy.

Without "the card," you will not be able to travel on airplanes, as this will become the new ID required to board domestic flights across the nation. [*Note:* Already airline personnel are demanding that your picture ID (now required to get on a plane) **must be government issued**—either state or federal.]

There is even a proposal by the Department of Health and Human Services, recommending the establishment of the "Unique Patient Identifier." It would have a person's entire medical record stored in a national database. The list of other daily activities for which the national ID card could be required is far too long to include here.

Biblically, the question comes to mind as to whether this is the mark of the beast as detailed in the book of Revelation: "And he had power to give life unto the image of the beast, that the image of the beast should both speak, and cause that as many as would not worship the image of the beast should be killed. And he causeth all, both small and great, rich and poor, free and bond, to receive a mark in their right hand, or in their foreheads: And that no man might buy or sell, save he that had the mark, or the name of the beast, or the number of his name" (Rev. 13:15–17).

Regardless of what Rapture version you believe, we must still consider this question. Is this the mark or a precursor? Honestly ask yourself, "How much further would it be to a microchip under the skin in the forehead or hand?" I think we would agree that it is not a giant leap.

An odd mix of groups combined in September 1998 to oppose the national drivers license ID (i.e., the ACLU, Christian Coalition, Libertarian Party, the CATO Institute, etc.) and the card program has been temporarily postponed. **In a state of emergency due to terrorism, etc., Clinton could quickly move to implement the ID card issuance in spite of present congressional objections.**

FDIC/Federal Reserve Proposal to Have
Banks Spy on You for Big Brother

The FDIC issued rules in December 1998 that, if implemented, will turn banks—to an even greater extent than they already are—into surveillance agents for the government. As the *Orange County Register* (12/15/98) reported in an article entitled "Enforcement Banking":

> The rules would make mandatory a similar, voluntary program called "Know Your Customers" at federally chartered banks and extend that program to state-chartered banks that aren't FDIC members but have FDIC insurance, and to other institutions.
>
> Specifically, the regulation "would require each nonmember bank to develop a program designed to determine the identity of its customers; determine its customers' sources of funds; determine the normal and expected transactions of its customers; monitor account activity for transactions that are inconsistent with those normal and expected transactions; and report any transactions of its customers that are determined to be suspicious, in accordance with the FDIC's existing suspicious activities reporting regulation," according to the FDIC's summary of the proposed rule. It was published Dec. 7 in the *Federal Register*.
>
> Members of an alliance forming against the rule include the conservative Free Congress Foundation, as well as the American Civil Liberties Union and the Electronic Privacy Information Center. The federal government already requires that banks report cash transactions of $10,000 or more, a requirement justified as a way to catch money-laundering drug dealers. In addition, banks are supposed to report patterns of suspicious activity, such as repeated cash transactions just under the $10,000 limit. But economist Richard Rahn, CEO of Novacon and author of the forthcoming book *The End of Money*, believes the regulations will substantially increase the cost of doing business and are another example of government asking the private sector to do its investigative work in catching criminals in the illegal drug trade. Do you really want your bank wondering whether or not your account activity is "suspicious" on an ever-larger variety of grounds?

On November 23, 1998, *WorldNetDaily* carried an article by David Bresnahan entitled "Big Brother Banks? FDIC Has Snooping Plans," in which he wrote:

> Are you a potential criminal? Are you a threat to banks, airlines, a potential spy, or perhaps an IRS tax protester? The government would like to know and they are about to force banks to be their detectives. The federal government wants banks to investigate you. Soon your banker will know more about you than anyone else in town. Banks must not only determine your correct identity, they must also know how you make your money, and how you spend it. Once you establish a pattern of deposits and withdrawals, banks must inform federal agencies when you deviate.
>
> Bank customers may soon find themselves explaining to the FBI, Internal Revenue Service, and the Drug Enforcement Agency why they made a $15,000 deposit to their bank account.
>
> According to the current Federal Deposit Insurance Corporation plans, banks will soon establish "profiles" of their customers and report deviations from those profiles. If you sell a car, for example, and place the proceeds in your account while you shop for a new one, a red flag may go off in the bank computer. Such a situation puts law abiding citizens in a situation where they must prove they are innocent, says Scott McDonald of the watchdog group Fight the Fingerprint.
>
> "The FDIC is proposing to issue a regulation requiring insured nonmember banks to develop and maintain 'Know Your Customer' programs," according to a FDIC information package sent to Congress to provide notice of proposed rule making, and to banks for comment.
>
> As the FDIC document wrote: "By requiring insured nonmember banks to determine the identity of their customers, as well as to obtain knowledge regarding the legitimate activities of their customers, the proposed regulation will reduce the likelihood that insured nonmember banks will become unwitting participants in illicit activities conducted or attempted by their customers. It will also level the playing field between institutions that already have adopted formal 'Know Your

Customer' programs and those that have not."

Many banks across the country have already begun to implement such programs, according to the FDIC. A quick search of the Internet found many stories in press accounts of problems reported at such banks. There have been a number of stories dealing with banks requiring fingerprints to open accounts and to cash checks. There are several lawsuits presently underway testing the right of banks to make that requirement.

The FDIC is selling the planned regulations by pointing out the need for prevention of financial and other crimes. "By identifying and, when appropriate, reporting such transactions in accordance with existing suspicious activity reporting requirements, financial institutions are protecting their integrity and are assisting the efforts of the financial institution regulatory agencies and law enforcement authorities to combat illicit activities at such institutions."

The proposed regulation is, according to FDIC spokesperson Carol A. Mesheske, authorized by current law. It comes from the statutory authority granted the FDIC under section 8(s)(1) of the Federal Deposit Insurance Act (12 U.S.C. 18189[s][1]), as amended by section 259(a)(1) of the Crime Control Act of 1990 (Pub. L. 101-647). The FDIC claims that the law requires them to develop regulations to require banks to "establish and maintain internal procedures reasonably designed to ensure and monitor compliance with the Bank Secrecy Act. Effective 'Know Your Customer' programs serve to facilitate compliance with the Bank Secrecy Act."

The proposed regulations will mandate that all banks insured by the FDIC must maintain an intelligence gathering department that screens out customers and keeps an eye on existing customers. Before you decide to move your money to a credit union, you should know that the FDIC is not the only federal organization making such plans. FDIC attorney Karen L. Main reports in the proposal: "Each of the other federal bank supervisory agencies is proposing to adopt substantially identical regulations covering state member and national banks, federally-chartered branches and agencies of foreign banks, savings associations, and credit unions. There also have been discussions with the federal regulators of non-bank financial institutions, such as broker dealers, concerning the need to propose similar rules governing the activities of these non-bank institutions."

Current customers will be subjected to the new regulation in the same way new customers will be scrutinized. The FDIC does not wish to permit any loophole which would leave any bank customer unidentified or unsupervised. Each bank will create profiles. The first profile will determine the amount of risk a potential customer might present by opening an account. The system of profiling potential customers will be different from one bank to the next, since the FDIC does not provide a uniform program. The purpose of the profile is to identify potential customers who might use a bank account for funds obtained through criminal activity.

The next profile will be one that is used by automated computers to determine when suspicious activity is taking place in an account. When activity in the account does not fit the profile, banks will notify federal authorities so they can investigate. Banks are expected to identify their customers, determine normal and expected transactions, monitor account transactions, and determine if a particular transaction should be reported.

The FDIC reassures banks that because the requirements will be universally applied to all banks it will not hurt their business and drive away customers. The proposal does not mention penalties for non–compliance, nor is there any mention of regulations to provide access to bank records by customers so errors can be found and corrections made. "If 'Know Your Customer' programs are required, insured non-member banks can more easily collect the necessary information because customers cannot turn readily to another financial institution free of such requirements," stated the proposal.

The above article referred to "automated computers to determine when suspicious activity is taking place." The Americas Software Corporation advertises on the Internet a software package called ASSIST to help banks implement their "Know Your Customer" rules and to monitor suspicious activity:

What is ASSIST? ASSIST or Americas Software—KYC Transactions Trend Monitoring is a Windows-based software that allows you to effectively manage suspicious account activity as required by the regulating authorities in the area of BSA/Know Your Customer and Transaction Trend Monitoring of Suspicious Activity.

ASSIST provides daily, weekly, and monthly reports of suspicious account activity based on irregular transaction volume and amounts.

ASSIST gives you the ability to create personalized client profiles based on transactional activity. The system automatically develops unique account profiles based on historical data.

ASSIST analyzes transactional activity to determine suspicious trends by account, branch, officer, dates, and types of transactions and/or country.

ASSIST maintains user-defined comment histories of client activity changes.

ASSIST maintains a history of all activity and reports performed for internal and external auditors.

ASSIST interfaces with formatted text files whether from a mainframe system or other PC driven systems.

With the advent of the "Know Your Customer" rules and banks being forced to spy on their customers and report them to the government, the last vestiges of financial privacy (and freedom) will quickly disappear. No one will trust their bankers or bank tellers, and bankers and bank tellers will not trust their customers. Would Hitler, Lenin, Stalin, Mao, or Castro have profited from having such a system? Would Bill Clinton utilize such a system—especially against those who are politically incorrect? What do you think? [*Note:* Due to massive public outcry against these new FDIC/bank spying rules, the U.S. Senate voted 88–0 on March 5, 1999, to postpone implementation of same until they can be modified. They will come back, however, in a more innocuous but still deadly form.]

Suspicious Transactions Can Result in Confiscation or Imprisonment
Mark Nestmann wrote in his June 1998 *ACCESS* newsletter:

The U.S. "Bank Secrecy Act" and similar legislation in most other industrialized nations and many offshore asset havens require banks and other financial institutions to report "suspicious activities" to a central authority. In many countries, insurance companies, securities brokers, gold dealers, casinos, and even attorneys must also spy on their clients, or risk imprisonment.

These laws impose Draconian penalties on financial institutions for not complying with Suspicious Activity Reporting (SAR) requirements. And funds "involved in" any suspect transaction may be frozen before trial or indictment. In some countries (particularly the U.S.), you must prove that the funds are not the proceeds of criminal activity to get them back. (Students of logic realize that proving a negative—in this case, that the funds have not somehow been tainted by illegal activity—is virtually impossible.) In some cases, a person convicted of the "crime" of engaging in suspicious transactions can even be imprisoned.

These initiatives, justified as always by the war on crime (and freedom), reflect a shift from the government's zealous protection of privacy to its aggressive, proactive intervention in all financial transactions. And they turn virtually every person who does business with the public into an involuntary informant.

In so doing, these initiatives breach the fundamental rule of law that every accused person is presumed innocent of a crime until proven guilty. They also violate human rights treaties such as the Universal Declaration of Human Rights that provide the same protections. (Governments get away with this chicanery by passing laws stipulating that you need not be charged with a crime to be deprived of your property.)

Banks Must Report Suspected Violations of "Any Law or Regulation"

The earliest Suspicious Activity Reporting (SAR) requirements came into effect in 1988 in the U.S. These requirements, constantly expanded, now require banks and other financial institutions to notify the Treasury Department's intelligence unit, FinCEN, and complete Form 90-22-47, "Suspicious Activity Report," whenever a customer engaged in one or more suspicious transactions that in aggregate exceed $5,000. The regulations read in part: "Every bank shall file with the Treasury Department . . . FinCEN . . . a report of any suspicious transaction relevant to a possible violation of law or regulation." **Any law. Any regulation.** And the penalties for banks not acting as informants are severe: fines as high as $25,000 a day for each offense. Individual employees, officers, or directors may face criminal prosecution even when all statutory requirements appear to be met.

You Are a Citizen—You Are a Suspect

How do banks identify suspicious transactions? Increasingly, by using "neural networking" software that identifies transactions that are not "reasonable" given your past account history. In other words, your bank's computers may be continuously trolling through your accounts, examining them for suspicious activity.

Not all banks are yet equipped with neural networking software. But even without it, banks have plenty of guidance to help identify suspicious customers.

Guidance—but not concrete guidelines. That's because the suspicious activities to which banks are instructed to be alert for are not themselves illegal. The Treasury asks banks to report to FinCEN persons who fit any of dozens of seemingly innocuous customer profiles; e.g., changing large bills to small bills, or vice-versa. Or engaging in transactions having "no business purpose." In other words, trying to protect their privacy. Indeed, one seventeen-year career IRS agent recently testified under oath that concern for reestablishing privacy in financial transactions was all the "proof" he needed to know that a person is engaged in criminal activity. Other suspicious activities, according to guidelines distributed by the U.K.'s Joint Money Laundering Steering Group (themselves adapted from U.S. Treasury Department guidelines) include:

- Not having sufficient identification.
- Presenting a letter of introduction from a bank in a "known money laundering center" (in practice, any major country).
- Paying down a delinquent loan all at once.

- Purchasing or selling unregistered securities made payable to the bearer.
- Changing currency from small to large denominations.
- Making deposits in currency, then having the money wired somewhere else.
- Ordering internal transfers between accounts, followed by large outlays.
- Engaging in transactions backed by secured loans.
- Making a transaction without counting the currency first.

Some of these suspicious activities could implicate anyone. No one wants to be deeply in debt, but paying off a loan may now mark you as a money launderer. And if you want to build up your credit with a secured loan (where you must deposit collateral in an account first), that action now brands you as a criminal.

George Orwell Would Be Impressed

Why don't national anti-laundering authorities simply issue concrete regulations on the types of transactions for which banks must be alert? According to *Communications Week* columnist Bill Frezza:

> The problem with making regulations precise is that what software algorithms can define, other algorithms can evade. Instead, regulation by "raised eyebrow" is becoming the norm. Federal bank examiners have been given significant latitude to invoke Draconian penalties against uncooperative banks. Because bank officers have few due process protections under this regime, it is no surprise that most of them have become sniveling toadies.
>
> The objective is to insure the banks "voluntarily" introduce even more aggressive, unpredictable, and intrusive monitoring than the government would ever dare mandate. **And to make sure nothing slips through the cracks, human surveillance will be supplemented with artificial intelligence agents that can perform pattern analysis on the aggregate flow of electronic transactions, flagging anything remotely suspicious. George Orwell would be impressed.**

Telephone Tapping in the U.S. and Abroad

It has been known for a long time that government agencies such as the FBI, CIA, NSA, etc. regularly tap phone calls—both domestic and international. The NSA eavesdrops and/or records most international phone calls to and from America, with over a hundred key words which trigger their recorders. For several years FBI director Louis Freeh and Janet Reno have been pushing for broad authority to tap most phones, faxes, and telexes in America. Though the "official" numbers show only 1,186 wiretaps (state and federal) in 1997, the real number (including illegal wiretaps by government agents) is far higher. For some time the FBI has been seeking the authority to track the location of cell phones (i.e., to know the precise location of cellular phone users) without having to get a court order.

It has long been known that cell phones are not private, that even amateurs with a scanning device can listen in on a cell phone conversation. But few users realize that a cell phone, when turned on, can be used as a homing or tracking device. On October 23, 1998, the Federal Communications Commission ruled that cell phone companies must make technical changes **so that the FBI and other law enforcement agencies can use cell phones like locator beacons.** As always, the excuse is to give the government better tools to track terrorists and drug dealers among America's 66 million cell phone users. Constitutional scholars believe that this unlimited access to track the location of 66 million U.S. cell phone users is a violation of the Fourth Amendment's protections against illegal searches. It is certainly one more tool in the surveillance arsenal of Big Brother.

But, there is one partial solution to the problem—simply leave your cell phone turned off except when making outgoing calls. Privacy experts believe that Americans who desire privacy will also have to learn as Europeans and people in communist countries have long known—never say anything of a highly private, sensitive, or controversial nature over the phone—not even in jest. Big Brother may be listening. In Europe, sensitive phone calls are often made from pay phones—although they may not always be private either. [*Note:* For a better sense of what it is like to live in a Big Brother/surveillance society, talk to someone who lived behind the former Iron Curtain, in Red China, or Cuba. Their experiences could be a preview of coming attractions for Americans.]

The Global Surveillance Network

Mark Nestmann, editor of *Access: The International Guide to Asset Protection and Privacy*, has written regarding international electronic surveillance: "With the touch of a button, governments can: track 'suspicious' transactions in bank accounts as they occur, worldwide; monitor telephone conversations; freeze international financial accounts."

Yes, you are being watched. Governments worldwide now monitor offshore financial transactions via sophisticated computer networks. International agreements require governments to freeze accounts on the mere suspicion of their association with crime. International "Deposit Tracing Systems," "Mutual Legal Assistance Treaties," and "Financial Intelligence Units" are just part of this complex and growing worldwide network of technology and law. To protect your privacy and wealth, you must now deal with global surveillance.

Big Brother Is Watching You

If you live or do business in the United States, Canada, the United Kingdom, Australia, or New Zealand, or any of their dependent territories or associated states, **your phone calls are automatically screened by intelligence agency supercomputers for words that might indicate clandestine financial activity.** Do you call your Swiss banker from the United States with investment instructions? Or your mutual fund manager in the Isle of Man from the United Kingdom? If you believe these conversations are "private"—hidden from government scrutiny—you're only fooling yourself. Another example: U.S. and U.K. banks must spy on their customers, or risk losing their licenses. This includes banks in most U.K. dependent territory tax havens such as Bermuda and the British Virgin Islands.

Echelon

According to Nicky Hager's book *Secret Power,* the 1947 U.K.–U.S.A. intelligence-sharing agreement was implemented in a global surveillance network called ECHELON. Within the NSA and other national intelligence agencies, a keyword analysis program called DICTIONARY has for decades been used to monitor global telephone traffic, and more recently, fax traffic:

> Keywords include all the names, localities, subjects, and so on, that might be mentioned. Every word of every message intercepted at each station gets automatically searched whether or not a specific telephone number or e-mail address is on the list. The keywords include such things as the names of people, ships, organizations, country names, and subject names. They also include the known telex and fax numbers and Internet addresses of any individuals, businesses, organizations, and government offices that are targets. . . .
>
> The best set of keywords for each subject category is worked out over time, in part by experimentation. The staff sometimes try a particular set of keywords for a period of time and, if they find they are getting too much "junk," they can change some words to get a different selection of traffic.
>
> The Dictionary Manager administers the sets of keywords in the Dictionary computers, adding, amending, and deleting as required. This is the person who adds the new keyword for the watch list, deletes a keyword from another because it is not triggering interesting messages, or adds a "but not ····" to a category because it has been receiving too many irrelevant messages.
>
> The computers used in ECHELON, according to Hager, can monitor conversations in hundreds of languages and can adjust for different tones and accents. **Calls containing keywords are identified, recorded, and routed to the appropriate intelligence analyst for further examination.**

Details of the ECHELON operation are classified, but its existence and the accuracy of Hager's account have been confirmed by the former prime minister of New Zealand, who wrote the preface for *Secret Power.*

Could these operations be extended to Internet traffic? Strassman and Marlow imply that it already has. Keyword searches on Internet search engines may be some of the most fertile fishing ground for NSA Internet monitors.

[*Note:* Mark Nestmann's excellent newsletter, *ACCESS,* should be subscribed to by those with a strong interest in privacy (P.O. Box 2697, London WIA 3TR, England, U.K.—Phone: (44) 171 447-4055; one year—$195).]

German Surveillance for the First Time Since the Nazi Era

On February 6, 1998, the Bundesrat, the upper chamber of the German legislature, gave final approval to a law that will allow police to bug private homes and offices in Germany for the first time since the days of Hitler (1933–45). **Proponents argued that the measures are similar to those already in effect in America.**

Nazi-Style Searches, Seizures, and Forfeitures

Each year in America, local, state and federal law enforcement officials seize several billion dollars in assets from about 250,000 Americans (about 5,000 per week)—including cash, homes, cars, boats, planes, property, businesses, jewelry, etc. (See Section D of *USA Today* each Wednesday for a list of 600 to 700 such forfeitures.) Less than ten percent of those seizures are drug related. Most are taken from honest, law-abiding citizens who have run afoul of one or more of the hundreds of thousands of laws, rules, and regulations on the books—most of which they have never heard of.

Seizure and forfeiture of cash is probably the largest category of government takings. **Anyone with a substantial amount of cash on his person (i.e., over $1,000) is now considered to be a money launderer, drug dealer, or other form of criminal.** Most of the "victims" are never charged with a crime or ever have their day in court. A high percentage of these seizures and forfeitures are simply legalized theft by government officials, judges, etc., whose departments or agencies get a share of the proceeds.

Chapter 4

The War on Cash:
Toward a Cashless Society

The socialist bureaucrats running America and most of the western world today hate privacy and they hate cash. Anyone who is a staunch advocate of privacy, or uses much cash, is considered by these government bureaucrats and law enforcement officials to be a criminal. If they are going to install a socialist America and New World Order (*a la* George Orwell's *1984*) they must be able to track, monitor, and control every aspect of a person's life. Cash is trackless and difficult to trace, so it must be eliminated. Hence, the goal is to ultimately do away with currency and to force every American into the computerized credit/debit/smartcard and banking system (into a cashless electronic funds system).

Present U.S. government attitudes toward cash and people who use it are reminiscent of Nazi Germany. Police agencies nationwide consider anyone carrying a large quantity of cash to be involved in criminal activity unless they can prove otherwise. For example, an Iowa man stopped for a traffic ticket pulled his driver's license out of his wallet, which also contained $7,000 in cash. He was on his way to a sale that required cash—much like the government's own auctions of seized property. The policeman confiscated the cash because he didn't think that a man dressed in overalls should be carrying that much cash.

A New Jersey resident reported driving down the New Jersey Turnpike in an eighteen-foot Hertz rental truck. He stopped at the last toll booth at the end of the turnpike near Wilmington, Delaware, and paid the toll with a $50 bill—the only cash he had on him. The attendant told him to wait a minute and then went to the front of the truck and wrote down the license plate number, a description of the man (who was driving) and his son (a passenger). While the driver asked about this, the attendant stapled the $50 bill to the government form and told him that this was the procedure for anyone paying with a $50 or $100 bill.

In Florida, the *Orlando Sentinel* carried a series entitled "Highway Robbery on I-95," which described how police seize your cash for even minor traffic violations on the basis that the cash is "probably proceeds of drug transactions." At airports, ticket agents and security personnel are alert to anyone carrying large quantities of cash. Why? Because if their tipoff leads to a seizure, they get a finder's fee of ten to twenty-five percent. In a seizure described on "60 Minutes," a DEA agent testified in court that the person he seized cash from was carrying $100s, $50s, $20s, and $10s, "which were all widely used in the drug trade." Of course, this only leaves $1s and $5s for everyone else.

Drug residue on your cash provides "probable cause" for its seizure. Tens of thousands of cash seizures are made each year because dogs allegedly identified the cash as containing drug residue. And yet, according to the DEA's own lab studies, it is the government itself (i.e., the Federal Reserve) that contaminated most cash in its currency sorting operations. Rollers on the Fed's cash sorting machines are contaminated with cocaine residue (twenty to one hundred times higher than those found on the average bill). Various studies dating back to 1985 show that anywhere between eighty percent and ninety-seven percent of cash circulating has drug residue on it.

What happens to the seized cash? It's deposited into a government bank account to be recirculated. No effort is made to take it out of circulation, according to affidavits from twenty-one agencies that participate in cash seizures. If you want your cash back, you must go to court to prove that the funds were earned legitimately. If you win, the government always appeals under the strategy that they will litigate until you run out of money. So, does this make carrying cash illegal? In effect it does! At the very least, it is becoming very politically incorrect to regularly use cash in transactions.

Even the Ultra-liberal ACLU Is Worried About Cash Confiscation

Ira Glassen, executive director of the very liberal American Civil Liberties Union, ran the following ad in the *New York Times* (12/11/98):

Let me ask you something. . . . Did you know there's a three out of four chance that the money you're carrying could be legally confiscated?

Why? Because seventy-five percent of American money is contaminated with cocaine. What's more astonishing is that the courts have ruled that cocaine residue is enough to warrant the forfeiture of your cash! In 1984 Congress gave police the right to keep and spend any "drug related assets" they seize. Police have since taken cars, homes, restaurants, and cash in epidemic proportions. And they can use these assets for anything from patrol cars to parties. Right now there is $2.7 billion in the federal government's "Asset Forfeiture Fund." And local police departments have filled their own coffers as well.

Most of the victims of forfeiture aren't criminals. Like the 75-year-old grandmother who lost her home because her drug-dealing son had once lived there. Or the landscaper whose $9,000 was seized at the airport because "only drug dealers carry that much cash." These people were never arrested or even charged with a crime. And they weren't entitled to a fair hearing, either.

It could happen to you. One leading historian has called this nothing less than a government "license to steal." The war on drugs has become a war on the Constitution. What kind of country rewards its police for shaking down its own citizens? Think about it.

A letter from a woman in New Mexico (one of dozens of such letters this writer receives each year) describes seizure/forfeiture activity in that state:

I have been watching our local situation for more than twenty-five years. I am not now nor have I ever been a drug user. I would not be if it were legalized tomorrow. But I am seeing more and more that the war on drugs is an excuse to roust people, steal their property, and profit from the forfeitures and seizures.

Our local sheriff's department, city police, border patrol, and New Mexico state police work in combined units and split the profits with the court system. Those who have their property seized are then put in the position of trying to retain an attorney (who are all "officers of the court") with no assets. If they get representation at all, it is usually from a court-appointed public defender. It has been my experience that public defenders are usually newly certified lawyers or those who cannot make it in private practice, and are unable to represent the defendants in any meaningful way. It is a fact that eighty-five percent of those who have their property seized are never even charged with a crime!

The Drug Currency Forfeitures Act

The Financial Privacy Report (P.O. Box 1277, Burnsville, MN 55337) recently described a new cash forfeiture initiative in Congress:

> If a bill now before the Senate Judiciary Committee becomes law, carrying too much money will soon be a crime. The law would allow police to seize cash from anyone in a "drug transit area" who's carrying $10,000 or more. A drug transit area is defined as any airport, highway, or port of entry to the United States.
>
> The police could simply take your money—and keep it—legally. You would have to prove that you're innocent before you could get it back. They would need no evidence of any wrong-doing. They would not have to get a warrant or show probable cause. The mere existence of a large amount of concealed money is sufficient rationale for them to seize it.
>
> This bizarre law is called the Drug Currency Forfeitures Act. It is a direct, full frontal assault on financial privacy. While police have been seizing large amounts of cash from business travelers and tourists for years, sometimes they would lose in court when the judge would rule that the seizure was improper.
>
> If this law passes, they will be able to seize your money—and keep it—and you would have to prove that you are not a drug dealer to get it back. How do you prove that you're not a drug dealer? Why should you have to? Isn't everyone in this country innocent until proven guilty? And what business is it of theirs how much cash you're carrying, anyway?

And why should they stop at $10,000 in cash? Why not $5,000? Or $1,000? Or $100 for that matter? If the existence of cash is a crime, then why should it matter how much you have?

One subsection of the law says that you are presumed to be guilty if you conceal the cash "in a highly unusual manner." So, if you're carrying $10,000 cash—and it's in a money belt to prevent you from being robbed—that's sufficient to justify a police seizure.

The socialists who run America, from Clinton and Gore on down, hate cash—which represents financial privacy and freedom. They want to drive all Americans into the computerized banking or credit/debit/smart-card system where all transactions can be monitored, recorded, and scrutinized. It's called people-control through financial control.

And in the future it is possible that Clinton or Gore will ration cash or bottle it up in the banking system—pushing us overnight into a near-cashless, electronic funds transfer system. Hitler would have loved it. Pity the man, that he didn't have computers and our high-tech surveillance systems.

Toward Electronic Money

Illustrative of the government attitude toward cash was the November 1992 article by David Warwick in *The Futurist* magazine entitled "The Cash Free Society." The article claimed that "cash has been the root of much of the social and economic evil. . . . Ridding society of its cash could make most criminal activity disappear, from purse snatching to drug trafficking. Electronic money systems promise to lead the way to a cash-free, crime-free society."

The article admitted that there are $300 billion in legitimate cash transactions in America each year, but argued that the 40 million Americans who primarily use cash must adjust. Warwick recommended the instituting of a federal debit card system for all transactions, down to buying gum or a newspaper, paying for a parking meter or toll phone call, or even leaving a tip. Electronic transfers would constitute legal tender. There would be no such thing as a withdrawal—only a transfer. A notable trial run is the government use of debit cards for food stamps and the paying of Marines at Paris Island via debit cards.

If one questions a government official or law enforcement officer about their suspicion of cash or their heavy-handed seizure techniques, they will simply argue that cash is the "mother's milk" of drug traffickers and money launderers and, therefore, "if we wish to stop drugs, we must make a small sacrifice, and stop cash." But we're not talking about a small sacrifice here. We are talking about the Constitution and Bill of Rights being dismantled one piece at a time. The incredible range of searches, seizures, and violations of due process that happen daily in America at present would make our Founding Fathers turn over in their graves.

The socialists and globalists hate cash because when you use cash, it is hard to track a person, to monitor their lifestyle and spending habits, for tax purposes, etc. Hence, the global socialists want to push us all into the computerized credit or debit card system or banking system where all of our financial lives can be completely monitored, recorded, and ultimately controlled. The ultimate goal of the global socialists is the total abolition of cash and all financial privacy on a global basis. Hence, the passage of a series of laws, rules, and regulations over the past decade or so to discourage and even criminalize the use of cash and concept of financial privacy.

Starting with the Bank Secrecy Act of 1986 and vastly expanding the definition of money laundering, structuring, and other crimes associated with non-reporting of cash or cash transaction, the government has begun to build a giant financial surveillance infrastructure over the past decade.

The push for computerized smartcards and a computerized national ID card is part of this major thrust toward a cashless society. The global socialists hope and plan to have this financial transaction-monitoring, people-controlling, cashless society in place and functioning within three to five years or less. Almost all the technology for such a system is now a reality. It is also very possible that the government will ration cash or bank withdrawals of cash from the banking system in the midst of a banking crisis.

As another major step in this direction, Microsoft and other companies have developed an electronic cash smartcard. Different from a debit card, the ECC does not take money out of your bank account. It has a certain amount of cash digitally encoded in a computer chip, and when it is fed into a machine reader at a retail outlet, the price of your purchase is deducted from the card itself. A similar card, the Mondex "electronic purse" card was first tested in Britain. MasterCard and Bank of America developed the technology and tested it in Australia and at the 1996 Olympic Games in Atlanta. They have been widely used for long distance phone calls.

The Establishment press is also conducting a media blitz to convince Americans that "cash is trash," is inconvenient, and should be replaced with electronic money. The *New York Times* carried an article entitled "An End to the 'Nightmare' of Cash," in which it said:

> Banks, credit card companies and even the governments of some countries are racing to introduce "electronic purses," wallet-sized cards embedded with rechargeable microchips that store sums of money for people to use instead of cash for everything from buying fast food to paying highway tolls or for phone calls.

Money Laundering Laws

In the former Soviet Union, if the government wanted to apprehend and imprison someone who had committed no crime, they charged him with the catch-all crime of "hooliganism." In America, the catch-all crime used against organized crime figures or other Americans has for years been RICO statutes or simply "conspiracy" [*Note:* presently being used against pro-life activists.] But in recent years the government has created a new catch-all crime, punishable by imprisonment, confiscation of property, heavy fines, or all three. It is called "money laundering."

Most Americans suppose money laundering refers primarily to the hidden, laundered movement of cash profits from drug deals. Wrong! It refers today to almost any "financial crime," broken financial regulation, use of cash, avoidance of government cash reporting laws, unreported foreign bank accounts, unreported transfer of funds, or virtually anything the government bureaucrats want it to mean. The definition is vague and ever-expanding.

Government agents are greatly accelerating money laundering cases in situations where there is obviously no criminal intent, and certainly no involvement whatsoever with drugs or drug money. Remember, the government considers money laundering to be any effort you make to disguise your assets or avoid completing a federal currency transaction or border crossing form.

If a tax case can be called money laundering, it is no longer civil, but criminal, with large potential criminal sentences and fines. The government's growing and expanding money laundering laws are becoming the basis for a total financial dictatorship in America—all under the guise of fighting the drug war. The first thing the Nazis did in the 1930s to establish control over their population was to establish money crimes that were punishable by forfeiture and imprisonment. Sixty-five years later, the same thing is happening here. The war on drugs is a classic government power grab.

Any non-reporting of cash transactions over $10,000 on a form 8300 (that now includes cashiers checks, money orders of any kind, and travelers checks) by a banker, stock broker, car dealer, jeweler, coin dealer, or any business accepting cash is considered a money laundering violation and can result in heavy fines, and even imprisonment. Personal checks, money market fund checks, and bank wires are not presently reportable on form 8300s. Note that murder, rape, and armed robbery now result, in many cases, in smaller and less frequent jail terms or fines than the new federal crime of money laundering. In fact, the penalties for money laundering can be ten times more severe than the same crime prosecuted as tax evasion.

Structuring Laws

"Structuring" is defined by the IRS as any effort to avoid reporting cash or other monetary transactions over $10,000 by breaking them down into smaller "related" transactions over any twelve-month period (defined by USC 31, Sec. 5322-5324—Money Laundering Control Act of 1986, as amended). A structuring violation carries with it a criminal penalty with a mandatory prison term, heavy fines, and confiscation of structured funds and money "connected" to them. (A civil penalty of up to a $250,000 fine with confiscation of structured funds also exists.) Monetary instruments included in structuring are cash, cashiers checks, money orders, and travelers checks.

Structuring is now defined as money laundering, and is a criminal offense. You can now go to jail for dealing in cash to protect your financial privacy if the IRS thinks you're trying to hide or structure your transactions or monetary instruments. Furthermore, it's against the law for a bank or merchant to tell you that you might be violating the law. This can get him prosecuted as part of your structuring "conspiracy." If they think your behavior is suspicious, they may fill out a form on you without your knowledge and file it with the IRS, who will promptly audit you or begin a criminal investigation.

A few examples of structuring violations include a series of "related" withdrawals or deposits over $10,000 (i.e., several in any twelve-month period) in monetary instruments without filing a cash reporting report (CTR) to the government, or making payments of $10,000 or more in monetary instruments on an installment loan without filing a CTR. One example this writer is familiar with is a high school principal who lived in the South, with no criminal record, no history of drug usage or dealing, or even a speeding record—he simply believed in privacy. He purchased $62,000 worth of Krugerands from a coin dealer and several days later mailed nine separate cashiers checks to the dealer, of sizes varying between $6,000 and $9,000.

He had accumulated $62,000 in cash (after taxes) over a fifteen- or twenty-year period, believing that privacy and Amendment IV of the U.S. Constitution were still in effect. He was wrong—they are not! The man went to nine separate banks to buy cashiers checks—three of those banks (thirty-three percent) turned him in to the IRS, the man was indicted on sixteen counts of criminal violation of Title 31 of the Bank Secrecy Act of 1986; was found guilty; fined $200,000; had his $62,000 forfeited to the IRS; and was sentenced to five years in the federal penitentiary—all for the new federal money laundering crime of buying nine cashiers checks with his own cash. That is the structuring law in action and that sounds more like Nazi Germany than the America most of us grew up in.

If the government's case is shakier (or less clear cut) than the principal's case (which, unfortunately, was a classic textbook Title 31 violation), their *modus operandi* will be to drop the criminal charges if you allow your assets to be seized without going to trial and/or pay a stiff fine. This is now very common in drug kingpin cases. The drug dealer goes free—the police keep his assets. Structuring is a strict liability statute. That means that even if there is no criminal intent, even if you earned the money legitimately, unless you can prove that the transactions were unrelated, the government keeps your assets.

If the government decides to prosecute you criminally, in addition to the mandatory prison sentence and fine, they can legally confiscate not just the money involved in the transaction, but any assets associated with the structured funds. For example, if you structure a withdrawal of $10,000 in cash (over any twelve-month period) from a $1 million bank account, the government can seize the entire $1 million. The seizure can proceed even without a criminal conviction or indictment—just like the forfeiture laws.

The average person might say, "Well, the government would never come after anyone who was totally innocent." But that's not true—that misses the point! The IRS admits that eighty-five percent of the people accused of structuring committed no other crime than seeking to protect their privacy. The courts have upheld numerous criminal structuring convictions for violations that concealed no criminal activity. If the government wins the conviction, the judge must sentence the "criminal" to a mandatory prison sentence.

This gives the lie to the argument that money laundering/structuring laws are enforced to get drug dealers and fight the war on drugs. The fact is that it is far easier to convict an honest, law-abiding citizen and confiscate his property than to go after a real drug dealer who has a battery of high priced lawyers and accountant, and who might even shoot back. Will these money laundering and structuring laws eventually be used selectively against politically incorrect Christians, conservatives, and traditionalists as they were in Nazi Germany? What do you think?

Chapter 5

Toward a National ID Card and
Implantable Biochip

> And he causeth all, both small and great, rich and poor, free and bond, to receive a mark in their right hand, or in their foreheads: And that no man might buy or sell, save he that had the mark, or the name of the beast, or the number of his name. Here is wisdom. Let him that hath understanding count the number of the beast: for it is the number of a man; and his number is Six hundred threescore and six.
>
> **— Revelation 13:16–18**

America today is rapidly becoming a total surveillance society, and privacy as we have known it since the founding of our country is now being abolished. Today there is virtually no financial privacy in the U.S. The government, credit bureaus, and insurance companies maintain financial dossiers on all Americans. Investigators can identify and locate a citizen's assets at the touch of a button. The more assets you possess, the greater the risk of government surveillance, lawsuits, or seizures. However, even greater surveillance measures are in store as the national ID card emerges.

American citizens who have little knowledge of history or have never been overseas cannot fully imagine the chilling implications of a mandatory national ID card. In countries where the national ID card is a way of life, presenting the government-approved card (or papers) is required for even the most routine transactions and matters. Police and military personnel can stop any citizen at will and demand that the "comrade" produce his or her "papers." Those who protest this invasion of privacy are treated as criminals, and woe to the person who doesn't have an ID.

Consider the nations where the national ID has been issued—Nazi Germany, the former Iron Curtain countries under Soviet rule, the former Soviet Union, Castro's Cuba, and communist China to name a few. This documentation (i.e., ID) has been an important tool used by tyrants for people-control.

As ominous as the prospect of a Nazi-style national ID is, today's computer and microchip technology can make a nineties version of the card into the ultimate people-controlling tool. The national IDs of the Nazi and Soviet eras were limited to basic information—name, address, workplace, party membership, and one or two other facts. Compare that to the kind of dossier that can be placed on a smartcard today. A high-tech national ID can contain your life history—with plenty of room left over for other information. With one swipe of the magnetic strip of the card, the police or other government officials could obtain your medical records, credit and job history, past residences, and just about anything else that might be sitting on a computer disk somewhere.

What would prevent Big Brother from creating a special file for politically incorrect people who had "dangerous" tendencies? How would you like to be listed as a constitutionalist, Christian, home schooler, all-around activist, conservative, food hoarder, non-conformist, pro-lifer, gun owner, or militia sympathizer, in the database of a power-hungry police state?

Does the above scenario sound like science fiction or an episode from "Twilight Zone"? Then you haven't been following the well–orchestrated bipartisan campaign for a national ID card. The Administration and their fellow national ID card boosters have skillfully used the Marxist Hegelian dialectic (thesis plus antithesis equals synthesis) to create a pro-ID climate. Under the Hegelian dialectic, a phony problem calls for a phony solution that advances the goals of the people–controllers and globalists. Note how the "crisis of terrorism" in 1996 became the excuse for the photo ID requirement for all air travelers in America—a forerunner of the national identity card.

The All-Purpose National ID (Smartcard)
The government has proposed four separate ID cards, but all are likely

to be ultimately merged into one all-purpose card: a) the national drivers license ID card (described in chapter three above) b) the INS ID card; c) the national health care card; and d) the U.S. Postal Service all–purpose card. (Good salesmen always give their target several choices—all of which the salesman can live with—and the administration is doing the same.)

The INS (Immigration and Naturalization Service) National ID Card

The U.S. Commission on Immigration Reform, the Clinton INS, and liberal politicians are pushing hard for a single, tamper-resistant INS card for all Americans (including your Social Security number, photo, fingerprint, and bar code) to verify employment eligibility. This card would be linked to a nationwide government database and would allegedly solve the problem of illegal aliens getting jobs.

Marc Rotenberg, director of the Electronic Privacy Information Center, said in *USA Today* (7/14/94) that "it will become a way to monitor people, like an internal passport." This Orwellian nightmare will, like the government's privacy/bank/cash reporting laws, allow the government to monitor 275 million Americans who are not illegal aliens, just as they monitor the cash transactions of 275 million Americans who are not drug dealers. Lucas Guttentage, of the ACLU (with whom this writer seldom agrees) said in the same *USA Today* article, "It won't work, it will cost billions, it won't solve the problems, and it will cause new forms of discrimination."

Steve Moore of the Cato Institute points out that just as the government has abused the once private Social Security number and now uses it as a national ID number which ties together dozens of U.S. databases on each U.S. citizen, so it will abuse this card. Moore observed: "Look at history and see the abuses—they used Social Security numbers to round up and incarcerate the Japanese-Americans during World War II." (And look how government has violated its promises and abused gun owners in New York and California who were naive enough to register their guns. In New York City they have confiscated many of those guns, and in California the 43,000 who registered sixty different firearms were computerized and are now closely monitored by numerous local, state and federal agencies.)

The National Health Care Card

One of the major side benefits for the Clinton Administration, of their socialized medicine program (in addition to giving the socialists control over eighteen to nineteen percent of the entire U.S. economy and over the health of every American) would have been forcing a national ID card down the throats of every American. During his drive for national health care, Bill Clinton was pictured holding up a card and pronouncing that everyone would have one from cradle to grave. Though their attempted slam dunk of the national health (socialized medicine) program did not pass the first time around, it has come back with a vengeance in Clinton's second term, being passed a piece at a time.

The high-tech national health care ID card is designed to keep permanent, accessible records of all aspects of your health care, including the details of every doctor visit, every drug store prescription, and every hospital treatment. The hype for this ID is that the card could be used to crack down on welfare fraud, trace deadbeat dads who refuse to pay child support, supplement our Social Security cards, our draft card, maybe our passports, and even to register voters and control voting fraud. The uses will be limited, not by technology (which is awesome and ever-expanding) but only by the imagination of government officials and their respect for our privacy.

To make this tracking system work, every one of us must have a number that can be fed into the national computer banks. That is why the National Health Board, which would have been set up by Mrs. Clinton's program, would enforce unique identification numbers for each American (probably an eighteen-digit number). This writer travels a lot, and has recently encountered a number of hotels and car rental companies that will not allow you to register or rent a car without a national credit or debit card and a photo ID (i.e., cash is not acceptable). Under the proposed Clinton health care program, it is likely that if you don't use the ID card, by law, you will not be allowed to receive medical service in America. "No one could buy or sell unless he had the mark."

The Postal Service All-Purpose "U.S. Card"

This general purpose smartcard could emerge as America's new national ID card—incorporating all the functions of the INS card, the health care card, the national drivers license ID, and much more. The Clinton Administration has been strategizing how they can create and introduce this smartcard (which will interact with any and all government agencies) to all Americans.

At a Card Tech/Secure Tech Conference several years ago, the Postal Service (which was directed by the Department of Defense several years earlier to develop a people-monitoring electronic card system) unveiled its general purpose U.S. Card. The U.S. Card would be designed to use either smartcards (plastic cards with an imbedded microprocessor carrying a unique number that can be read by an electromagnetic scanner and linked to computerized records stored on a network), or PCMCIA cards which can contain megabytes of information.

Postal Service representative Chuck Chamberlain outlined how an individual's U.S. Card would be automatically connected with the Department of Health and Human Services, the U.S. Treasury, the IRS, the Veterans Administration, and all other government agencies (i.e., ATF, FBI, CIA, OSHA, EPA, FDA, etc.), the banking system, and a central database of digital signatures for use in authenticating electronic mail and transactions.

The Postal Service has acknowledged that it is prepared to put more than 100 million of the cards in citizens' pockets within months of administration approval. This means that this project for the computerized control of all Americans is not only on the fast track, but is much further advanced than most people would suppose. And it is not being done with congressional approval, but rather through a series of presidential Executive Orders.

There will ultimately be one U.S. Card for every member of your family. In the not-too-distant future, you may find harmless looking smartcards in the mail in an official envelope. Without the U.S. Card (or whatever the smartcard is ultimately called) you won't be able to own property, receive government benefits, get medical attention, conduct bank or credit card transaction, travel across state lines or international border, etc. Without it, you can't do anything! Your life will be complete-ly controlled by the device if the Administration adopts the Postal Ser-vice (or some other similar) proposal. Executive Orders have already been drafted to adopt the cards and force them on Americans without congressional approval.

The Clinton Administration hopes to reduce every American to total dependence on this card and near total surveillance. It is a super smart-card—a Tesserea card prototyped by the Defense Department and per-fected by experts in the Postal Service, the Treasury Department, the IRS, and the National Security Agency. (The various U.S. security agen-cies—which believe that they need an enemy to justify their existence in the post-communism/post-Cold War era—have found their new ene-my—the American people! This whole people-control/smartcard project was birthed by the U.S. security agencies, who are simply using the Postal Service, INS, and health care programs as a cover. The Defense Depart-ment has deployed this system among many of its personnel in recent years via its so-called MARC card.

The word *Tesserea* (as in the Tesserea smartcard) has an interesting Latin origin. It means "a piece of mosaic." It is the name given by an-cient Roman conquerors to identify chits they issued to conquered peo-ples and slaves. It was adopted as the code name for the smartcard de-velopment project, apparently by the Defense Messaging Agency. The Tesserea cards developed in that program years ago were the precursors of the all-encompassing mandatory device now being proposed by the Postal Service and other federal agencies.

The U.S. Card is designed to mediate information about you (like a magic key) in every government database that contains information about you. But without your magic key, you will be out in the cold. You won't be able to file tax returns, collect your pension or Social Security, con-duct bank or credit card transactions, or function in your business or personal life. (Now do you see why the government hates cash and pre-cious metals? They make it difficult or impossible to control you—espe-cially your financial life.)

It appears that the government databases are already far more inte-grated and the system far more developed (i.e., to the point of almost instant deployment) than most knowledgeable observers would have supposed. If the Postal Service could mail 100 million of these cards within months it is very late indeed!

William Murray, an information system security consultant to Deloitte and Touche, said in a *Digital Media* article entitled "Ever Feel You're Being Watched? You Will"

> There won't be anything you do in business that won't be collected and analyzed by the government. This national information infrastructure is a better surveillance mechanism than Orwell or the government could have imagined. This (blank, blank) thing is so pervasive and the propensity to connect it is so great that it is unstoppable. . . .
>
> Most of this shift in privacy policy is apparently being done by Executive Order at the initiative of the bureaucracy and without any congressional oversight or concurrence. They are not likely to fail. You know, Orwell said that bureaucrats, simply doing what bureaucrats do, without motive or intent, will use technology to enslave the people.

But, there is motive and intent. It is called people control! It is called a socialist police state! It is called world government!

The MARC Card—Already in Use by the U.S. Military

The prototype for the national ID card is already being used by the U.S. military. The MARC card (Multitechnology Automated Reader Card) is a smartcard now being issued by the Department of Defense (DoD) to U.S. military personnel. This smartcard uses several media: a standard 3-of-9 bar code, magnetic stripe, embossed data, printed information (including a digital photograph), and an Integrated Circuit (IC) computer chip.

The combination of several media on one credit card-sized device gives the MARC its versatility—it can interface with a variety of technologies and systems from rudimentary imprinting machines to computer systems that use IC chips as data carriers. The Department of Defense Information Technology Policy Board initiated the MARC project several years ago to have the ability to instantly track and control all U.S.

military personnel worldwide. It is a prototype for the national ID card to be issued to every member of the U.S. civilian population.

The MARC card and its IC chip will be used by DoD to manage *all* medical information on *all* U.S. military personnel worldwide (i.e., it will store *all* medical information on each card carrier in its IC chip). It will store *all* personal information on each carrier, *all* legal information, *all* family information, and *all* personal data (i.e., educational background, police record, religious background—everything you would expect to be on a highly detailed job resume).

The DoD considers one of the most important aspects of the MARC system to be its ability to continually track the location of each cardholder worldwide, using the IC chip and bar code, and keeping track of the present status of all personnel. The MARC card will replace the traditional meal card, will keep track of all meals eaten, and without it, the carrier cannot get their meals at military bases or installations, or buy food or other goods at base exchanges. Without the card, which carries all the medical data on the carrier, the person cannot get access to military treatment facilities.

The DoD and the civilian project coordinators have been evaluating the MARC card for use in paying personnel (i.e., linking it to an electronic banking system where the military card carrier will never see his paycheck or use cash for anything [i.e., all financial transactions will go through the computerized banking system]). This has been tested at Parris Island and other military facilities in recent years. It has also been evaluated for use in welfare payments, day care, peacetime medical applications, and a host of other civilian applications.

This writer has seen and closely examined one of these MARC cards. It is real, it is high, high-tech, and its implications for people control of the American civilian population in the not-too-distant future are most frightening indeed.

Is the National ID Card the First Step to an Implanted Biochip?

This writer first acquired several computerized biochips and the injector several years ago. The tiny transponders (the size of a grain of rice) are presently being injected into pets, cattle, sheep, goats, and other livestock by veterinarians and ranchers all across America as a means of computerized identification and location of lost or stolen animals. Originally introduced by Infopet, the tiny transponders are now being reduced to about one-sixth the size of a grain of rice (or more the size of a splinter). Several years ago the DoD began to experiment with tiny microchip implants in GI's fillings in lieu of dog tags.

The government's proposed national drivers license, health care card, electronic benefits card (EBT), Social Security card, immigration card, and postal "U.S. Card" are nothing less than disguised **national identity cards** for all Americans! They are in reality devices for tracking and controlling the lives of all citizens. These new citizen ID cards will allow our (and other) governments to maintain computerized, electronically digitized, permanent, and accessible records on every man, woman, and child in America (and eventually, all over the world).

These proposed government cards are a devious new means of further consolidating and computerizing all available information on each of us into a new electronically digitized, centralized government database that will ultimately lead to a complete loss of privacy, and government control of the citizenry. To make this system work, each of us must have a unique ID number that can be fed into various local, national, and international computer data banks. That is why the National Health Board, which would have been set up under Hillary's socialist health care program, would enforce unique identification numbers for all consumers, according to government literature. This is already being done in Canada and some other countries.

The Clinton's national identity card, whether it takes form as a national drivers license, a health card, electronic benefits card, or whatever card, will become so ubiquitous, so necessary, in order to comply with various government regulations, that we will be forced to carry it with us at all times: it will be like always having your billfold or purse, drivers license, and some cash with you at present. That leads to a very serious problem. What if we lose it? What if someone steals it? Will we be able to function without it? Probably not!

But don't fret, the globalists have a solution. You see, there is a new, more advanced, and sophisticated system of identification that cannot be lost or stolen! It will make the ID card obsolete. It's a syringe–implantable ID transponder biochip that goes into your body. A tiny microchip, the size of a splinter, is simply injected under the skin of your right hand. Unlike laser-light bar code marking systems, biochip implants utilize low frequency FM radio waves (125 kHz) that pass through objects. These ID biochips are therefore much more effective than any previous method of verifying one's identity. Such ID implants will eventually replace all existing forms of identification for people.

These amazing, relatively simple biochip radio transceiver implants are battery-free passive devices that will have everyone's unalterable, international eighteen-digit ID number electronically encoded into them. Once they have been injected under our skin, we will have been electronically branded for life! Liken it to a modern, electronic technological tattoo if you will. Of course most of us (especially Christians) will find such a surgically implanted government microchip unacceptable and repugnant, but it may be forced on us nevertheless. In fact, many people will be easily coerced into this new totalitarian system of identification because without accepting it no one will be permitted to buy or sell anything, anywhere in the coming cashless, global economy. (Remember, for over twenty years Americans have not been able to open bank, S&L, stock brokerage, or almost any kind of financial accounts without a Social Security number. This concept is now to be vastly expanded.)

Transponder ID/debit chips may not only replace cash, checks, and credit cards, they may supplant all existing forms of identification. The implants may become our passports, driver's licenses, credit cards, ATM cards, health care cards, Social Security cards, etc. In other words, they may become our universal ID and ATM debit chips all in one. **One World, One Biochip!** AT&T has advertised its new contactless, electronic smartcard as **"One World, One Card."**

Simply pass your right hand over a radio-frequency (RFID) scanner and you will be identified instantly and processed automatically wherever you are. A radio wave will pass through the skin of your hand, activate your ID transponder, and transmit your unique ID number back outside the skin to the scanner. This entire process will take less than two seconds. Computers in the new, digitized, fiber-optical information superhighway infrastructure will do the rest. In the future, all of our buying and selling could be conducted and controlled in this manner. Scan your hand and debit your account.

Tim Willard, executive officer of the World Future Society, a Washington, D.C.-based New Age organization that claims 27,000 members globally (including *Future Shock* author Alvin Toffler), was quoted in 1989 as saying:

> The technology behind such a biochip implant is fairly uncomplicated and with a little refinement, could be used in a variety of human applications. . . . Conceivably, a number could be assigned at birth and follow that person throughout life. Most likely, it would be implanted on the back of the right or left hand so that it would be easy to scan at the store. Then you would simply scan your hand to automatically debit your bank account. . . . The biochip implant could also be used as a universal type of identification card that would replace all credit cards, passports, and that sort of thing. It could also become our medical care ID chip. It could even replace house and car keys someday.

Martin Anderson, a senior fellow at the Hoover Research Institution at Stanford University in Palo Alto, California (and a top advisor in the Reagan Administration), summed it up this way in an April 7, 1993, article in the *San Jose Mercury News,* San Jose, California: "Unless this move to force a national identity card on Americans is stopped quickly, we may live to see the end of privacy in the United States. All of us will be tagged like so many fish!"

In another article by Anderson on October 4, 1993, in the *Washington Times,* he said this about an ID biochip implant in our bodies:

> There is an identification system made by the Hughes Aircraft Company that, unlike your national identity card, you cannot lose. It's the syringe-implantable transponder. According to promotional literature, "it is an ingenious, safe, inexpensive, foolproof, and permanent method of . . . identification, using radio waves." A tiny microchip the size of a grain of rice is simply placed under the skin. It is so designed as to

be injected simultaneously with a vaccination, or alone.

    This tiny microchip transponder is sort of like a technological tattoo, and far more effective than the numbers the Nazis marked indelibly on the arms of concentration camp victims. . . . There is no difference in principle between being forced to carry a microchip in a plastic ID card in your wallet or in a little transponder pellet injected in your arm. The principle that Big Brother has the right to track you is inherent in both. The only thing that differentiates the two techniques is a layer of your skin!

Anderson concluded the article with the following statement: "Once you denigrate the idea of privacy, all kinds of innovative government controls are possible, things that didn't even occur to Aldous Huxley when he wrote his chilling novel *Brave New World.*" Currently, farmers, pet owners, and manufacturers are using radio frequency biochips, or transponders, to track and control their animals and equipment. But one day soon, every human being on earth may also be tracked and controlled in like manner using this technology. In the coming global government we will all have become chattel assets of the Establishment (or perhaps even of the Antichrist).

Conclusion

The national ID card is almost a reality and could be implemented soon by the Administration via Executive Order—making a total end run around the U.S. Congress. The technology is now perfected, the physical capacity to mass-produce hundreds of millions of these ID cards and link them to presently existing government databases now exists, socialist/globalist types are now in almost complete power in America (and many, if not most, other governments around the globe), and with the new millennium now upon us, the Establishment is moving toward a national ID card/people-control system at mach ten speed.

    Could the national ID card be a stepping stone to a computerized biochip transponder as Martin Anderson suggests? This writer certainly doesn't know, but the technology for same now exists and the people-control motives of our leaders seem very clear. This writer knows that the whole concept of a national ID smartcard and implantable biochip seems far out, bizarre, implausible, and like something out of science fiction, except for one thing: Our government is working feverishly to develop and deploy these people-control systems right now!

Chapter 6

Attacking Parental Rights: The Global Socialists Want Your Children

The German schools from the first grade through the universities, were quickly Nazified. . . . When an opponent declares, "I will not come over to your side," I calmly say, *"Your child belongs to us already. . . . What are you? You will pass on. Your descendants, however, stand in the new camp. In a short time they will know nothing else but this new community."*

> — Adolph Hitler, Nov. 6, 1933, as quoted by William Shirer in *The Rise and Fall of the Third Reich*

This new Reich will give its youth to no one but will itself take youth and give to youth its own education and its own upbringing.

> —Adolph Hitler, May 1, 1937

Children belong to the general family, to the state, before belonging to private families.

> —Bertrand Barere, a member of the French Revolutionary Committee on Public Safety during the French Revolution

The communists, the socialists of the French Revolution, the Nazis, and today's socialists knew (know) that if they could gain control of children (and their minds); if they could separate children from the anti-socialist, reactionary, traditionalist religious influence of their parents and families, that they could control the next generation and those to follow it— that they could control the future.

John Dewey, the secular humanist "father" of modern American education, understood the concept. He once said that if the schools could keep the children from 7:30 a.m. to 3:30 p.m., if they could keep the children preoccupied with sports from after school until 6:00 p.m. (or so), if they could keep them busy with homework all evening, that they could keep the parents from having more than thirty minutes to an hour per day with their children, and that *within a generation the schools could break the influence of the parents and their religion on the children.* Has this happened in America via our government/socialist-controlled school system? Indeed it has!

The communists in Russia, China, Cuba, South Africa, etc., have also proven that children can be very useful tools in a communist revolution. In China, Cuba, and Russia, children were taught to spy on their parents and report to school or government officials reactionary, anti-revolutionary, or Christian teachings or tendencies on the part of their parents. Tens of thousands of Chinese parents were turned in to the communist government by their own children, and some were even executed by their children under the watchful eye of the Red officials.

Children were taught by the communists during and after the revolution to rebel against and hate everything their parents stood for—their traditional values, their religion, their discipline, etc. During the South African revolution, black children were taught by the communist (ANC/SACP) cadres to hate their parents, to rebel in every way against their parents and their beliefs and values, to report parents who opposed the revolution and the communists, and even to kill parents. Hundreds (perhaps thousands) of black parents (or other adults) were killed by children ranging from ages seven to fifteen during the South African revolution. Communist cadres would incite the children against the "reactionaries" and the children would execute the parent (or adult) via the infamous "necklace treatment," whereby they would place a gasoline-filled tire around the victim's neck, light it with a match, and dance in glee around the victim while he or she died an excruciating death over twenty to thirty minutes.

The global socialists who wish to establish a world dictatorship over the next five to ten years, which **they** call the New World Order or New Civilization (or the New International Order), know that many adults and parents, who are steeped in the old, "outmoded" nationalist, constitutionalist, traditionalist, religious values **cannot** be re-educated for the new dispensation.

But they believe that if they can break the hold and eliminate the influence of the parents on their children; if they can instill in them secular humanist, non- or anti-religious thinking; if they can weaken them through promiscuous (or hedonist) sexual behavior or drugs; if they can program them to be obedient, passive, citizens (or is it serfs?) in the emerging global neighborhood, that they can control (as Hitler so aptly put it) "the next generation and the future."

Hence, a whole series of initiatives are emanating from the political left across America on a local, state, and federal level; from the government education system (including the leftist National Education Association); from the one-world globalist establishment; and from the United Nations which will eliminate parental rights, traditional freedoms, and religion (or Christianity) as we have known them.

Just as the crisis of terrorism, the environmental crisis, the drug crisis, the money laundering crisis, the firearms crisis and numerous other crises (real, imagined, or manufactured) have been used by governments, the global socialists, and the political left as an excuse to put Draconian, freedom-strangling controls on Americans, so the crisis of child abuse is to be used in the same way.

The political left all over the world are now escalating the drumbeat regarding the global crisis of child abuse in an effort to pass and implement national and international laws emancipating children; restricting parents' rights to raise their children as they see fit; converting the primary responsibility for raising children from parents and family to government; and breaking the parents' influence (especially religious) over their children.

Since 1989 the global socialists have been pushing the United Nations Convention on the Rights of the Child. It has been ratified in 189 countries, has been signed by the Clinton Administration, and will be submitted to the Senate by Clinton for ratification when he thinks he has enough votes. The U.N. convention will utterly destroy all parental rights, control, or influence over their children, making children in America (and all other countries who have signed the U.N. treaty) virtual property of the state—just as is the case in hard-core communist countries such as China, Cuba, North Korea, etc. Under this treaty, traditionalist parents who resist the state's control over their children will be "re-educated" if possible, and if not, they will be jailed, fined, have their children taken from them, or all three.

Since there has been stiff political opposition (from conservatives, traditionalists, and Christians) across America to this U.N. children's treaty, the political left is trying a second approach—to pass the key elements of the treaty on a state-by-state basis in the various state legislatures, and even on a local basis. So they are pushing from the bottom up and from the top down to destroy parents' rights and convert our children to wards of the state.

This chapter will discuss the U.N. treaty's various global/socialist anti-parent initiatives, as the political left presses forward to take over our children. Hillary Clinton, who has written a book on the government control of children (i.e., *It Takes a Village*) has been helping to lead the charge. Protecting children from child abuse will be how the left will package this takeover, and traditionalist, conservative, religious, Christian parents will be the primary targeted child abusers.

Three Ways Socialists Control People and Advance Their Agenda

The global socialists (from the Clintons and Gores, to the communists; from the United Nations to the National Education Association; from the ACLU to the Children's Defense Fund) attempt to control people (and especially politically incorrect Christians) in three ways: 1) through the issuing of licenses or permits; 2) by usurping parents' control of their children; and 3) by regulating employment (i.e., who can work, and where).

The **first** of these people-control techniques is *the issuing of licenses or permits*. The permit signifies that the requirements set by the government have been met and approved of. This legal mechanism can be found in every form of government (i.e., democracy, socialism, dictatorship, communism, fascism, etc.). Therefore, through the issuance of licenses or permits, or the denial thereof, a government (free, democratic, or totalitarian) can control virtually any human activity it chooses.

Religious practices in the former Soviet Union were *not* outlawed—they *were* controlled and precluded through the use of licenses and permits, which were denied to all true believers and issued only to those who followed the party line. Such licenses or permits were the people regulators in many areas of Soviet society, as they are now becoming in many (if not most) areas of American life.

Soon churches, religions, private religious schools, (including home schools), grass roots lobbying, writing of newsletters, radio talk shows, firearms ownership, parents and children, access to national parks or wilderness areas, and a host of other human activities and endeavors are likely to be regulated by the global/socialist people controllers via legal registration, licensing, or permits. Remember, Hitler first registered all the Jews before he arrested them and herded them into concentration camps.

Politically incorrect conservatives, Christians, and traditionalists will thereby be controlled (just as in the former Soviet Union) not at the point of a gun (at least not at first) but through a series of state, federal, and international laws, and court rulings. If the U.N., the Clintons, and the global socialists have their way, all children, parents, guns, and churches will be *registered* in America and *licensing* of guns, parents, and churches may become a reality. All of these are being advocated regularly at globalist/U.N. meetings, such as Habitat II, the U.N. Conference on Population Control, the U.N. Women's Conference, etc. In the November 1996 elections, Colorado was the first state to propose an amendment to the Colorado Constitution to give the state the authority to tax church property. (It did not pass.) If the government can tax and license churches, it will soon control them. The threat of the loss of tax exempt status will be a very effective tool in controlling churches and watering down the content of their message.

There is growing intolerance for Christians in America and their lifestyles—and this includes Christian parents and how they raise their children. Pressure is growing for Christians to accept the state's authority over their church property, their freedom to gather, and the indoctrination of their children with a state-sanctioned concept that refutes the biblical teachings of *one* God, *one* Savior, and *one* set of rules for human conduct.

The **second** way Nazi, communist, and socialist governments control people in general (and especially Christians) is *to usurp control of their children.* The concept is called *parens patriae*—the "parenthood of the state." By classifying children as a national resource, the state took over the position of managing the upbringing and education of all children. The sanctity of the family unit was displaced by an overriding national interest to manage this resource (i.e., the children) for the political and economic betterment of the nation. Eventually religion was classified as harmful to children (i.e., harmful to the national interest) and parents in many countries were forbidden to tell their children about their religious beliefs. Today, the parent/child control initiatives coming out of the U.N./globalist conferences, state legislatures, the Congress, and the judiciary are proliferating rapidly—and most are directed against Christian parents and their religious beliefs and practices.

The **third** means of control is *the government's regulation of employment.* By characterizing Christians as uncooperative or anti-government, they are able to deny them employment (as well as higher education). The Nazis did the same thing to the Jews in Germany in the 1930s. New laws, rules, and regulations are being promulgated at this writing (just one example is President Clinton's Goals 2000 plan) which will enable federal agencies to control the nation's workforce.

Congressman Henry Hyde (R-IL) in a "Dear Colleague" letter dated May 9, 1996, described the socialists' emerging new school-to-work program for the nation (as embodied in such laws as Goals 2000 and the Improving America's Schools Act):

> School-to-Work . . . when carried to its logical extreme, will choose careers for every American worker. Children's careers will be chosen for them by Workforce Development Boards and federal agencies "at the earliest possible age" (i.e., as early as the third grade). . . . Forcing children to work where and how federal agencies deem necessary is not the way to go.

> Goals 2000 utilizes America's educational system as the infra-

structure for *nationalization of the labor force in the U.S.* Our schools will be restructured to teach labor skills *and to focus on changing attitudes and social behavior.* The results will be to create *a controlled workforce for the global economy* and our children will be the *"human resources"* for this plan. . . . Emphasis will be placed on "social engineering."

The Improving America's Schools Act (IASA) signed into law in 1995, *extended the time for learning each day and longer school year programs.* [*Note:* Remember John Dewey's admonition that the state needed to "minimize" the time children have with their parents or families."] . . . States are now busy complying with Goals 2000 and School-to-Work federal mandates. . . . *Of course, they will decide* where these human resources will reside. They will have to live where the "state" chooses, according to what skills the "state" has chosen for them to learn.

[*Note:* And this is exactly how the state chose (or denied) education and eventual employment for all children from kindergarten through the university in the former Soviet Union. It was mandatory to be part of this system, and if you were Christian, religious, or politically incorrect, you, your family, and your children were frozen out of the system and relegated to poverty, menial jobs, and a sort of internal exile. For two excellent booklets on Goals 2000 and School-to-Work, *Paychecks and Power* and *The Dawning of the Brave New World* by Donna Hearne, write to: The Constitutional Coalition, P.O. Box 37054, St. Louis, MO 63141 (fax: 1-314-878-6294).]

All three of these socialist people-control mechanisms are presently being pushed hard across America at the federal and state levels, and via government and media propaganda, are beginning to gain public support. As Jeanne Bignall, a Colorado Christian/conservative political activist and syndicated columnist, has written regarding these three government control mechanisms:

Church, children, and employment. They may seem like totally unrelated matters. But, let's put it another way—faith, family, and finances. If you were denied the ability to exercise your freedom in any one of the three, what would your life be like? That's why the issue of tax exempt status of churches is *not* just about paying taxes. That's why parents' rights to direct the upbringing of their children is *not* just about children. That's why the government's upcoming move into the field of employment is *not* just about jobs. These three mechanisms are about freedom (or the lack thereof), they are about "Big Brother government" and the management of a highly controlled society.

The Globalization of Parent/Family/Child Control—
The U.N. Convention on the Rights of the Child
"Every child is our child"—the UNICEF slogan

Globalist education will require early and diligent efforts to correct many of the errors of home training which cultivate attitudes running directly counter to international understanding . . . attitudes such as nationalism, chauvinism, and sclerosis of the mind. . . . As long as the child breathes the poisoned air of nationalism, education in world-mindedness can only produce precarious results.

—From *Towards World Understanding,* a 10-volume series by UNESCO (U.N. Education, Scientific and Cultural Organization).

Over the years, this writer has written much about the United Nations— its domination by communists and globalists since its inception in 1945; its agenda for population, environmental, economic, and people control and global socialism; its New World Army (i.e., the U.N. army to be used to impose global government on the peoples and nations of the world); and how the U.N. is to be the primary vehicle for imposing the coming global government on planet earth.

A series of U.N.-sponsored conferences (i.e., World Conference on Education, Thailand, 1990; the Earth Summit, Rio, 1992; the U.N. World Conference on Human Rights, Vienna, 1993; and the Global Tribunal on Violation of Women's Human Rights; the 1993 Parliament of World Religions in Chicago; the U.N. Women's Conference, Beijing, 1995; the Gorbachev Forum, San Francisco, 1995; the 1995 Global Conference on the International Year of the Family, Salt Lake City; the U.N. World Conference for Social Development, Copenhagen, 1995; the U.N. Conference on Human Settlements (Habitat II), Istanbul, 1996; etc.) are all signs of the accelerating fast track agenda of the global socialists toward imposing a world socialist dictatorship over the next five to ten years.

The objective of all of these conferences and the current frantic activity of the globalists is abolition of national sovereignty, global governance, building our global neighborhood; U.N. management of our global village; sustainable development (i.e., the socialization [or Sovietization] of the world economy); and the training of the masses for global citizenship.

To implement these objectives, U.N. programs are being (at the present time) set up to train, monitor, and control the global workforce; to control the global environment; to control consumption, population, gender equality, and where and how people live (i.e., Habitat II focused on forcing populations into dense, highly populated urban areas—where people-control can be more easily facilitated); the training of every person to embrace global spirituality (a pantheistic blend of occult spirituality and the world's earth-centered religions); *and the control of families (i.e., parents and children) via the nationalization of all children.*

As Berit Kjos wrote in the *Colorado Christian News:*

The Habitat II and other U.N. reports suggest that biblical Christianity and other traditional gender roles are out, along with capitalism, cars, and the U.S. Constitution. Global socialism is in! No one would escape the watchful eyes of the U.N. agents. As the Habitat agenda writes: "Build capacity for monitoring and evaluating compliance at all levels. . . . Establish global information networks on human settlements in the form of permanent and electronic conferences."

Solidarity is essential. Young and old must be taught, trained, and tested through "life-long learning"—a UNESCO vision written into Goals 2000, the education law of our land. The global, U.N.-controlled data bank would track *personal* and communal "progress" toward global unity. . . . As Hillary Clinton reminds us, "it takes a village" to press each person into the twenty-first century mold.

As Kjos writes: "U.N. leaders know it is far easier to reprogram people in planned cities than in scattered groups." [*Note:* Which is one more compelling reason why this writer has long advocated that readers, if possible, move to the country or a small town. You will be harder to control or herd into the corral (or feedlot)!]

> Urbanization and the environment it creates predisposes the populace to new attitudes, to social change and awareness, to early access to new ideas and to innovation and change, states a 1995 report from the U.N. Center for Human Settlements. No wonder the Habitat agenda encourages "optimal density in the occupation of available serviced land." [*Note:* It's called people control.]

Does the U.N. agenda sound too radical to be real? If you doubt its influence in America, compare its plans with those of our political leaders. Start with Goals 2000 and study its blueprint for a "global neighborhood." Notice how the two plans fit together. Compare them with Hillary Clinton's book, *It Takes a Village.* The process is already well underway.

The U.N. Convention on the Rights of the Child

A classic illustration of the U.N.'s globalist, people-control agenda is this nefarious treaty, which, if adopted in America while the Clintons or Al Gore are in power, will destroy *all* parental rights, and make all American children the possession of the state.

The U.N. Convention on the Rights of the Child was adopted by the U.N. General Assembly on November 20, 1989, was signed by Madeleine Albright (the U.S. Ambassador to the U.N.) on February 16, 1995, and will be submitted to the U.S. Senate for ratification when Clinton thinks he has the votes. The Clinton Administration has made ratification of the children's treaty a major policy objective. [*Note:* Public opposition to this treaty may continue to preclude its Senate ratification, so Clinton (and the political left) may try to implement it either piecemeal, or via executive orders.]

This U.N. treaty, already ratified (and therefore the law of the land) in 189 countries, will allow the government (or the world government under the United Nations/New World Order) to dictate to you how you raise your children, what you can and cannot do, and the role that the state will have in raising your children.

If ratified, the U.N. Convention on the Rights of the Child will be implemented in the United States and virtually destroy the parental rights we presently enjoy. This treaty will give all children the "right" to freedom of association, freedom of expression, freedom of religion; the right to privacy (which includes the right to abortion); the right to choose public schools; the right of access to media materials (including TV); etc. Any parent who infringes on his/her children's "rights" in these areas could be prosecuted with the possibility of having the children removed from the home. The treaty virtually prohibits corporal punishment of children.

Spanking of children is specifically defined as criminal child abuse and the treaty mandates that such child abusers must be jailed and have their children taken from them. In France, in the first few days following the ratification of the treaty, seven families had their children taken from them and the parents jailed for the new international crime of child abuse (i.e., spanking their children).

The Bible has much to say about discipline of children, and why it breaks the rebellion (found in all of us) at a young age. As **Proverbs 22:15** says: "Foolishness is bound in the heart of a child; but the rod of correction shall drive it far from him." **Proverbs 29:15** says: "The rod and reproof give wisdom: but a child left to himself bringeth his mother to shame." **Proverbs 13:24** says: "He that spareth his rod hateth his son: but he that loveth him chasteneth him betimes." And **Proverbs 23:13–14** says: "Withhold not correction from the child: for if thou beatest him with the rod, he shall not die. Thou shalt beat him with the rod, and shalt deliver his soul from hell."

Many millions of Christians and Jews worldwide follow these teachings, and are now (with the ratification of the U.N. convention) to be branded instant criminals—subject to losing their children and going to jail. The socialists and the New World Order may have set the greatest trap of all with this treaty. They know that millions of Christians, Jews, and traditionalists will disobey this treaty—and many will become instant targets of the government child grabbers.

Background on the U.N. Convention

An agreement was reached in 1989 which for the first time created a comprehensive charter advancing the agenda of the children's "liberation" movement. What the children's rights advocates have for over two decades been unable to accomplish through the normal legislative process, may now be realized in one sweeping blow should the Clinton Administration push the Senate to ratify the United Nations Convention on the Rights of the Child. Under the guise of a "child's rights" measure, this wolf in sheep's clothing will, if passed, totally undermine the authority of parents to exercise vitally important responsibilities toward their children if these responsibilities infringe on the child's "right" to autonomy and self-expression as defined by a panel of "experts" appointed by the United Nations.

If ratified, this treaty could undermine the family by granting to children a list of radical "rights" which would be primarily enforced against the parents. These new "fundamental" rights would include the right to privacy, the right to freedom of thought and association, and the right to freedom of expression. A fundamental presumption of the treaty is that parental responsibility exists only in so far as parents are willing to further the independent choices of the child.

The impact of the convention is particularly ominous in light of the fact that the United States Constitution declares treaties to be the law of the land. Thus, the U.N. convention would constitute legally binding law in all fifty states. Otherwise valid state laws pertaining to education, the family, etc., which conflict with the provisions of the treaty will be subject to invalidation. If this convention is enforced, the United Stated would be required to alter large portions of long established law to cater to the demands of the United Nations and the panel of "experts" (i.e., the International Tribunal for Children's Rights [ITCR]) they select to define international standards for child's rights.

Children's rights advocates realize that calls and letters from concerned citizens who oppose the treaty are increasing. Thus, they are turning up the pressure on government. Over 150 groups have indicated their support of the U.N. Convention on the Rights of the Child, including the National Education Association (NEA), the National Council of Churches, the Children's Defense Fund, American Council for Social Services, National Committee for the Rights of the Child, Planned Parenthood of NYC, International School Boards Association, American Bar Association, International Council on Social Welfare, and the Girl Scouts of America.

Summary of the Articles of the Convention

Article 3: "In *all* actions concerning children," the courts, social service workers, and bureaucrats are empowered to regulate families based on their subjective determination of "the best interest of the child." This shifts the responsibility of parental judgment and decision making from the family to the state (and ultimately the United Nations).

Article 4: Signatory nations are bound to "undertake all appropriate legislative, administrative, and other measures, for the implementation of the rights" of the convention. In fact, the U.S. would be required to "undertake measures to the maximum extent of available resources . . . within the framework of international cooperation" in order to restructure society.

Article 7: All children must be immediately registered after birth, to ensure state and U.N. control over their development. Computerized tracking will follow. [*Note:* Home births via midwives are likely to increase dramatically as a result of this in the coming years.]

Article 13: Parents would be subject to prosecution for any attempt to prevent their children from interaction with pornography, rock music, or television. Little children are vested with a "freedom of expression" right that is virtually absolute . . . NO allowance is made for parental guidance. According to a Canadian study, the North American Man-Boy Love Association (NAMBLA) believes the treaty "could be used to support its position that children as young as six have the right to choose to have sex."

Article 14: Children are guaranteed "freedom of thought, conscience, and religion." They can object to all religious training. They can assert their right to participate in occult or contrary services.

Article 15: "The right of the child to freedom of association." If taken seriously, parents could be prevented from forbidding their child from associating with people deemed to be objectionable companions. Children could claim this "right" and join gangs, cults, witch covens, racist organizations, and associate with drug addicts over parental objections. Parent's rights and responsibilities are not mentioned.

Article 16: Mandates the creation of an intensive bureaucracy for the purpose of "identification, reporting, referral, investigation, treatment, and follow-up" of parents who, in violation of the child's rights, treat their children negligently. This could include spanking, teaching them from the Bible, teaching them against homosexuality, or "alternate lifestyles," or other "psychologically damaging" religious or traditionalist ideas or dogmas.

Article 24: The governments of each signatory nation are required to provide "the highest standard of health care facilities, including family planning [i.e., abortion] and education services." Section 3 of Article 24 instructs governments to "take all effective and appropriate measures with a view to abolishing traditional practices prejudicial to the health of children." Note that a practice need not be proven to be injurious, but instead only "prejudicial" to the health of children. What traditional practices might be prejudicial to the health of children in the view of the U.N.'s global/socialist experts? Discipline? Religious instruction? Criticism of the government, the New World Order, or a minority group (i.e., homosexuals)?

Article 26: Parties must recognize the right of every child to benefit from Social Security and social insurance.

Article 27: Parents are required to implement "conditions of living necessary for the child's development." These conditions of living are to derive from state-determined standards for his "physical, *mental, spiritual,* moral, and *social* development."

Article 28: Compulsory Education. All nations are challenged to unite in the creation of an internationalist approach to education. All school-age Americans would be "encouraged" to be part of the school system. The content of what must be taught to all children is pre-scribed. These include anti-American one-worldism, anti-family and anti-traditional values, multiculturalism, and environmentalism. [*Note: The home school movement could be massively attacked or terminated by this article!*]

Article 29: It is the goal of the state to direct the education of the people it governs toward the philosophy of the New World Order as "en-shrined in the charter of the United Nations." This philosophy in-cludes occultic, anti-Judeo/Christian values, authoritarianism and intolerance.

Article 32: The state is responsible to prevent children from providing labor which would interfere with the child's education, or be harm-ful to the child's "health or physical, mental, spiritual, moral, or social development." What? No more household chores?

Article 37: Every child "deprived of his or her liberty" shall have access to free legal counsel and access to the courts to make such a chal-lenge. Parents will have to pay new taxes to support the legal pro-cesses against themselves! (The ACLU lawyers are lining up!)

Article 43: An international committee of twenty "experts" (the Inter-national Tribunal for Children's Rights) is to be established to over-see the progress and implementation of the treaty. These experts will be chosen by secret ballot by all signatory nations. They will be children's rights social engineers. There is no assurance that ANY American will even be on the committee, and if they are, they will be appointed by Bill or Hillary Clinton or Al Gore.

In Summary. The U.N. Convention on the Rights of the Child would do the following:

a) The convention would give children the right to disregard parental authority.

b) The state will determine child's best interest.

c) The provisions of the treaty *must* be enforced.

d) All children must be registered from day of birth forward.

e) Severe limitations are placed on the parent's right to direct and train their children.

f) The convention would further entrench the right of teenagers to abort their babies.

g) The state must assist parents in the raising of children.

h) Parents who don't comply may be prosecuted.

i) A prohibition on corporal punishment (i.e., spanking).

j) Our children will be educated for world government (i.e., the New World Order).

k) International social engineers will parent our children.

This U.N. children's treaty, if ratified by the U.S. Senate, will make the Congress, the Clinton Administration (and its bureaucracy), and the U.S. courts the national guardians of our children, charged with seeking "the best interest of the child" (Article 3); and answerable to the United Nations. But, the government and the global/socialists' definition of a child's best interest is often very different from a parent's definition.

For instance, the convention allows the government to take a child from their parents if the child has been "abused" or "neglected" (Article 9) but does not clearly define child abuse. Since many state, local, and international organizations define child abuse as spanking, there will be severe legal implications for Christians or traditionalist families who spank. Indeed, Social Services in a number of states across America are already seizing children who have been spanked or "psychologically abused" and in some instances are jailing parents.

And now the socialists are expanding the definition of child abuse to include psychological (or mental) trauma due to strictness, rigidity, intolerance of others' views or religions, exclusivism, homophobia, etc. [*Note:* Criticism of the government or opposition to the New World Order, or other politically incorrect prejudices will soon make the list (i.e., be included in the expanded definition of child abuse).]

The convention also usurps parental authority by advocating the view that children are autonomous agents who are capable, in all areas, of making adult decisions and dealing with adult situations. This radical legal doctrine stands in stark contrast to the traditional concept, upheld in America and throughout most of the free world that children are minors, in need of parental guidance and protection.

The great danger of this treaty is that it will codify the assumption that government is the primary custodian of children—it will give the United Nations power over parent/child relationships to a degree unheard of in the field of human rights. To put the United Nations and government bureaucrats in charge of parent/child relationships, where there are huge differences of culture, history, customs, conventions, and traditions among nations and people is to open up an avalanche of socialist controls over parents everywhere.

Just look at the Chinese communists' controls over families, abortion, baby killing, one-child-per-family, education of children, the banning of religious teachings, etc. for a preview of coming attractions. **The U.N. leaders laud the Red Chinese family/children controls and believe they should be implemented on a global basis.**

Shorn of its rhetoric, the U.N.'s "family" agenda is intended to destroy the traditional family through redefinition (i.e., families now include cohabitating unmarried couples, homosexual couples, communes, etc.), and make the home an administrative unit of a global government. From the U.N.'s point of view, the one significant function of families is to help promote world government and the socialist and humanist values enshrined in the U.N.'s human rights documents. With one of the key elements of its thrust for world domination—the control of families and children—the U.N.'s campaign to corrupt, subvert, and eventually destroy the family is accelerating dramatically.

End Run: Implementing the U.N. Children's Convention Through State Legislatures and Agencies

The global socialists, the political left, and the U.N. have been frustrated for almost ten years in not getting ratification of the U.N. Children's Treaty through the U.S. Senate. Opposition from Christians, conservatives, and traditionalists is high. So, they will resort to subterfuge, trickery, and piecemeal passage of the elements of the treaty on a state and local basis until they can muster enough support in the Senate for ratification.

The political left in America are not reticent to using backdoor methods when frontal assaults fail. For example, in 1995 the global socialists made a failed attempt to stage a constitutional convention (ConCon), called a Conference of States, at which they planned to replace our Constitution with a new socialist/globalist constitution. Conservative opposition derailed this plan. So now, the globalists have pushed term limits amendments in all sixteen states which opposed the ConCon (amendments which are supported by the vast majority of conservatives and many moderates and liberals as well). But now they have sneaked into the fine print a cleverly disguised call for a constitutional convention. This has passed in Colorado and a number of other states.

The Clintons did the same thing by sneaking gun control legislation into the thousand-page omnibus spending legislation six hours before Congress voted for the spending bill and adjourned in late October 1996. Such treachery, stealth, and subterfuge will also be used to pass key elements of the U.N. Children's Treaty on both national and state levels.

It Takes a Village:
Big Brother's (or Sister's) Plan to Raise Your Children

The Lord created fathers and mothers as children's primary nurturers, educators, protectors, and guides—to train and raise them up. But today the liberals, the socialists, and the globalists believe that the government has an equal, if not more important role in the child's life. Hillary Rodham Clinton has articulated the socialist desire to control children in her book *It Takes a Village and Other Lessons Children Teach Us.*

She believes that children are society's responsibility, and argues that because of our increasingly violent, unstable society, government should take a much greater role in every child's upbringing. Mrs. Clinton based her book on the African proverb, *"It takes a village to raise a child,"* and justifies her radical ideas as being in the best interest of children. "We can see to it," she has said, "that even *parental rights and adult prerogatives take a back seat* to the love and security children so deeply need."

Newsweek described the purpose behind Mrs. Clinton's book: "Throughout her political and legal career she has lobbied for children's rights. With families breaking down and children increasingly consigned to poverty, it is up to society [translation—the government!] to step in.

That is the central message of her new book." With our culture crumbling under the strain of social problems like abortion, divorce, pornography, crime, promiscuity, and illegitimate births, Mrs. Clinton reasons that government should take on the job of parents to solve these problems.

Under this "village" philosophy, the Clinton Administration advocates policies that undermine families and the rights of parents to guide their children. That is why they signed the U.N. Children's Rights treaty in 1995 and both Clintons have pushed so hard for its adoption since 1989. The treaty would make Congress the ultimate guardians of our children—assigning the bureaucrats the role of seeking the best interests of our children.

This "village" parenting concept is not just at the federal level either. In recent years, a growing number of local and state courts have removed children from their homes because parents spanked them, required attendance at religious services, or forbade immoral behavior. In fact, the court's abuse of the child protection laws has been so rampant that Congress has introduced legislation to restore and protect the rights of parents to direct their children's education, health care, discipline, and religious training.

Hillary Clinton argues in her book that "for the sake of our children, let us use the government, as we have in the past, to further the common good." [*Note:* Stalin, Hitler, Mao, or Castro could have argued the same thing.] *USA Today* columnist Barbara Reynolds wrote: "Clinton's book is a wake-up call *that other peoples children are our own.* She encourages the private sector, parents, and the government *to move past empty rhetoric about family values,* and take up programs that value people."

As Beverly LaHaye has written: "The wake-up call is that some of the most influential leaders of our country believe that children belong to everyone. Our children **do not** belong to everyone else. First and foremost, they are the responsibility of their own parents."

The concept of "common ownership" of our children comes straight from communism. In the Peoples Republic of China, in Cuba, and in the "former" Soviet states, ownership of everything—property, businesses, farms, and *even children* "belonged to the people"

(i.e., to the state). That so-called common ownership was in fact no ownership at all. Hillary's mission to promote "the village" is really not just about children. It's about the conversion of America to socialism and people control. It just starts with children and the family—and also socialized medicine.

As Christopher Lasch noted in *Harper's*: "Hillary Clinton doesn't believe parents should direct their children's lives; she proposes that children should have equal rights with their parents before the law, and she is opposed to the principle of parental authority in any form." [*Note:* If carried to its bizarre conclusion, children who share equal legal rights with their parents should be able to vote at age five or six; they should be able to make contracts; sue in the courts (including lawsuits against their parents—with the help of the ACLU, of course); marry; divorce; serve in the military; drive cars, etc. It's called socialist emancipation! Or is it called destruction of the family and of society?]

In her legal writings (prior to *It Takes a Village*) Hillary was not restricting herself to abused children, but was "talking about everything from compulsory school attendance to driving privileges to nurturing/ child rearing requirements." As she wrote:

> Decisions about motherhood and abortion, schooling, cosmetic surgery, treatment of venereal disease, or employment, and others where the decision or lack of one will significantly affect the child's future, **should not be made unilaterally by parents.** Children should have a right to decide their own future if they are competent.

Hillary Clinton has been in the forefront of the movement for forced inoculations for all American children from the day of birth to adulthood, with computerized tracking of *all* children to ensure parental compliance. **Hillary and the socialists would charge parents who resist those inoculations (for religious or medical reasons) with criminal child abuse—with fines, imprisonment, or loss of children as penalties.** The Clintons and their comrades pushed such forced inoculations very hard early in their first term.

Carol Baker, an unpaid lobbyist who works with the state legislature in Arkansas, wrote in *Christianity Today* about Hillary's "village" idea in action:

> I have worked . . . to try and stop some of the programs and liberal agenda of Ms. Rodham and Mr. Clinton. Some of those programs— all of them attacks on the family and parental authority—were: school-based sex clinics, with abortion referral and three-year-olds required to go to kindergarten. . . . During Mr. Clinton's tenure as governor, we dropped from twentieth to twenty-fifth of the twenty-eight states taking the same tests.

In *It Takes a Village*, Hillary Clinton argues that these are "terrible times when no adequate parenting is available and the village itself [i.e., the state] must act in place of parents. The village accepts those responsibilities in all our names through the authority we vest in government." [*Note:* Instead of the people's republic, it will be the "people's children."]

The June 3, 1996, issue of *Time* magazine reported that Mrs. Clinton "has been more forceful than some people in arguing for severing parental rights in certain cases. . . . At some point a child's rights deserve careful attention, and some parents do not deserve continual authority over their children."

Social workers around the country apparently share Mrs. Clinton's view, as they have taken thousands of children from their homes and parents because of spanking, "emotional abuse," or teaching of traditional (politically incorrect) values, or rigid "religious repression." These activities illustrate the anti-family ideology of our government and the liberal Establishment—and it has grown geometrically in the latter half of the 1990s. The Clintons, the global socialists, and their U.N. Convention on the Rights of the Child, if we allow them to, are about to formally designate the government as the primary custodians of all children in their campaign to demolish parental authority and nationalize (or globalize) American children.

In the biblically inspired world view of our Founding Fathers, parents received their mandate to raise and nurture their children from God, and the function of the state was to support the family in this divinely ordained mandate. But the socialists and globalists of our day line up much more closely with the philosophy of the French Revolution that "children belong to the general family, to the state, before belonging to private families." Louise-Antoine de Saint-Just agreed that "children belong to the state," and recommended that children be seized from families and raised entirely by the state after the age of five.

By laying custodial claim to all children in the name of the state, Mrs. Clinton is promoting the doctrine of *parens patriae*—"the parenthood of the state." Arrayed around Mrs. Clinton in this takeover of our children are a host of leftist/socialist/globalist groups including: the National Education Association, the National Parent Teachers Association, the American Association of School Administrators, the American Academy of Pediatrics, the American Civil Liberties Union, the National Abortion and Reproductive Rights Action League and, of course, the United Nations and its "educational agency," UNESCO. [*Note:* Readers who grew up in the forties, fifties, or even sixties may have a hard time believing that groups like the National PTA, NEA, American Association of School Administrators, etc. have been co-oped by the political left, but indeed, while most of us slept, this has happened.]

Conclusion

Welcome to Hillary Clinton's "village"—to the parenthood of the state. If one will closely examine the United Nations agenda (including the U.N. Convention on the Rights of the Child, Habitat II, the UNESCO and UNICEF agendas, and the U.N. Commission on Global Governance report entitled *Our Global Neighborhood*); Hillary Clinton's book *It Takes a Village*; the various state initiatives to control parents and children; the present thrust of the U.S. government educational system; and the long-term strategies of the communists and the political left worldwide, a very ominous picture will be seen to be emerging.

The global socialists and the political left want control of our children and their minds as a major element in their quest for a Brave New World. **Parents (especially conservative Christian traditionalists who believe in and teach their children "the old ways"), stand in the globalists' way—just as such parents did when the communists took**

over China, Russia, Cuba, etc. This parental control must be neutralized by the socialists and transferred to the state. This neutralization and transfer is now taking place at mach ten speed and will increase dramatically over the next few years. This battle for our children will be part of the impetus behind the coming persecution of Christians and traditionalist families in America.

What can concerned Christian, traditionalist parents do about these attacks?

First, take your children out of government schools and home school them (while it is still legal to do so, which may not be for long if Hillary and the United Nations have their way).

Second, support efforts in your own state legislature to deflect initiatives to install piecemeal the U.N. children's treaty on a state-by-state basis.

Third, oppose the U.N. Convention on the Rights of the Child in every way possible. Put pressure on your U.S. senator to oppose it. Get your church to oppose it. Get fellow home schoolers to oppose it. Write letters to the editor in your local papers opposing it. Express your opposition by calling local and national radio talk shows.

Fourth, support efforts by certain congressmen, senators, and state legislators to pass federal and state legislation and state amendments defending and protecting parental rights against *parens patriae* and the socialists' plans for your children. **Hillary's "village" concept is not just a book—it is a socialist strategy to attack the family, neutralize parental rights, and seize control of our children.**

Fifth, and finally, decide what is your choke point. How much will you let Big Brother take control of your children before you draw a line in the sand and say, *"No more—you go no further!"* [*Note:* i.e., a growing number of parents who "understand the times" are having home births of babies, via midwives, in order to avoid government registration and tracking of newborns.] What is your choke point? As Dr. James Dobson has written, is there anything left in America that's worth fighting for, or dying for? How about our children? What do you think?

Chapter 7

Toward a State of National Emergency and Martial Law

Is it possible that in the midst of the coming financial crisis, when there could be panic in the financial markets, bank runs, power failures like we saw in December 1998 in San Francisco, rising unemployment, food shortages, and social unrest in large American cities, that Bill Clinton (or Al Gore) would declare a State of National Emergency and martial law to deal with the crisis?

What if the financial crisis is compounded by one, two, or a series of terrorist attacks, or the threat of such attacks by terrorists such as Osama bin Laden, Saddam Hussein, or some terrorist group—Islamic, Bosnian, communist, or former Soviet? What if one or more of the dozens of Soviet-made "suitcase" nuclear bombs that are believed to have been smuggled into the U.S. over the past ten to fifteen years were detonated in, for example, New York City or Washington, D.C.?

In December 1998, *Time* magazine reported that terrorist groups affiliated with embassy bomber Osama bin Laden are planning to strike on U.S. soil. New York City and Washington were cited as likely targets in the *Time* report.

Would Americans surrender major freedoms in such a crisis (i.e., in a terrorist crisis, perhaps compounded by a financial collapse)? Of course they would! Since a series of terrorist hijackings in 1970, we have willingly submitted to airport searches and electronic screening (i.e., for almost thirty years). Since the TWA 800 crash in July 1997 (at first thought to be a terrorist attack but later officially pronounced as a "bad fuel pump") we have submitted to showing photo IDs at all airports—*and now they must be official government IDs.*

When the Los Angeles riots of 1992 paralyzed that giant metroplex, the people begged for martial law "to stop the pain," and it was declared and implemented via Operation Rio and Joint Task Force 6, even though it involved the suspension of the peoples' constitutional rights. When Americans are in pain, in danger (real or imagined), in danger of losing their cherished wealth or affluence, or are simply frightened, they will willingly give up some or all of their freedoms to a government which promises to end the pain, protect them, preserve their wealth, etc.

Americans willingly yielded major freedoms to Franklin Roosevelt and the government in the Great Depression in 1933—when FDR declared a State of National Emergency. In that same year the German people willingly surrendered their freedom to Adolph Hitler in a State of Emergency after Hitler and his Brown Shirts burned the Reichstag (German parliament) and blamed it on the communists.

Would President Clinton or his successor, Al Gore, and the legions of socialists they brought to power with them, use the emerging terrorist crisis (whether real or manufactured), and/or the emerging financial crisis as an excuse to seize a tremendous amount of political power, advance their socialist/globalist agenda, declare a State of National Emergency and martial law in America, and impose Draconian people-control measures on the American people?

Could the Clintons, Gore, and their comrades use such a crisis to attack their political enemies ("the dangerous religious right") such as they did after the Oklahoma City bombing in 1995 or as Hitler did after the Reichstag fire in 1933? Could the Clintons' present push for hate crime legislation; a national ID card; bank monitoring of customers' financial affairs; government monitoring of all medical records; telephone, fax, and Internet surveillance; unconstitutional searches, seizures, and forfeitures; new restrictive gun control measures; and a rash of new Executive Orders which give the president (with the stroke of a pen) total dictatorial control over every aspect of Americans' lives—all be part of moving America toward martial law and a socialist police state?

There is growing evidence that this is precisely what is happening and that Bill Clinton or Al Gore could emerge from the coming period of crisis (financial and terrorism) as an all-powerful dictator. *Remember, quantum change always takes place in a period of (or under cover of) extreme crisis.* On September 28, 1998, Rep. Bob Barr (R-GA), one of the leading early exponents of impeaching Bill Clinton, released information exposing a huge police state power grab by Bill Clinton and his attorney general, Janet Reno. As Rep. Barr wrote:

> Attorney General Janet Reno and the Department of Justice intend to obtain massive new enforcement powers in the closing days of the 105th Congress.
>
> Barr obtained the information from a confidential source within federal law enforcement. Among other things, the Department's "wish list" for new authority includes:
>
> • *A vastly expanded definition of terrorism to include domestic crimes having no relationship to terrorism.*
>
> • The power to seize commercial transportation assets for federal use.
>
> • The ability to commandeer personnel from other federal agencies without reimbursement.
>
> • Expanded wiretap authority to allow "roving" wiretaps, and wiretaps without any court authority.
>
> • Enlarged asset forfeiture provisions to allow the FBI to seize personal property in both criminal and civil matters.
>
> • The establishment of a permanent "FBI Police Force."
>
> • Loosening of *posse comitatus* restrictions *to allow more military involvement in domestic law enforcement.*
>
> • Authority to force telephone and Internet companies to divulge information on their customers.

These requests belong in some bizarre conspiracy novel, not in serious legislative documents being circulated at the top levels of federal law enforcement. *"These proposals represent a sneak attack on the most cherished principles of our democracy. If they become a part of our law, freedom and privacy in America will be permanently and severely diminished,"* said Barr. Barr also noted the Justice Department and the FBI are "shopping" this wish list in an effort to get the items placed in a spending measure without hearings or debate. (For additional information, visit Barr's web site at *www.house.gov/barr.*)

It is noteworthy that Clinton and Reno want a vastly expanded definition of terrorism. Remember, Reno has defined pro-life demonstrators praying in front of abortion clinics as terrorists. Will the entire right-wing religious conservatives, gun owners, politically incorrect opponents of present government encroachments all soon fall under some expanded definition of terrorist?

A totalitarian police state came in like a flood (virtually overnight) in Germany in the 1930s. The German people had been prepared or conditioned for it for the prior fifteen years and were in such a state of moral, political, and financial collapse that they had no resistance to Hitler's overtures when they came. Is America about to follow in Germany's footsteps? This writer fears that it is!

The Clinton Dictatorship: Ruling by Executive Orders (EOs)

Stroke of the pen, law of the land—kinda cool.

—Paul Begala, Clinton advisor

We have allowed the executive branch, through various Executive Orders, to usurp what is legitimately and constitutionally our right and responsibility.

—Senator Tim Hutchinson (R-AR), September 18, 1997

All legislative (law making) powers herein granted shall be vested in a Congress.

—Article 1, Section 1, Clause 1, U.S. Constitution

Congress has a choice to make, in writing this chapter of history. It can choose partisanship or it can choose progress. Congress must decide. However, I have a continuing obligation to act to use the authority of the presidency to advance America's interest at home and abroad.

—Bill Clinton, July 6, 1998

Law consists of two lines above my signature.

—Iraqi dictator Saddam Hussein

The U.S. Constitution grants the president no lawmaking authority, yet throughout his term in office Bill Clinton has preferred to rule by decree (through the writing of hundreds of Executive Orders and Presidential Decision Directives) rather than carry out his constitutional duty to execute laws properly enacted by Congress.

The most corrupt president in U.S. history, stymied by Congress in the passage of his socialist agenda, has assumed dictatorial powers never intended by the Constitution, our Founding Fathers, or the American people. He could, in a period of crisis due to a financial collapse or a series of terrorist attacks, assume dictatorial powers via martial law and a State of National Emergency—completely suspending the Constitution, the power of Congress, and possibly the year 2000 elections. A president who will bomb another country, costing the lives of thousands of innocent Iraqi victims, as Clinton did, in an effort to forestall a vote of impeachment and retain his power, is a man who will do anything (even if it destroys the country) to retain his hold on the presidency.

Clinton's Executive Order Strategy

Bill Clinton came to office with a strategy to rule by executive decrees (or fiat) rather than with Congress and through the legislative process. As he said in his 1992 acceptance speech at the Democratic National Convention: "President Bush: If you won't use your power to help people, step aside. **I will!**"

In his first two days in office, with the stroke of a pen, he signed five Executive Orders: allowing homosexuals in the military; extending U.S. aid for U.N.-sponsored abortion and population control; ordering abortions to be performed in U.S. military hospitals; rescinding the ban on the use of fetal tissue (i.e., dead babies) in federally sponsored research; and abolishing the Bush Administration Council on Competitiveness, which gave businesses and large corporations a way to obtain exemptions from government regulations. **None** of these unilateral decrees would have been passed by Congress.

Clinton and his subordinates have made no secret of their strategy to bypass Congress and rule by Executive Orders or Presidential Decision Directives. *Shortly after his second election, Clinton bragged: "I will run the country by Executive Orders." That's exactly what he is doing.* As the *Los Angeles Times* (7/4/98) reported in an article entitled "Clinton to Bypass Congress in Blitz of Executive Orders":

> The president will use his strategy to move his domestic agenda past GOP resistance. Frustrated by a GOP controlled Congress that lately has rebuffed him on almost every front, President Clinton plans a blitz of Executive Orders in coming months, part of a White House strategy to make progress on Clinton's domestic agenda with or without congressional help.
>
> "He's ready to work with Congress if they will work with him. But if they choose partisanship, he will choose progress," said Rahm Emanuel, senior policy advisor to the president. "The president has a very strong sense of the powers of the presidency, and is willing to use **all** of them," said Paul Begala, another senior advisor. . . . The president also hopes his Executive Order offensive will pressure Congress to enact his legislative priorities. . . .
>
> The latest series of Executive Orders is illustrative of a president who has used his unilateral authority more robustly and frequently than almost any of his predecessors. Clinton has rewritten the manual on how to use executive power with gusto. His formula includes pressing the limits of his regulatory authority, signing Executive Orders and using other unilateral means to obtain his policy priorities when Congress fails to embrace them.

As the *Wall Street Journal* (8/6/98) wrote:

> President Clinton has pursued an "Executive Order Strategy" that goes way beyond trying to guide federal agencies in how to implement laws. **Instead it seeks to actively put in place policies Congress would never adopt.** Last week, the White House admitted that a May Executive Order gutting major powers of state and local governments had been drafted in secret without consulting them.

The History and Background of Executive Orders in America

The Founding Fathers of this nation established a republic with a highly effective system of checks and balances precisely *because they desired to avoid, at all costs, the consolidation of power in any single individual.* The presidential Executive Order was, at one time, a genuine exercise of power based upon law that was already in existence. It was a presidential proclamation that carried the force of law, and was to give the president rule-making authority over the executive branch (over government agencies). Unfortunately, Executive Orders have been distorted into tools for illegitimate creation of new laws, which the Congress would never pass.

When a president creates a new law by decree, representative government is completely averted. Any concept of checks and balances or separation of powers is no longer involved in the legislative process. The catalyst for the issuance of an Executive Order has, until recent years, been some form of emergency, such as when FDR seized the property of 100,000 Japanese-American citizens in 1941, arrested them, and threw them into concentration camps until the end of the war—under Executive Order 9066.

Throughout this century, but especially since FDR, presidents have unconstitutionally exercised legislative power by use of Executive Orders, which they have issued during presidentially-declared States of National Emergency. Franklin Roosevelt declared a State of National Emergency in 1933 (ostensibly to deal with the Great Depression—and later World War II) and over the next 12.3 years, wrote 3,522 Executive Orders (285 per year).

In truth, through that State of Emergency and those Executive Orders, FDR had almost total dictatorial power over America—power which the Congress unconstitutionally relinquished to him. So, once a national emergency is declared, presidents use Executive Orders to exercise emergency powers. Thirteen thousand Executive Orders have been issued since we became a republic. Many are still in effect.

Executive Orders were the means by which Germany was converted from a republic into a Nazi dictatorship in just three months. Executive Orders are issued by the president and appear in the *Federal Register* for thirty days. If there is no challenge by Congress, the order then becomes law. Similar to EO's are Presidential Decision Directives, such as the secret PDD-25, which allows for the use of U.S. troops in U.N. operations without congressional approval—in violation of the Constitution.

There have been thousands of Executive Orders written by presidents since the 1940s. Most of these consist of administrative housekeeping. *However, a few orders involve much more than the efficient management of the nation. They virtually suspend constitutional rights and provide dictatorial powers to the executive branch of the government in a time of real or contrived emergency.* There is no provision for how long a state of emergency can last.

If the president were to declare an emergency, for whatever reason, congressional consent **is not** required. *Executive Orders give the government the power to act as an unaccountable dictatorship.* In addition, authority does not flow from the president to the governors of the various states during the emergency, but rather through the director of the Federal Emergency Management Agency (FEMA) and his regional directors. The states are totally bypassed. *A few years ago, Bill Clinton quietly moved FEMA out from under the authority of Congress and under his own authority (i.e., directly under the National Security Council).*

The authority to issue Executive Orders grants the occupant of the Oval Office imperial, dictatorial control—power, raw unadulterated power, vested in one individual, *with only a claim* that there is a domestic, financial, or social crisis needed to trigger its use. Can Bill Clinton, Al Gore, or any U.S. president be trusted with such unrestrained power? Would Clinton use such power to keep himself in office?

Presidential Decision Directives (PDDs)

PDDs are issued by the president outlining broad changes in future policy. PDD-25 (formerly PDD-13) is an example of Clinton PDDs which make broad policy changes with no congressional approval. *PDD-25 created the framework for moving the U.S. military under United Nations command, and is the basis for U.S. military participation in U.S. peacekeeping operations.* Despite the fact that the Congress has the exclusive constitutional authority to make rules and regulations for our land and naval forces, members of Congress have never been able to see PDD-25—which Clinton has had classified. *Clinton has issued sixty-three such PDDs since coming to office—all classified in whole or in part.*

PDD-63 is another example of Clinton's power grab. Issued on May 22, 1998, it establishes a new federal bureaucracy called the National Infrastructure Protection Center, which includes the FBI, the Secret Service, other federal law enforcement agencies, the Department of Defense, and the intelligence agencies, and sets up the bureaucracy to help manage the crisis in coordination with the Defense and Commerce Departments and intelligence agencies.

PDD-63 will facilitate the setting up of more computerized files on each American, the sharing of these files between agencies, etc. This classified PDD sounds ominously like it may be used to facilitate a State of Emergency and martial law.

EOs Now in Effect Which Threaten Americans' Freedoms

Several dozen Executive Orders passed under Presidents Kennedy, Johnson, Nixon, Ford, Carter, Reagan, Bush, and Clinton, if implemented in a coming State of Emergency, *would turn America overnight into a totalitarian police state*—a dictatorship not unlike those under Lenin, Stalin, Hitler, Mao, or Castro. The following Executive Orders, now recorded in the *Federal Register* and therefore accepted by Congress as the law of the land, can be put into effect at any time an emergency is declared by President Clinton or his successor with the mere stroke of a pen. [*Note:* Some of these may have been revised, updated, had their numbers changed, or consolidated under other omnibus EOs. Most of them are still in existence at this writing, in some form, however.]

- **EO 10995**—All communications media seized by the federal government. Radio, television, newspapers, magazines, CB, HAM, short wave, telephones, satellites, and the Internet. The First Amendment would be suspended.
- **EO 10997**—Seizure of all electrical power, fuels, including gasoline, and minerals.
- **EO 10998**—Seizure of all food resources, farms and farm equipment. **Anti-food hoarding regulations would go into effect.**
- **EO 10999**—Seizure of all kinds of transportation, including your personal car, and control of all highways, seaports, waterways, rail-

ways, airports, and public storage facilities. The government can seize any vehicle.

- **EO 11000**—Seizure of all civilians for work under federal supervision.
- **EO 11001**—Federal takeover of all health, education, and welfare, including hospitals, pharmaceuticals, and schools.
- **EO 11002**—Postmaster General empowered to register every man, woman, and child in the U.S.A.
- **EO 11003**—Seizure of all aircraft and airports by the federal government.
- **EO 11004**—Housing and Finance authority may shift population from one locality to another. Housing may be seized.
- **EO 11005**—Seizure of railroads, inland waterways, and storage facilities.
- **EO 11051**—The director of the Office of Emergency Planning authorized to put Executive Orders into effect in "times of increased international tension or financial crisis." He is also to perform such additional functions as the president may direct.
- **EO 11490**—Presidential control over all U.S. citizens and businesses (including churches) in time of emergency.
- **EO 11921**—The government would seize control over education, welfare, mechanisms of production and distribution, energy sources, wages, salaries, credit, and the flow of money in U.S. financial institutions and impose total censorship.
- **EO 12919**—Directs various cabinet officials to be constantly ready to take over virtually all aspects of the U.S. economy during a State of Emergency—at the direction of the president.
- **EO 13010**—Directs FEMA to take control over all government agencies in time of emergency. [*Note:* FEMA is now directly under the control of Bill Clinton and his National Security Council.]
- **EO 13011**—Creates a national information system, a massive new bureaucracy with authority to manage "Federal Information Technology." (Signed by President Clinton on July 16, 1998.) It links the data gathered by the Health, Education, and Labor Departments to the data assessable to the FBI, CIA, EPA, and other federal agen-

cies. It gives the unified information system the power to control people through a vast, federal data bank and monitoring system.

- **EO 12919**—On June 6, 1994, President Clinton issued this Executive Order entitled "National Defense Industrial Resources Preparedness." This Executive Order effectively puts the entire U.S. under the control of FEMA and the various cabinet secretaries. It asserts that the president can require any person in the country to accept and give priority performance of contracts or orders.

It gives the president complete power to seize or allocate all public and private materials, services, facilities, food resources, food resource facilities, distribution of farm equipment and commercial fertilizer; construction materials; health resources; all forms of energy; and all forms of civilian transportation. Under this Executive Order, the president's National Security Council will be in charge of controlling and distributing **ALL** U.S. resources.

FEMA will function under the National Security Council, but the director of FEMA will report directly to the president. The director of FEMA is responsible for executing presidential policy regarding essential civilian needs, supporting national defense, continuity of government, and related activities. *The comprehensive power set forth in Executive Order 12919 currently rests with the president, his cabinet, and FEMA, who therefore have the structure in place to exercise plenary power over this nation whenever the president chooses to do so.*

[*Note:* There is a lot of overlap and redundancy in these various Executive Orders, but this one, **EO 12919, may be the primary one under which Clinton may attempt to implement a State of National Emergency and martial law.** It encompasses most of the other Executive Orders. It is reminiscent of the Depression/wartime era powers which Roosevelt seized when he declared a State of National Emergency. Actually, that State of Emergency and the one declared by Clinton on November 14, 1994, are still in existence. Thus, the plans and programs outlined in EO 12919, which are at this writing apparently well developed, could be implemented (perhaps by another Executive Order) without congressional approval **at any time** (e.g., in a financial or terrorist crisis which could eventuate in the coming months). **Voilá! We have an instant dictatorship!]**

The Present State of Emergency

The Executive Orders discussed in this section are only those covering a potential State of National Emergency, martial law, and complete power grab. They have been enacted by several presidents over the past thirty-five years. Clinton has enacted several hundred other Executive Orders covering everything from A to Z, which space constraints will not allow us to discuss.

Other Dangerous Clinton Executive Orders

a) **EO 13083—Ripping Federalism from Its Constitutional Roots—** On May 14, 1998, President Clinton issued **EO 13083** (while in England) entitled "Federalism." It was to replace President Reagan's **EO 12612** which was designed to **protect** the Tenth Amendment. That Tenth Amendment reserves all powers not expressly given to the federal government to the states. **EO 13083** would have effectively given all states' powers to the federal government in a breathtaking executive power grab.

In essence, EO 13083 claims the authority to dispense with constitutional limitations, the separation of powers, and the reserved powers of individual states when the president or his subordinates in the executive branch believe such action is necessary. For the Clintonites, federalism is defined by consolidation of arbitrary power in the central government, rather than diffusion of power among the various state, county, and local governments, and limitation of all government power through a written Constitution.

There was no effort by the Administration to solicit input from state or local governments. They simply sneaked it into the *Federal Register* and hoped that nobody would notice. But a number of congressmen, senators, and governors did notice after a huge public outcry, and Clinton was forced on August 5, 1998, to suspend (not cancel—just suspend) the Executive Order. He will try to slip it back in later.

b) **The Implementation of Human Rights Treaty (EO 13107)** — On December 10, 1998, while America focused on the impeachment, Clinton quietly signed a seditious new Executive Order that would create a massive and intrusive federal bureaucracy to monitor and enforce compliance with the United Nations human rights regulations and treaties. One of those treaties, the unratified Convention on the Rights of the Child (described above) would be included. These U.N. treaties and regulations could have been written by global socialists (or communists) in Russia, Red China, or Cuba, and are totally destructive of Americans' freedoms.

Reagan's 1988 Executive Order Paves the Way for a Dangerous Federal Power Grab

Howard Phillips wrote the following in his November 30, 1998, *Issues and Strategies Bulletin:*

Executive Order 12656, "Assignment of Emergency Preparedness Responsibilities," which President Reagan signed on November 18, 1988, states in part that: "Whereas the Congress has directed the development of such national security emergency preparedness plans and has provided funds for the accomplishment thereof: Now, therefore, by virtue of the authority vested in me as President by the Constitution and laws of the United States of America, and pursuant to Reorganization Plan No. 1 of 1958 (72 Stat. 1799), the National Security Act of 1947, as amended, the Defense Production Act of 1950, as amended, and the Federal Civil Defense Act, as amended, it is hereby ordered that the responsibilities of the Federal departments and agencies in national security emergencies shall be as follows: . . .

Clinton Would Set Policy During "Technical Emergency"—Unless Congress Objects—"A national security emergency is any occurrence, including natural disaster, military attack, technological emergency, or other emergency, that seriously degrades or seriously threatens the national security of the United States. Policy for national security emergency preparedness shall be established by the President. . . ."

Education and Labor in Service to the State—"[T]he Secretary of Education shall: . . . Develop plans to support the Secretary of Labor in providing education and training to overcome shortages of critical skills; . . ."

Federal Takeover of Local Law Enforcement?—"[T]he Attorney General of the United States shall: . . . Coordinate Federal Government/domestic law enforcement activities related to national security emergency preparedness, including Federal law enforcement liaison with, and assistance to, State and local governments; . . . Coordinate contingency planning for national security emergency law enforcement activities that are beyond the capabilities of state and local agencies; . . . Develop intergovernmental and interagency law enforcement plans and counter-terrorism programs to interdict and respond to terrorism incidents in the United States that may result in a national security emergency or that occur during such an emergency. . . ."

What "Is" a Civil Disturbance?—"Develop intergovernmental and interagency law enforcement plans to respond to civil disturbances that may result in a national security emergency or that occur during such an emergency. . . ."

Will Local Police Work for the U.N. and the IMF?—"Support the Secretaries of State and the Treasury in plans for the protection of international organizations. . . ."

Will You Be Able to Move Your Assets In and Out of America?—"Support the Secretary of the Treasury in developing plans to control the movement of property entering and leaving the United States; . . . ."

Will American Workers Be Employed by a Fascist State?— "[T]he Secretary of Labor shall: . . . Develop plans and issue guidance to ensure effective use of civilian workforce resources during national security emergencies. Such plans shall include, but not necessarily be limited to: (a) Priorities and allocations, recruitment, referral, training, employment stabilization including appeals procedures, use assessment, and determination of critical skill categories; and . . . "

Wage and Price Controls Will Be Imposed—"In consultation with the Secretary of the Treasury, develop plans and procedures for wage, salary, and benefit costs stabilization during national security emergencies; . . ."

Your Child May Be "Conscripted"—Along with You—"Support planning by the Secretary of Defense and the private sector for the provision of human resources to critical defense industries during national security emergencies; . . . Support planning by the Secretary of Defense and the Director of Selective Service for the institution of conscription in national security emergencies. . . ."

Federal Government "Shall" Control Your Travel In and Out of America—"The Secretary of State shall: . . . Assist the Attorney General of the United States in the formulation of national security emergency plans for the control of persons entering or leaving the United states. . . . Coordinates with the State and local highway agencies in the management of all Federal, State, city, local, and other highways, roads, streets, bridges, tunnels, and publicly owned highway maintenance equipment to assure efficient and safe use of road space during national security emergencies; . . ."

Imposition of Currency Controls Is Anticipated—"[T]he Secretary of the Treasury shall: . . . Develop plans for encouraging capital inflow **and discouraging the flight of capital from the United States.** . . . Develop plans, in coordination with the Secretary of Commerce and the Attorney General of the United States, to control the movement of property entering or leaving the United States; . . . Cooperate with the Attorney General of the United States on law enforcement activities, including the control of people entering and leaving the United States; . . . Support the Secretary of Labor in developing plans and procedures for wage, salary, and benefit costs stabilization; . . . Support the Secretary of State in plans for the protection of international organizations and foreign diplomatic, consular, and other official personnel and property or other assets in the United States. . . ."

Signed, Sealed, and Delivered by the "Great Communicator"—"Executive Order Nos. 10421 and 11490, as amended, are hereby revoked. This Order shall be effective immediately. Ronald Reagan, The White House, November 18, 1988."

Combining the **Reagan Executive Order** with the other Executive Orders (briefly described above)—and especially Clinton's EO 12919, *the* *legal machinery for a complete government takeover of America and es-tablishment of a totalitarian police state and dictatorship is now in place.* Would Clinton or Gore push the button? What do you think? All we need is the right major crisis (real or manufactured)! The coming finan-cial collapse, or a series of terrorist attacks such as Oklahoma City, the World Trade Center, TWA 800, etc., all would be justification for a giant power grab.

If Bill Clinton declares a State of National Emergency, let's say due to chaos or a series of terrorist incidents, and moves to institute the EOs and PPDs described above, the Constitution will be suspended during the emergency. Once enacted, Congress, which has allowed Clinton (and other presidents) to amass this power via the EOs and PPDs, will be helpless to stop him.

In such a crisis, FEMA will be empowered to act on a national basis (backed by the U.S. military, National Guard, or U.N.) and "in the in-terest of national security" the year 2000 elections could be suspended and Clinton or Gore could remain in office on a more or less permanent basis. (People who know Clinton *intimately* believe he has no intention of leaving office in the year 2000.) This is how Hitler and the Third Reich dictatorship came to power.

The Ominous Parallel with Nazi Germany

The *New American* (8/17/98) reported in an article entitled "The Impe-rial President":

> The attempted preemption of state and local governments by EO 13083 offers an ominous echo of the campaign of *gleichschaltung*—"coordi-nation"—through which Germany's National Socialist (Nazi) Party abolished federalism and created a totalitarian state in 1933. "The plan was deceptively simple and had the advantage of cloaking the seizure of absolute power in LEGALITY," wrote liberal historian William Shirer in *The Rise and Fall of the Third Reich.*
>
> The Reichstag would be asked to pass an "enabling act" confer-ring on Hitler's cabinet exclusive legislative powers for four years. *Put more simply, the German Parliament would be requested to turn over its*

constitutional functions to Hitler and take a long vacation. But since this necessitated a change in the constitution, a two-thirds majority was needed to approve it.

Like Bill Clinton, Hitler urged the German Parliament to choose "progress" over "partisanship." He also exploited a terrorist attack (the burning of the Reichstag in February 1933) to obtain legislative support for expanding his executive powers. **And, like Bill Clinton, Hitler pursued his consolidation of power through executive decrees.**

Beginning on March 9, 1933—two weeks before passage of the Enabling Act—Hitler's government evicted sitting state governments and installed Reich commissars to replace them. On March 31, using the powers granted through the Enabling Act, Hitler dissolved all state diets or assemblies (except for the previously Nazified diet in Prussia). On April 7 Hitler issued a law appointing Reich governors in all states and granting them power to reconstitute state and local governments. Each new governor was a National Socialist Party member and was required to follow the general policy laid down by the Reich chancellor.

"Thus," concluded Shirer, "within a fortnight of receiving full powers from the Reichstag, Hitler had achieved what Bismarck, Wilhelm II, and the Weimar Republic had never dared to attempt: he had abolished the separate powers of the historic states and made them subject to the central authority of the Reich, which was in his hands. He had, for the first time in German history, really unified the Reich by destroying its age-old federal character."

By January 30, 1934, Hitler fully consummated his triumph over Germany's federal constitution by issuing a "Law for the Reconstruction of the Reich." Under that measure, according to Shirer, "'Popular Assemblies' of the states were abolished, the sovereign powers of the states were transferred to the Reich, all state governments were placed under the Reich government, and the state governors put under the administration of the Reich Minister of the Interior"—that is, under the head of Germany's nationalized police. As Interior Minister Wilhelm Frick triumphantly observed on that date, "The State governments from now on are merely administrative bodies of the Reich."

The parallels between Hitler's executive tyranny and that being fashioned by Bill Clinton are inexact, but instructive nonetheless. In fact, it may be said that President Clinton's bid to consolidate executive power and abolish federalism by decree actually displays greater audacity than Hitler's, given that Hitler's most decisive actions were taken after the German legislature had formally surrendered power through the Enabling Act.

The U.S. republic is in grave danger from Bill Clinton (who appears to have no intention of yielding his power), Al Gore, and the Executive Orders and Presidential Decision Directives which could be used to turn America into a dictatorship literally overnight. It is absolutely essential for Congress to:

1. Nullify all existing Executive Orders and PPDs.
2. Require that in the future any such orders be authorized by the Congress by a two-thirds vote of both houses.
3. Require that such orders be made public in the *Congressional Record* and to the general public immediately after congressional authorization.
4. Require that they may not go into effect until at least thirty days following congressional authorization unless otherwise authorized by two-thirds vote of both houses of Congress.

Toward a State of National Emergency and Martial Law in America
Until recently, the concept of martial law in America was as foreign and unthinkable to most Americans as the idea of putting a man on the moon would have been in 1940. However, with the rapid approach of chaos (economic, financial, and social) it is likely to engender, and the growing threat of terrorist attacks within the continental United States, the concept of martial law is no longer so farfetched.

Two Potential U.S. Crises
Either of two crises taken separately or happening concurrently can be enough to justify a State of National Emergency and martial law: 1) a

financial collapse like we almost saw in September–October 1998, accompanied by a nationwide bank run; 2) Terrorist attacks such as those warned of in *Time* magazine (12/98), wherein foreign terrorists unleash weapons of mass destruction (i.e., nuclear, biological, or chemical in some major city); or several large buildings are bombed *a la* the World Trade Center and Oklahoma City; or several airliners are taken down by terrorists.

When the breakdown begins, the public will demand that the government do something to protect them and stop the pain. That's exactly what the people of Los Angeles did during the Los Angeles riots of 1992 and martial law was declared. They will cry out for help and the president will act. He will mobilize the troops. Governors will do the same. **When it's a choice between chaos and loss of freedom, most people will choose loss of freedom.**

What Is Martial Law?

Martial law is purely and simply rule by the military. It comes into existence when civil government can no longer maintain law and order; it requires no proclamation to be invoked; and exists so long as it is necessary to restore conditions to where civil government can function.

Under martial law, the Constitution is suspended and the legal protections we enjoy under the Constitution, such as the *writ of habeas corpus* (i.e., right to trial by jury) can be suspended. People can be arrested and imprisoned indefinitely without charges under martial law. Freedom of speech and freedom of assembly can be suspended under nationwide martial law and **censorship of the media (the press, television, the airwaves, and the Internet) imposed.**

Gun Ownership Will Come Under Attack Under Martial Law

Under martial law or some future civil disturbance, or under any (or all) of the three conditions described above, house-to-house searches for firearms and seizure of same by the military, National Guard, or foreign troops would be conducted. The National Guard has been practicing the same for several years. Firearms have already been seized in Great Britain, Australia, and even in New York, where guns were registered several years in advance of the laws that banned them.

The Brady law's five-day waiting period for gun purchases was replaced on November 30, 1998, by a national computerized instant check of gun buyers' backgrounds. During negotiations over the 4,000-page federal budget agreement, language that would have prevented the Feds from retaining purchase records generated by the new system was stripped out. Timid Republicans were frightened that Clinton would veto the budget and make them look bad, so they gutted the anti-registration provision inserted by Sen. Robert Smith (R-NH). *As a result, the Justice Department will know where you bought your gun, when you bought it, and where to find it when they decide to confiscate it.*

Terrorism or the Threat of Terrorism Could be the Trigger for a State of Emergency and Martial Law

Bill Clinton's "wag the dog" attacks on alleged terrorist camps in Afghanistan and Sudan and his bombing of Iraq in 1998 (both attacks killing substantial numbers of innocent civilians) have triggered incredible hatred throughout the Islamic world for America and Americans. In late 1998 warnings began to mount around the world of coming terrorist retaliatory attacks against Americans in Kuwait, Saudi Arabia, Bahrain, the United Arab Emirates, New York, Washington, and elsewhere.

U.S. military personnel throughout the Middle East have been put under curfew and told not to gather in public places. *Time* magazine has warned that Osama bin Laden may be planning a strike with weapons of mass destruction in New York and Washington in an eye-for-an-eye retaliation. One State Department official told *Time*: "We've hit his headquarters, now he hits ours."

The U.S. military says there are 120 major U.S. cities that are potential terrorist targets and at least until recently those were listed on the "Domestic Preparedness" web site at *db.sbccom.army.mil/fs_120c.html.* **These are the most likely target cities for martial law, since they encompass eighty percent of the U.S. population.** Some of these cities are being stockpiled with anthrax vaccines by order of the president (from early 1998). Federal workers and the military are being trained in techniques such as how to dispose of large numbers of dead bodies, how to keep people off the streets and prevent them from using highways, how to bring emergency supplies to those still alive, and other unpleasant topics.

Martial Law: An Assessment of the Military Response

In studying military publications such as *Legal Aspects of Domestic Employment of the Army* by Thomas R. Lujan (published in *Parameters*, Autumn 1997); DoD Directive 3025.12—*Military Assistance for Civil Disturbances* (MACDIS) February 4, 1994, USD(P); the White Paper on PDD-63; Operation Garden Plot—the DoD's Generic OPLAN, and other such government documents—*there is growing evidence that high priority preparations are underway for the declaration and implementation of martial law in America.*

The **legal authority** for such martial law is the various Executive Orders and PDDs discussed earlier. So, the **legal** machinery for martial law has been assembled, the **military** machinery for martial law is being moved into place at this writing, with deployment of advance teams or military assets in over fifty cities at this writing, and is about fifty to seventy percent complete. All that stands between us and martial law is a terrorist crisis (real **or staged**) and the whim of a president who desperately wants to hang on to his power at all costs.

The following section will focus exclusively on the government's likely response and how it will affect you. This section was written with the assistance of an individual with years of intimate, very high level contacts within the military and intelligence community; relies heavily on information already published in military, intelligence, and other government publications; and contains no classified information.

The government is formulating its contingency plans, investigating ways for it to not only hold on to power, but expand that power broadly, until the people can no longer seriously impede anything it desires to do. This is perhaps the most serious threat that faces the citizens of this country, beyond the immediate issues of food, water, and shelter in a terrorist crisis.

While many of the plans are shrouded in secrecy, no large-scale planning and preparation can occur without a lot of information being leaked through personnel or through troop movements, training exercises, and other deployments that occur throughout the course of preparatory deployment. We will examine information from many sources to draw a picture that should cause concern to every citizen of this country.

What the Government Will Demand—The primary reason for a government's existence is to protect the nation from both external and internal threats. This, when coupled with the enforcement of law and order, should, according to our Founding Fathers, constitute the bulk of our government's responsibilities. Unfortunately, our government has increasingly taken authority upon itself to deal with a plethora of other issues, thereby expanding its power at an almost geometric rate. This has been done largely through crisis management. Crises give the government broad powers to act essentially as a dictatorship should it so desire. Under a State of Emergency, it is not directly answerable to the people, and that is precisely what the Clintonites are banking on.

The government, as it was originally founded, envisioned the people of the country to be the final check and balance in the greater system of checks and balances within the government structure itself. This is why an armed populace was seen as an indispensable part of a free society. It was seen as nearly impossible to oppress an armed populace, and so this was the last line of defense against the kind of dictatorial tyranny the from which the founders fled. This is by definition a confrontational relationship. The government knows that the single greatest threat to its grand socialistic designs is the armed populace of America. This is why there has been such a war on private gun ownership over the last thirty years. Major steps are now being put in place for the absolute destruction of the Second Amendment.

Operation Garden Plot—The DoD's OPLAN for Martial Law—The global socialists must remove or minimize the threat posed by an armed populace. According to Department of Defense documents, in time of national emergency the government sees and will treat the general public as the enemy. The following are excerpts from Operation Garden Plot, the DoD's generic operations plan (OPLAN) for **Civil Disturbance Doctrine**:

If any civil disturbance by **a resistance group, religious organization, or other persons considered to be non-conformist takes place,** Appendix 3 to Annex B of Plan 55-2 hereby gives all Federal forces total power over the situation if/when local and state authorities cannot put down said dissent.

Under section D, a Presidential Executive Order will authorize and direct the Secretary of Defense to use the Armed Forces of the United States to restore order.

POR:SGH.JCS Pub 6, Vol. 5, AFR-160-5 Hereby provides for America's military and the National Guard State Partnership Program to join the United Nations personnel in said operations. This links selected U.S. National Guard units with the Defense Ministries of "Partnership for Peace." This has been done in an effort to provide military support to civil authorities in response to civil emergencies.

Partnership for Peace is an international agreement whereby the U.S. and other nations will exchange troops to put down disturbances in each other's country (i.e., U.S. troops could be sent to Eastern Europe, Europe, or Russian or Chinese troops could be sent to America to help "restore the peace"). [*Note:* Check the Internet under: *USAF Civil Disturbance Plan 55-2* to find the "Operation Garden Plot" text.]

Under PDD-25, this program serves to cement people to relationships between the citizens of the United States and the global military of the U.N. establishments of the emerging democracies of Central and Eastern European countries. National Guardsmen will hence be under the direct jurisdiction of the United Nations.

What should be particularly disturbing to the reader is that the definition of dissenters, non-conformists, and religious cults are sufficiently broadened to define nearly anyone the government chooses to label as a criminal and an enemy of the state. These definitions will allow the government the legal authority to imprison anyone they wish for however long they wish, especially those seen as being a thorn in the side of the government forces enforcing Executive Orders.

People Control in the Coming Crisis—The Clinton Administration has laid the legal groundwork (through Presidential Executive Orders and Presidential Decision Directives) for a possible widespread seizure of power. A financial collapse—replete with a bank run or terrorist attacks on U.S. soil (or some combination thereof)—will be their "reason." Now we need to look at what their plans will likely be.

The government needs to control the people. Well over eighty percent of the nation's population is now located within 120 major cities (1990 U.S. Census statistics). This provides the government with 120 areas where they can corral the majority of the U.S. populace and keep them from becoming a major problem. There are, however, problems with this strategy.

The people of this country would not readily stand for a blatant government takeover, using troops to quell and subjugate the masses. This kind of overt action, without a major crisis, would only lead to civil war. They need an acceptable justification for such action, and they already have it.

One of the things being talked about on the evening news these days is the threat of WMD (weapons of mass destruction). These are defined as NBCs (nuclear, biological, or chemical weapons). Public statements are now being made warning of the inevitability of a terrorist strike, and inoculations are being given to the armed forces as a precautionary measure.

I believe the proliferation of weapons of mass destruction presents the greatest threat that the world has ever known. We are finding more and more countries who are acquiring technology—not only missile technology—and are developing chemical weapons and biological weapons capabilities to be used in theater and also on a long range basis. So I think that is perhaps the greatest threat that any of us will face in the coming years.
—Secretary of Defense William Cohen, January 1997

Experts tell us it's not if, but when.
—Acting Secretary of the Army, Michael Walker, on the likelihood of a WMD attack on U.S. soil, March 17, 1998

On March 17, 1998, the Telecom News, American Forces Press Service, quoting Defense Secretary William Cohen, wrote the following:

> Saying the "front lines are no longer overseas," Defense Secretary William S. Cohen announced *a new DoD program March 17 to respond to domestic attacks with weapons of mass destruction.* Under his new initiative, National Guard and Reserve forces will receive training to help states and local governments respond in case of attack. *Ten Rapid Assessment and Initial Detection elements will be trained and equipped beginning in fiscal 1999.* Cohen said the initiative is the "cornerstone of our strategy for preparing America's defense against possible weapons of mass destruction. The larger meaning of this moment is that we live in a world where more powerful weapons are in the hands of more reckless people who are more likely to use them . . . terrorist, religious zealots, or organized crime groups who also seek these weapons."

[*Note:* Over the past few years, it has been in vogue for the political left and the liberal media to lump Islamic fundamentalist radicals and religious right activists (in America) together as religious zealots, extremists, or terrorists. Hence, it is only a short jump to label Christian activists as terrorists, as Janet Reno has so labeled pro-life demonstrators.]

Cohen continued:

> Under PDD-39 the SICG (Senior Interagency Coordination Group) will offer training **to the nation's 120 largest cities** over the next several years in support of established U.S. government counterterrorism response procedures. . . . DoD will lead interagency assessment teams which will liaise with city officials and emergency response personnel. Initial assessment of the first twenty-seven cities should be completed by the end of fiscal year 1997. The National Communication System, DoD, FEMA, and eight other federal organizations are members of this interagency group.

This talk is meant to "educate" the public, and frighten them to a degree that will cause them to accept government preparations and actions they would not under normal circumstances accept. The Clinton Administration (or Gore Administration) cannot possibly execute all of its planning and preparation without offering some defendable rationale for its activities, both to the general public and the men inside the military itself, who are still American citizens who love freedom.

Weapons of mass destruction are the rationale, and while the threat is indeed real, it is being played for all it is worth to further the Clinton agenda. The above recently announced WMD training **in 120 major cities** around the country speaks to the census information on population distribution and demographics perfectly—the numbers match. It is as if they took the census information and formulated their operational plans from it. This training program came straight from the top through PDD-39, and involves ten federal agencies including FEMA and the DoD.

This program will set up coordination with local law enforcement, establish interagency command structures, set up working relationships between National Guard and Army Reserve units, unify overall training efforts between federal and local assets, as well as collecting much needed regional intelligence. Once hierarchies (who answers to whom) have been established, then the intelligence gathered would be analyzed (likely using the aforementioned FBI profiles) to determine the greatest possible threats in that locality. The first twenty-seven cities had already conducted their initial assessments as of the end of fiscal 1997 and by early 1999, fifty-two cities had completed assessments and have had the groundwork laid for martial law.

It is important to remember that many of the average citizens of this country live lives that the Clintonites perceive as threatening to their own dominance. (So much for the idea of serving the people.) The Clintonites will take what steps they can well in advance to prepare to neutralize these perceived threats. The Clintons see non-conformists (whatever that means) as enemies of the state, and will authorize, during the coming crisis, deadly force to be used to put down these threats.

This intelligence gathering approach is referred to in military parlance as IPB (Intelligence Preparation of the Battlefield). These activities were conducted in-depth by JTF-LA during the LA riots, with information being passed on to intelligence analysts at Fort Ord, California

(*U.S. Army Newsletter*—Civil Disturbance Doctrine 7/93).

Once they have established their operational structures, and ensured that commanders of local military and civilian forces will cooperate, they will wait until the Executive Order is given by President Clinton to begin Operation Garden Plot.

Over the past six to twelve months and the next six to twelve months, the infrastructure for the enforcement of this presidential Executive Order has, or is being put into place. There are many seemingly innocuous adjustments taking place in the way things are organized both within the executive branch and the military coordination with civilian law enforcement. As the *Washington Post* wrote (3/28/98):

> *The White House has proposed an overhaul of counterterrorism strategy that would concentrate greater power in the National Security Council* . . . the proposal would shift key assignments among federal law enforcement agencies, including FBI, CIA, and the Defense Department, while giving the NSC more power and control. The NSC would have authority over everything from the development of yearly budget plans to rescue efforts after an extremist attack.
>
> "When money was going to the war on drugs, we created a drug czar. Now money is going to counterterrorism and so we'll have a czar for that, except this one will have real power," said an administration official.

[*Note:* It should be remembered that the National Security Council is directly under the authority of President Clinton. *He is consolidating more and more power under his authority!*]

In analyzing the above news report and the proposal it describes, it becomes clear that the Clinton Administration wants and needs to take prosecutorial powers away from traditional law enforcement agencies, and give them to those within the immediate command structure of the National Command Authority (NCA). In other words, they need to be able to arrest (without the objections of the involved military or government personnel) whomever they wish, for whatever they deem as a threat, whether legal, ethical, fair, or not.

This move is designed to remove any possible interference from those within the justice system who might have a problem with the Draconian actions that will be taken. *This streamlines the whole process of the government assumption of power, coordinating all the command structures through the NSC (National Security Council) under Bill Clinton,* which is more able to handle the operational demands of an operation of this size than FEMA.

It should also be noted that FEMA is largely a disaster management agency, and is not equipped to handle civil disorder and counterterrorism activities (CT). CT activities are the purview of the FBI, which has the power in many CT operations to request and receive aid from the DoD. This interaction is becoming more commonplace every day. It was utilized in the government operation against the Branch Davidian compound in Waco, Texas, in 1993. FEMA is primarily oriented toward dealing with an event after it has happened, rather than working to prevent it.

Part Two

The Rising Persecution of Christians and Traditionalists in America

Most Americans have very little concept of religious or political persecution, because in our 223-year history we have never experienced real persecution in our country. Discrimination, yes, but persecution because of our political or religious beliefs, no.

Most Americans (including American Christians) have paid very little attention or read very little regarding the persecution of Christians around the world, from the martyrdom of Stephen to the present, and most know very little about the persecution of the Jews under the Nazi Third Reich or the Christian church in Russia, the former East bloc countries, or in China, North Korea, Vietnam, Cuba, Sudan, Saudi Arabia, or the other Islamic countries today.

This section will explore past and present persecutions around the world; the incredible parallels between Nazi Germany in the 1930s and America today; and how the pattern of escalating persecution against the Jews under Naziism is very similar to the pattern of escalating persecution against Christians and traditionalists in America today.

It will examine how the political left in America, which controls the major levers of power in the U.S., is systematically building a consensus against Christians and conservatives by stereotyping, marginalizing, vilifying, slandering, and discriminating against them and setting the stage for criminalizing the activities of these groups. Outright persecution will follow—within a very few years.

Until the last few years, the U.S. Constitution would have protected any political or religious group against persecution, but over the last decade or two the liberals and the political left in the U.S. judiciary and government have ignored, neutered, and virtually shredded that Constitution. So, there is a growing possibility (indeed probability) that like the Jews of the 1930s, the politically incorrect Christians and traditionalists of our day, who have been trying to take a stand against the evils of our day, could be the new targets of discrimination and outright persecution.

Chapter 8

Global Persecutions: Past and Present

> Blessed are they which are persecuted for righteousness' sake: for their's
> is the kingdom of heaven. Blessed are ye, when men shall revile you,
> and persecute you, and shall say all manner of evil against you falsely,
> for my sake. Rejoice, and be exceeding glad: for great is your reward in
> heaven: for so persecuted they the prophets which were before you.
>
> —Jesus, Matthew 5:10–12

The thrust of this book so far has been an emphasis on the increasing
nature of socialist people-controls over the American people; the accelerating loss of freedom which is occurring; the potential for an emerging
police state in America; and the thesis that God's judgment and a withdrawal of His hand of protection over America may now be becoming a
reality. This chapter attempts to remind us that historical and current
persecution is more the norm than not for conservative Christians, unlikely as this may seem to most Americans today.

Most American Christians are not sensitized to persecution. This
may be considered a blessing with a downside. The blessing is the obvious benefit of relative freedom to worship and practice one's faith. The
downside is the temptation we have to normalize our existence and therefore anesthetize ourselves to reality. The reality is that suffering and persecution are the more normal Christian existence, whereas the scenario
we have experienced in America is an anomaly in history and even in
much of the world today. George Otis, Jr., a widely traveled missionary
and son of a missionary, has referred to modern America as Disneyland,
in comparison to the rest of the Christian world.

In the introduction to their book *By Their Blood: Christian Martyrs
of the Twentieth Century,* James and Marti Hefley note that more Chris-

tians have died for their faith in this century than in any other comparable era in history. One estimate is that this number is in the range of 120 million people, which of course only includes those who died. Many times this number have experienced persecution of a less terminal sort such as imprisonment, starvation, loss of jobs, state seizure of children and property, harassment, beatings, and prohibitions to meet for worship or Bible study.

This chapter will illustrate one particular source of this persecution that was brought on by repressive governments. This will be done primarily by reviewing some of the more notorious regimes of the century: the Soviets, the Nazis, and the Red Chinese. Some of the most horrendous stifling of Christians today, however, is done by the Muslims. Islamic theocracies, which comprise an ever increasing portion of the world population, pose a growing resistance to the advancement of the Gospel. (Fortunately, there are breakthroughs, as documented in George Otis's book, *The Last of the Giants.*)

A Biblical Perspective

Even the most committed Christian, who affirms the priority of the Scriptures and who claims that he or she receives their direction for faith and life read the Bible through tainted lenses. We are incapable of a pure reading since we filter the Word with our understanding, background, and culture. This means that we unconsciously study the Bible in our frame of reference of present-day America and its (at least until now) religious freedom and prosperity. The "Health, Wealth, and Prosperity" or "Name It and Claim It" gospels could only originate in America. The normal state of God's people in much of the Bible is suffering and persecution. Much of the history in the Bible and much of teaching, doctrine, exhortation, and prophecy reflect this reality. Since we do not relate to this, we look past it and try to find what we can relate to. We miss the norm again. Given the thesis of this book, let's review a few past persecutions.

The people of God throughout the Bible have experienced suffering and persecution. The dominant story of the first five books of the Bible is the Exodus—meaning "the way out." The early Hebrews were distinctly God's people. They were in bondage, performing slave labor under oppressive taskmasters for 430 years in Egypt. They were not persecuted explicitly because they were special to God, yet one can suspect the implicit spiritual dynamic causing the Pharaohs to repress them is the same which caused Hitler to rampage against the Jews.

Moses led the people out through the miracle-working hand of Almighty God. They eventually found themselves in the Promised Land with emphatic instructions from God not to adopt the pagan religious practices of the surrounding peoples. They failed and within a few short generations were overrun by foreign oppressors. Thus began a centuries–long cycle of religious decadence, leading to God's judgment in the form of foreign oppression, followed by crying out to God for deliverance, only to fail once again after being delivered.

Finally the Hebrews had a king, but were only united under the second king, David. David's son Solomon ushered in the ultimate glory years for the nation with peace on the borders and great opulence and splendor seen within the land. Yet even this period at the height of the history of the Jewish people was not all it appeared to be on the surface. The magnificence of the new Temple and the king's surroundings came with a cost. He taxed and worked his subjects to the limit, creating an oppressive government.

After Solomon's illustrious reign, his son Rehoboam took the throne and proceeded to immediately make life even more unpleasant for his subjects. He threatened them saying: "My little finger shall be thicker than my father's loins. And now whereas my father did lade you with a heavy yoke, I will add to your yoke: my father hath chastised you with whips, but I will chastise you with scorpions" (**1 Kings 12:10–11**). In short order the kingdom split asunder, with the Northern Kingdom (called Israel) straying far from God for its duration. A succession of evil kings accelerated the decline of Israel until it was finally conquered by Assyria in 712 B.C. and the people deported and scattered.

The Southern Kingdom (Judah) had more kings with hearts after God, but still drifted far from Him. While there were times of occasional national repentance, such as in the reign of Josiah, the outcome was still destruction and deportation under the Babylonian armies, in what was to be called the time of the exile.

Much of Old Testament literature is comprised of the writings of the prophets who spoke for God during the time of the kings. Their message was multifaceted, containing identification of sin, calls for repentance, predictions of God's judgment, and hope of God's mercy and restoration. Thus, while the Old Testament is not about Christians and is not primarily about people suffering under oppressive government, it is about God's people, it is about suffering, and it is about God's judgment falling on people straying from God. We can learn much reading about God's relationship to His people through his Old Testament actions and the writings of the prophets.

New Testament

The New Testament is about Jesus. Jesus experienced suffering and persecution under the rulers of His day. Beginning early in His ministry, He said provocative words about suffering for the faith. His first recorded teaching is the famous Sermon on the Mount which begins with the Beatitudes. Robert Schuller has written a book on the Beatitudes, calling them the "be happy attitudes." What Jesus was saying in the last two of the nine beatitudes, however, was not how to be happy. He was talking about strength and hope while under persecution. He knew this was a vital message for the believers for all time.

The scope of this chapter does not permit an exhaustive cataloging of all Jesus said about persecution of believers, but this emphasis is very real in His teachings and His life. He told us to take up our cross and follow Him. He warned His followers that they would be like sheep among wolves. His comments on the times of the end contain many warnings of persecutions and calls to be ready.

The New Testament was written out of the life of the first century church; they knew persecution first-hand. Initially the Jewish leaders were the primary source of opposition, but later Roman rulers became even more antagonistic to the church. Nero Caesar was notorious, having been known to burn Christians at the stake along Roman highways to provide light at night. Stories abound of Christians being thrown to the lions or gladiators in Roman coliseums. To avoid the authorities, believers often met in the catacombs or tunnels beneath the city.

Tradition has it that most of the original twelve closest disciples of Jesus met death as a result of their faith. As one reads the Book of Acts one finds the messengers of the Gospel meeting opposition for their faith regularly. Their understanding of persecution is certainly evident in their writing, as exemplified in Peter's first letter. The common thread through this letter is suffering, presumably suffering for Christ. Revelation has frequent reference to persecution of believers. In fact, he wrote this book based on visions he received while imprisoned in a penal colony on the Greek island of Patmos. Some of the book is future oriented, while some has to do with Rome's activities. Chapters two and three are letters to real churches encouraging them to persevere and be overcomers in their struggles.

Much of the New Testament is written by the Apostle Paul, who was himself in the business of persecuting the church before his dramatic conversion to Christ. Once he embarked in the apostolic work, he ran into much resistance himself. In the eleventh chapter of his second letter to the church at Corinth (**2 Cor. 11:23–27**), he describes what he has been through:

> . . . in labours more abundant, in stripes above measure, in prisons more frequent, in deaths oft. Of the Jews five times received I forty stripes save one. Thrice was I was beaten with rods, once was I stoned. . . . In journeyings often, in perils of waters, in perils of robbers, in perils by mine own countrymen, in perils by the heathen, in perils in the city, in perils in the wilderness, in perils in the sea, in perils among false brethren; In weariness and painfulness, in watchings often, in hunger and thirst, in fastings often, in cold and nakedness.

An Historical Perspective

The biblical perspective obviously contains an historical perspective of persecuted believers. Persecution continued after Bible times and has continued up through the present. The early church spread far and wide as committed missionaries fanned out to spread the Gospel. Throughout the Roman Empire there was continued oppression, and yet the church grew. Finally in the fourth century the Emperor Constantine had a vision, before a critical battle, to conquer in the name of Christ. He won the battle and essentially nationalized Christianity. Curiously enough, the precursor to the monastic movement, the hermits, came about by believers who felt the new church was impure and that they personally were not living out the true Christian life when they were not persecuted.

While much history developed in the millennia or so, the Christian faith as contemporary conservative Christians know it was not a major factor, especially in the Dark Ages. Once the Protestant Reformation was underway in the sixteenth century, religious persecution took place from many sources. Even liberal U.S. history books must admit that many of the early settlers of our country came here to gain religious freedom, meaning they suffered for their faith where they came from.

This brief summary has obviously not done justice to over 1,500 years. Our primary purpose is to observe some of the regimes in our century where there has been an existing group of believers with relative freedom of worship who lost it after a change in government—because the same thing can happen here.

Russia

The state of the church in Russia was a complex one when the communists took over in 1917. The principle church body was the Russian Orthodox Church, which was to celebrate its thousandth year in Russia in 1988. The Orthodox Church was more than a church, it was part of the very fabric of what it meant to be Russian. It was deeply intertwined with the culture, and in many cases, the government. It was part of the establishment and consequently when the Bolsheviks ousted the czarist regime, they intentionally put pressure on the Orthodox Church as well.

Evangelicals were a relatively new and relatively minor presence. They had not had all smooth sailing under the czars since they were not part of "the church." (Note that the czars often executed *pogroms* against the Jews. **Where Jews are persecuted, evangelicals often receive similar treatment.**) In 1905 Czar Nicholas II issued a decree allowing for religious liberty—so the situation for evangelicals improved markedly over the next decade or so. Then came the Revolution.

The Orthodox Church was actually first in experiencing the impact of the new regime. On January 23, 1918, the Bolsheviks issued a decree which proclaimed the separation of church and state [*Note:* Sounds like America today!], and church and school, and nationalized all church property. With the stroke of a pen the Orthodox Church was deprived of the lands from which much of its income was derived, on which the monasteries were particularly dependent; it lost its network of parish schools; and it lost the right of priests to teach the catechism in government schools. Initially the Bolsheviks were too busy to enforce this edict so the churches remained open for a time.

For evangelicals and other non-orthodox denominations the decree was less damaging since the evangelicals in particular had little land and few schools. For the first time, in fact, they were much more free of persecution from the Orthodox Church. Also, the Bolsheviks were at first friendly, since history had left a legacy of persecution by the czars, and the new regime felt uttermost that anything the czars were against was acceptable. Evangelicals actually prospered and reached their height in the decade of the 1920s.

In the 1930s, Josef Stalin, who was a former seminary student, really began to tighten his grip on the church. In fact, 1928 was the last year Scriptures were to be legally published until 1956. April of 1929 saw the enactment of the Law on Religious Associations. In keeping with Marx's adage that "religion is the opiate of the people," religious believers were treated as though they were registered drug addicts: pending a cure for their religious faith they were allowed to "satisfy their religious needs," as the law put it, in worship services held inside a registered church building, but were not permitted to do anything that might spread the "addiction" to others.

In the notorious purges of the 1930s, Stalin removed all real, potential, and imaginary opposition to his rule. The remaining clergy and many ordinary members of all religious denominations were prosecuted under the catch-all Article 58 of the Russian criminal code, which covered all forms of counterrevolutionary activity. [*Note:* Similar to our RICO (racketeering) statutes today.] The Special Department of the NKDV (predecessor to the KGB) secret police compiled lists of people who for one reason or another were suspected of being in opposition to the regime. They were categorized under various headings, which included AS (anti-Soviet), TS (*tserkovnik*—active church member, i.e., Orthodox, Catholic, and Lutheran) and S (sectarian—member of a religious sect, i.e., Baptists, Pentecostals, etc.).

When Lithuania was occupied by the Soviets in 1940 the suspect part of the population amounted to twenty-three percent. Overall, throughout the USSR, it is estimated that during the purge period of 1936–39 between five and six percent of the population were arrested. Ten-year sentences were routine, and many were summarily sentenced to be shot. In many cases, mortality in the camps was high, as prisoners were used as slave labor until they were so exhausted they could do no more work. Imprisonment was thus tantamount to a suspended death sentence.

During World War II, Soviet oppression of Christians lightened somewhat, especially in those areas directly involved with German occupation. 1944 saw the creation of a state body called the Council for the Affairs of Religious Cults to deal with non-Orthodox denominations and religions. One of its key functions was to register churches. Registered churches were legal, but constrained by myriads of regulations. [*Note:* Throughout most of the communist era the various red regimes in Russia, Eastern Europe, etc. had their Ministry of Cults which was the ministry to control and repress fundamental/evangelical Christians. It is ominous that Bill and Hillary Clinton, Attorney General Janet Reno, FBI director Louis Freeh, and the political left in America regularly refer to fundamental/evangelical Christians, or the Christian right as "dangerous religious cults." The U.S. Justice Department is rapidly becoming the equivalent to the former communist Ministry of Cults.]

In 1953 Stalin died, to be replaced by Nikita Khruschchev, who allowed something of a thaw in persecution as he tried to position himself as "the reformer of Stalin's atrocities." The situation took a sharp turn for the worse, however, in 1959 when Khrushchev launched a much more active anti-religious policy. Churches were closed, Christians of all denominations were imprisoned, and anti-religious propaganda was stepped up. The campaign was part of the program to establish a fully communist society by 1980, by which time religion would be entirely superfluous. Religion would be relegated to museums as a relic of the past and Khrushchev boasted that he would show the last Christian on television.

Many times when Christians were taken to court, all kinds of allegations were made against them ranging from hypocrisy, dishonesty, ruthless exploitation of believers, and child sacrifice. These were reported by the media as facts endorsed by the court, though they did not relate to the substance of the true charges of church activity. The official propaganda line had to be maintained that there was religious freedom and that those on trial were charlatans and criminals and not genuine believers. The media was quite successful in instilling this distorted image of evangelical Christians, reinforcing a deep-seated prejudice which persists to this day.

One sure technique for disturbing Christians (or most anyone) is to focus the consequences on the children. When prominent pastor Georgi Vins and other families in his Kiev church had their children turned away from church, they wrote a letter of protest to the authorities. The response was they would be expelled from the church if they did not renounce their protest letter. They were told: "Children and young people belong to the government, not to you. [*Note:* This is Hillary Clinton's "it takes a village" concept.] The Soviet authorities do not permit religious upbringing of children or teenagers." (These families were eventually expelled, but formed a fellowship which met in the woods.)

One of the most fiercely persecuted congregations in the 1960s was an independent Pentecostal congregation in Chernogorsk, Siberia. In addition to the usual harassment, on more than one occasion the authorities attempted to disperse their meetings by calling in the fire truck from the local mine and driving worshipers out of their prayer house with high pressure hoses. Children from Christian families were mocked and denigrated at school, so that some parents decided to withdraw them from school. Some of the children were then taken away by force to be brought up in state children's homes. Two of the families involved later sought refuge in the U.S. Embassy and ended up spending almost five years seeking asylum there. They gained great notoriety, becoming known as the Siberian Seven.

As the decades wore on, one of the most significant issues facing believers was the question of being part of a registered church or not. Registered churches were legal, so worshiping in them was legal. The catch was that they were so heavily restricted and monitored that the members had very little real freedom anyway. Registered churches also were known to have the organizational structure which monitored them infiltrated with KGB personnel.

Unregistered churches did not have to follow certain restrictions in the same sense. **Everything they did was illegal.** They had a certain freedom, the freedom of the outlaw. The catch here was facing the consequences if caught, therefore they often had to be very secretive about their activities and meeting places. They eventually became known as the "underground church."

Chapters can be written documenting the change of treatment by the government of both registered and unregistered churches as years passed and issues varied. For example, after years of heavy persecution, the unregistered church was still growing, leading the government to desire that more of these believers be registered and therefore subject to control. This led to an easing of control on the registered churches in an attempt to entice more registration. At other times the government would pursue the policy that the only way to curb the unregistered churches was to crack down even harder.

Finally the modern era of *glasnost/perestroika* and the achievement of the current level of freedom were reached. Yet even the apparent breakdown of communism is not as hopeful as many in the West might believe. Dr. Ernst F. Winter, a retired Austrian diplomat who still lectures at the Diplomatic Academy in Vienna, writes in a private letter of some of his observations of students from the former Eastern bloc countries.

They are unfortunate products of communism. Communism not only tried to destroy the faith, it really destroyed man. The Western attraction to money, egotism, consumerism, etc. is falling on most fertile soils, because of the communist philosophy which is not dead. In fact, I fear new global dangers developing in Russia. This time, it will be worse than under communism, because of the total frustration of the people. They can be easily manipulated. The West has introduced most primitive capitalism and thus gain for thousands and misery for millions. You have no idea how bad the situation is.

The relaxation of persecution since *glasnost/perestroika* (actually the sixth such period of *glasnost/perestroika* since 1920) may soon be over, with the window of opportunity for taking the Gospel into Russia beginning to close at this writing. As hardened communists (or nationalists) reassert themselves, pressure and persecution against the church in Russia and the other former East bloc countries are likely to return.

Nazi Germany

Adolf Hitler's Third Reich only lasted thirteen of the thousand years he predicted, yet it caused the massive suffering and deaths of millions. The most well known of the manifold atrocities is the "final solution," the extermination of six million Jews now referred to as the Holocaust. Countless others suffered profoundly in concentration camps. The army and SS troops were guilty of massive acts of terror and horror in the field as they conquered and pillaged en route to seeking more *lebensraum*, or living space for the Fuhrer's master race. The reign of terror on the common German citizen wrought by the Gestapo is legendary. Christians predictably did not fare well in the Reich.

Of course, as Hitler took the reins of power in January of 1933 he was making all kinds of promises to respect the rights of the church. Within months Catholics were severely harassed, arrested, and suppressed. Protestants met a different fate. There were about 45 million Protestants in Germany, with all but about 150,000 in some form of Lutheran or Reformed church. By July of 1933 most of the Protestant groups had sent representatives to formulate a constitution for a new Reich Church. In an act of outrageous insult, the Nazis strong armed the election of their man as the first bishop, who was officially installed in the same church where Martin Luther had nailed his ninety-five theses to the door four centuries earlier.

A few months later a key leader of this new group proposed the abandonment of the Old Testament, "with its tales of cattle merchants and pimps," and the revision of the New Testament with the teaching of Jesus "corresponding entirely with the demands of National Socialism (Nazi)." Resolutions were drawn up demanding "One People, One Reich, One Faith," requiring all pastors to take an oath of allegiance to Hitler. This sort of thinking did not sway the masses of church people initially, but would become the state standard soon enough.

In his excellent book, *The Rise and Fall of the Third Reich,* William Shirer summarizes the sad state of the German people.

> It would be misleading to give the impression that the persecution of the Protestants and Catholics by the Nazi State tore the German people asunder or even greatly aroused the vast majority of them. **It did not.** A people who had so lightly given up their political and cultural and economic freedoms were not, except for a relatively few, going to die or even risk imprisonment to preserve freedom of worship. What really aroused the Germans in the thirties were the glittering successes of Hitler in providing jobs, creating prosperity, restoring Germany's military might, and moving from one triumph to another in his foreign policy.
>
> Not many Germans lost much sleep over the arrests of a few thousand pastors and priests or over the quarreling of various Protestant sects. And even fewer paused to reflect that under the leadership of Rosenburg, Bormann, and Himmler, who were backed by Hitler, the Nazi regime intended to eventually destroy Christianity in Germany, if it could, and substitute the old paganism of the early tribal Germanic gods and the new paganism of the Nazi extremists. As Bormann, one of the men closest to Hitler, said publicly in 1941 "National Socialism and Christianity are irreconcilable."

In the midst of the widespread sellout of much of the Protestant church, a relatively small group of pastors stood up and said no. Led by Martin Niemoller and Dietrich Bonhoeffer, they formed what became known as the Confessing Church. This name came about in 1934 when a document drafted by Karl Barth was adopted called the Barmen Confession.

Bonhoeffer and Niemoller remain heroes of the true church to this day.

Bonhoeffer left Germany for a few years, but later returned and was involved in an illegal seminary where he sought to truly live out life in Christian community. He was a brilliant man and prolific writer. He was later arrested and spent many years in prison where he wrote his *Letters and Papers from Prison,* smuggled out to his good friend Eberhard Bethge. Perhaps his most famous work is *The Cost of Discipleship,* containing his famous quote: "When Christ calls a man, he bids him come and die." Indeed at the specific orders of no less than Heinrich Himmler, head of the SS, Bonhoeffer was hanged just months before the Allied liberation of Germany in 1945.

While Martin Niemoller was also imprisoned, he survived the war and lived until 1984. He left us with the timeless quote:

> First they came for socialists [communists], and I did not speak out because I was not a socialist. Then they came for the trade unionists, and I did not speak out because I was not a trade unionist. Then they came for the Jews and I did not speak out because I was not a Jew. Then they came for me, and there was no one left to speak out for me.

China

Russia has changed at least for the moment, and Nazi Germany was defeated over fifty years ago, but China is still the communist state it has been for fifty years. Despite some openness economically, and increased trade with the West, the government's pressure against Christians has changed very little. The astonishing fact is that in spite of five decades of heavy persecution, there are probably more evangelical Christians in China than in any other country. The Chinese regime admits to 15 million Christians, but realistic estimates are as high as 100 million!

China's Christian presence is even more remarkable in light of its history. Unlike Russia with its thousand years of Christianity, and Germany, home of the Protestant Reformation over four centuries earlier, China had a relatively insignificant Christian community at the time of Mao Tse Tung's revolution in the late 1940s. China's major religions were Taoism, Confucianism, Buddhism, and ancestor worship. Christianity was limited to the influence of the various mission efforts and made up a very small percentage of the total.

Since Christianity was such a minor religion at the time of the revolution, it would be less instructive for Americans to review the history of the change in policy toward the church than it has been with Germany and Russia. There is plenty of current persecution, however. In fact, China has more Christians in prison than any other nation in the world. Protestants are arrested and tortured for holding prayer meetings, preaching, and distributing Bibles without state approval, and Roman Catholic priests and bishops are imprisoned for celebrating mass and administering the sacraments without official authorization.

There are thought to be tens of thousands of Christians now imprisoned for their faith in China's religious *gulag.* In several dragnet operations known to have recently been carried out, hundreds of Christians have been arrested at a time. Some are serving sentences of up to a dozen years or more on counterrevolutionary charges, simply for their faith. Others are being held indefinitely, thrown behind bars by administrative decree, without standing trial. Many Christian prisoners are forced to work in the *laogai,* the reform-through-labor camps where prisoners must toil as slaves for twelve hours a day, seven days a week, in automotive and chemical factories, brickmaking plants, in mines, and on farms.

The mechanism for Beijing's control of religion is the Religious Affairs Bureau, controlled by the Department for a United Front, which in turn is controlled by the Central Committee of the Communist Party. The Religious Affairs Bureau registers, oversees, and controls all Christian churches within a framework provided by its Three-Self Patriotic Movement for Protestants and the Catholic Patriotic Association. Those with ultimate power for controlling religion in China are atheists—they are required to be so by Communist Party regulations. State religious policy, as explained by Chinese president Jiang Zeminn in the March 14, 1996, edition of the *People's Daily,* is to "actively guide religion so that it can be adapted to socialist society. . . ."

The Three-Self churches are the registered churches. This system is very similar to the registered churches in Russia, as one might suspect in another communist land. Those Christians and churches who do not register are illegal and meet in underground, or house churches. There has been increased pressure by the government to register churches since January of 1996. This has been particularly aggressive in Shanghai and the provinces of Anhul and Xinjiang, with hundreds of unregistered churches being raided and dozens of house church Christians being arrested, detained, and fined. The *Far Eastern Economic Review* reported that between February and June 1996, "police destroyed at least 15,000 unregistered temples, churches, and tombs."

Analysts such as Hong Kong-based evangelical preacher Rev. Jonathan Chao believe one motivation for the crackdown is the Communist Party's belief that Christianity, which continues to grow rapidly in the vast country, is the principle threat to China's political stability. Beliefs such as the Christian tenet of individual human dignity remain anathema to communist officials who seek a monopoly on absolute power. [*Note:* In like manner, and for good reason, the dictators of the Roman Empire feared Christianity—which history shows ultimately triumphed over the might of the empire.]

Other Areas of Persecution

Though not in the headlines, Christians continue to be persecuted in other current communist countries such as Cuba, North Korea, and Vietnam. Some of the most brutal persecution of Christians, however, is now taking place in Islamic countries.

In Saudi Arabia no public expression of Christianity is permitted. It is even illegal to wear a cross necklace, to read a Bible, or to utter a Christian prayer in the privacy of your own home. Freedom of religion simply does not exist in Saudi Arabia. Under the law, conversion to Christianity by Saudi citizens is a criminal offense punishable by death. Christian foreign workers have been beaten and arrested for attempting to conduct clandestine worship services.

Persecution of Christians in Saudi Arabia has increased dramatically since the Gulf War. The Saudi government has even made demands to the United States restricting Christian worship by American citizens on U.S. Embassy grounds there. American officials have apparently capitulated to some of these demands by, for example, restricting Christian services at the embassy in Riyadh and prohibiting Christmas services for U.S. troops defending Saudi interests during the Gulf War.

Perhaps one of the most tragic places today is the Sudan. This country has been undergoing a civil war for years with Islamic forces in the north trying to subdue rebel forces in the largely Christian and animistic south. The northern Moslems are fanatical in their faith, as are the Saudis, and require their subjects to be Moslems. Many children are being kidnapped by Moslems in a widespread, government-sponsored campaign of cultural cleansing. They are summarily detained in high security closed camps for children where they are given Arabic names, indoctrinated in Islam, and forced to undergo a military-style training. Within the camps, disease is rampant and food scarce.

The northern government has also performed scorched-earth and forced starvation tactics as it prosecutes its religious war in the south. This has resulted in the deaths of over two million people and the displacement of more than three million more. Individual Christians, including clergy, have been assassinated, imprisoned, tortured, and flogged for their faith. Some have even been crucified or thrown out of airborne planes. These atrocities are but the tip of the iceberg. Similar stories can be told in Pakistan, Egypt, Burundi, and Nigeria.

As an interesting footnote, some Chinese Christians are praying that persecution will break out in America so that the American church will wake up out of its complacency and have true revival.

Considerations for American Christians

Our primary response to the current persecution of Christians around the world should be threefold. We should first learn more and be up-to-date on the magnitude and breadth of the problem. We should next be on our knees in prayer for those who are suffering for their faith. We can pray for strength, provision, hope, and relief for those being persecuted. We can also pray for those doing the persecution that they would find Jesus as their Savior and Lord as well. Finally we can advocate for these people by using every means available to put international pressure on those regimes perpetrating these most heinous of human rights violations.

We can also be learning from situations past and present. This includes being watchful and sober, as Jesus said, and understanding the times we live in. As this book chronicles, we need to be aware of the trends in our own country which are setting the stage for persecution, and not remain apathetic, complacent, and asleep until it is too late, as did the Germans.

Finally we can learn from history, in order to be prepared. For example, it is not inconceivable that we may see a situation where we have approved denominations and those that are not, in the same sense as the communists have registered and unregistered churches. Mainline denominations have a current fascination with ecumenism and are flirting with "covenanting" with each other under the auspices of the Council on Church Union (COCU). Pay attention to this. We may have to choose where we will worship: approved church or not. The unapproved churches will eventually be labeled as cults and come under government pressure. Sensitivity to God's leading is essential here.

Another decision may be how visible we are in a persecution scenario. Dietrich Bonhoeffer was highly visible. He was imprisoned and hanged. His close friend Eberhard Bethge was very secretive about his faith and actually ended up serving in the army of the Third Reich. Yet God used them both, as Bethge was the recipient of Bonhoeffer's letters from prison, which have been published and benefitted millions of believers. In other words, do we openly stand up for Christ, with potentially harsh and painful consequences, or do we work underground to further God's Kingdom in that fashion? Some will be called to the former, some to the latter. Having searched our heart ahead of time may be valuable.

Hong Kong could prove to be a tremendous laboratory for us to study in the near term, in the wake of the Chinese communists' takeover in July 1997. How they treat the church and how the church prepares and responds could teach us much. Already the Christians in Hong Kong are diligently developing small group ministries. They recognize that their places of worship may become nationalized and therefore taken from them, so they are gearing up to be able to continue ministry without reliance on the building.

Christians in Hong Kong are also concentrating on discipleship to prepare the individual for the rigors ahead. They are particularly concerned about deepening relationships so that there will be less likelihood of divisive and destructive quarrels breaking out as the heat is applied from the communists in various ways. Christians need to be strong in their faith, to not place the state ahead of Christ—as Hitler desired and as the Chinese government currently does. The Christians also have to be very wise and wary since the communists are extremely clever in their methods of undermining the church.

Out of this transition from freedom to a totalitarian dictatorship, the underground church will ultimately emerge in Hong Kong. Herein may be some excellent lessons for American Christians who could face something very similar over the next few years. This could apply to South African churches and many others around the world as well as the New World Order emerges.

An excellent source of information on the persecuted Christian church around the world (past and present) is Voice of the Martyrs, which is headed by Richard Wurmbrand, who was head of the underground church in Romania, and was imprisoned and tortured by the communists for fourteen years. (A list of his books on persecution and the underground church can be found in appendix A of this book. To contact Voice of the Martyrs, or to receive their fine newsletter, write: P.O. Box 443, Bartlesville, OK 74005.)

(Subsequent chapters will give more specific ways Christians can be spiritually prepared for persecution.)

Chapter 9

The Ominous Parallels Between Nazi Germany (in the 1930s) and America (in the 1990s)

In Germany, the Nazis first came for the communists, and I didn't speak up because I wasn't a communist. Then they came for the Jews, and I didn't speak up because I wasn't a Jew. Then they came for the trade unionists, and I didn't speak up because I wasn't a trade union- ist. Then they came for the Catholics, and I didn't speak up because I was a Protestant. Finally they came for me, but there was no one left to speak up.

—Martin Niemoeller, a Lutheran Pastor who was sent to
the Dachau Concentration Camp in 1938.

There are some very ominous parallels between the emergence of Nazi- ism in Germany in the 1930s and the emergence of socialism and glo- balism in America in the 1990s.

Naziism, fascism, and communism had a number of common de- nominators: an all-powerful totalitarian dictatorial government which controlled all aspects of their subjects' lives; massive numbers of rules, regulations, and laws enforced by an all-powerful bureaucracy; and a preoccupation with death. All three were secular humanist (i.e., wor- shipped and elevated man versus God) to the core. All three were based on man's reason and a rejection of God, His authority, and His law.

Socialism (which America is presently plunging into) is simply com- munism or Naziism minus (at least for the present) the total dictatorship or *gulag*—as in Sweden in recent decades. Socialism is simply a small

step away from communism or Naziism. As the head of the Labor Socialist Party (who was also a communist) in England, John Strachey,
once said in the 1930s: "We cannot go directly from capitalism to communism. Socialism is a necessary stepping stone or transition. Hence,
all communists should work for socialism." Lenin, Stalin, Hitler, Mussolini, Gorbachev, Castro, Daniel Ortega, etc. are (or were) all, first and
foremost, socialists. (So are Bill and Hillary Clinton and Al Gore and
most of their subordinates in their Administration.)

Most people condemn Naziism because of its gross manifestations
(i.e., the Holocaust, the extermination of millions of Jews and others,
the death and destruction of World War II, etc.) instead of because of its
essence. Naziism was much more than killing Jews and starting wars. It
was rejection of God, His authority, and His law.

To understand Naziism and where we are headed today in America,
we must understand western thought in the twentieth century. The acceptance of what passed for scientific knowledge led to weakened spiritual faith and the blatant rejection of Christianity, which is the stabilizing
force in this world. Man has elevated himself to the position of a god
(the essence of secular humanism), determining that he can better understand the forces of nature than the God who established them.

The 1920s and early 1930s in German's Weimar Republic saw rampant inflation and debt accumulation, monetary, economic, social, political, moral and spiritual decline on a scale unprecedented in German
history. America since 1980 has experienced quite the same thing.

There are a number of ominous parallels between Nazi Germany in
the 1930s and America in the 1990s which should be contemplated:

1. A Preoccupation with Death

In the 1930s the German people began to have a preoccupation with
death. Via abortion they killed forty percent of all babies conceived. Then
they moved on to euthanasia, then to the killing of the crippled, de-
formed and handicapped, and then to the killing of Jews. At one point in
the 1930s, the Nazis emptied out hospitals, clinics, and sanitariums, and
killed up to 275,000 old, sick, crippled, retarded, or otherwise handicapped persons. This was well before the Nazi death camps opened.

As in America today, the disposal of the unwanted was rationalized as making room for the more capable, competent, or productive. As Germany evolved into a culture of death, most Germans barely took note of it, or saw anything wrong with it. Extermination of Jews, Christians, and any other undesirables was a natural progression of this preoccupation with death in Germany.

In America, we kill 1.6 million babies per year via abortion (i.e., over 40 million in the past twenty-six years); we are moving rapidly toward euthanasia; we see massive gratuitous violence and murder on television and in movies and most people barely take note of it or see anything wrong with it. Drive-by or freeway shootings and violent murder have become a way of life in America. We have even seen Dr. Kevorkian perform an assisted suicide (i.e., murder) on television. We have become anesthetized to violent death.

2. Thousands of Laws, Rules, and Regulations Were Passed

The Nazis passed thousands of laws, rules, and regulations to regulate and control every aspect of the German peoples' lives—so many, that virtually anyone could be branded (or labeled) as a criminal and have their property seized, be jailed, or executed at the whim of the Nazis. Highly complex financial, currency, cash reporting, and privacy laws were passed which almost no one understood. Christians who sent money out of the country to missionaries had their assets seized and were often jailed (or worse) under Nazi money-laundering laws. Raids on homes (often in the middle of the night) by the Gestapo became commonplace, along with widespread property seizures.

The same thing has happened in America in the 1990s as at least 2,500 new laws are passed each year by Congress. The bureaucracy, consisting of dozens of alphabet agencies (i.e., EPA, FDA, OSHA, BATF, FBI, IRS, DEA, etc.), then write over 86,000 pages of regulations each year to implement these new laws. These laws, rules, and regulations carry criminal as well as civil penalties and have led in recent years to the seizure and forfeiture of the property of roughly 250,000 Americans per year, who have inadvertently violated one of these regulations. Raids on homes by the BATF, FBI, and other federal agents (often at dawn) have become commonplace along with widespread property seizures.

Hence in the 1990s every American has become a potential criminal (just as in Nazi Germany) and is probably in criminal violation of a number of regulations at any time—and doesn't even know it. And just as in Nazi Germany, anyone who is politically incorrect can be fingered, arrested, and jailed—or stripped of their assets. As in Germany, it is all done legally.

3. A Preoccupation with Environmentalism and Animal Rights

The Germans in the 1930s were preoccupied with environmentalism and animal rights, with the Nazis passing all sorts of laws, rules, and regulations to protect the environment (while restricting the rights of their people) and to protect animals (wild and domestic). America has a very similar preoccupation with environmentalism and animal rights today, with the government passing all sorts of laws, rules, and regulations to protect the environment and animal life, while restricting the rights of the people (from the wetlands, clean air, clean water laws, to the Endangered Species Act and the protection of snail darters, northern and Mexican spotted owls, golden cheeked warblers, kangaroo rats, a myriad of insects, etc.).

There is an ominous parallel between the animal rights legislation in the Third Reich and the Endangered Species Act in America today. The book *Understanding Nazi Animal Protection and the Holocaust,* by Arnold Arluke and Boria Sax, explains the Nazi's perverted and occultic attitudes toward animals:

> In close evaluation of prominent Nazi military and political figures, it is suggested that there was a strong affection for animals, but an equally strong enmity toward human beings. . . . Perhaps in their twisted point of view, their dedication to the welfare of animals excused their inhumane treatment of Jews.
>
> The most interesting facet of Naziism is the abolition of moral distinctions between animals and people. (A rat is a pig is a dog is a boy.) They believed it was possible to increase the moral standing of animals and decrease the moral standing of people, thus integrating human characteristics to animals.

Immediately after the Nazis came to power, laws were passed that forbade the experimentation and dissection of animals for research. In their fervor for animal protection, they even addressed the shoeing of horses and the suffering of lobsters and crabs being boiled alive.

Around 1935, the Nazis shifted their concentration on protection of farm animals and pets to include wildlife. They talked of "establishing conservation and breeding programs," and passed laws governing hunting.

Incredibly, the Nazis were not satisfied with merely centralized regulation, but sought **to extend their control of animal protection throughout the world**.

Nazis believed that *"returning to the animal nature within man, communing with nature, and elevating animal life to the level of cult worship, as alternatives to modernity, technology, and urbanization . . . would lead to the spiritual and ideological changes necessary . . . for a new national self-identity."*

Hitler said: "I want violent imperious, fearless, **cruel** young people. . . . The free, magnificent beast of prey must once again flash from their eyes. . . . I want strong and beautiful . . . and athletic youth. In this way I shall blot out thousands of years of human domestication. I shall have the pure nobel stuff of nature."

German zoologist Ernst Haechel attacked religion, especially Christianity, for its reverence to human beings. He believed that man and animals shared the same natural and moral status. Animal protection was to be used to reform human society.

Naziism rejected the killing of animals for hunt or sport. Meat eating was symbolized as part of a decaying society. Vegetarianism became the identification of the new, pure civilization.

Does any of this sound familiar? We are hearing many of these ideas today from animal rights activists and environmentalists— many of whom, like the Nazis, are socialists and involved in the occult.

4. There Was an Occultic Dimension to the Third Reich

The Nazi Third Reich was not just a political movement or regime—it was also a supernatural, occultic movement and was in strong opposition to Bible-based Christianity and Orthodox Judaism. The religious foundation of the Nazi Third Reich was from the same Eastern religions that are the foundation for the present-day New Age movement, which now permeates the Liberal Eastern Establishment and energizes or provides the occultic dynamic behind the New World Order.

It is interesting how the Nazis had a low respect for human life, but revered animals, nature, etc. and how today's abortion movement, environmentalists, animal rights activists, etc. have low respect for human life (they are almost fanatical about population limits, control, reduction, abortion, euthanasia, etc.) but are concurrently fanatical about preserving trees, plants, animals, fish, birds, insects, planet earth (called Mother Gaia), etc. The extremes of low regard for people but high regard for animals and nature at first seems inconsistent, but not if one considers the occultic nature of both the Nazis and our present-day hardcore environmental and animal rights activists.

These apparent inconsistencies are very consistent within the context of the occult and Eastern religions. Remember, in India, the breeding ground of the Eastern religions, cows and rats are worshipped as gods and cannot be killed or eaten, while insects cannot be killed because they could be some reincarnated friend or loved one. The Eastern religions made more of an inroad into Nazi Germany in the 1930s and likewise into America in the 1990s than most people might suppose. This helps to explain several of the parallels described above.

The globalists and their fellow travelers—the environmentalists, the secular humanists, the abortionists, the radical feminists, the homosexual movement and the communists—have several common denominators. They hate traditional American values, they hate the U.S. Constitution, they hate the traditional family, and they hate fundamental, evangelical, Bible-believing Christians—whom they consider to be a great threat to their socialist/globalist, homosexual, or environmental agendas for the planet. Some globalists refer to fundamental Christians and Orthodox Jews as a "virulent virus" that has to be purged.

So, just as there was a supernatural, occultic, satanic dynamic behind the Nazis, there is also a supernatural, occultic dynamic behind the

New World Order and the present American social, cultural, and political freefall.

Many of the leaders in the globalist establishment today are occultists or Lucifer worshippers. The reverse side of the globalist coin is the New Age religion which is based upon the same Eastern mysticism and occultism which were the foundation of the Third Reich. This preoccupation with the occult is one of the major factors in the growing Establishment's hatred for evangelical Christians in America and will be one of the major factors in the coming globalist persecution of American Christians—which is now beginning to accelerate.

5. Ignoring the Constitution

Hitler completely ignored the German Constitution, just as our politicians and courts are doing today in America. Whenever he wanted to do something, he would just do it. He would often write a note, as he did when he wrote a note to the Nazi doctors instructing them to begin widespread euthanasia, and they did. How does this differ from the five Executive Orders which Bill Clinton issued at his whim on his third day in office in 1993, the hundreds he has since issued, or the thousands issued by other presidents in recent years. As discussed above, these Executive Orders are setting the stage for a State of National Emergency and martial law in America, just as similar orders written by Hitler in 1933 set the stage for the Nazi seizure of power and the dictatorship which followed.

These Executive Orders, hundreds of new laws, thousands of new regulations, and many of the actions of our government are as unconstitutional as Hitler's notes, orders, and edicts in the 1930s.

6. Rejection of Their Heritage

The German people, before and during the Nazi's rise to power, began to reject their Christian heritage, their history, their national heros, and their traditions. The Nazis accelerated this obliteration of their history and heritage as they came to power. And this is precisely what the liberals, socialists, and the globalist crowd in America have been doing in recent years. Our heritage, history, heros, and traditions are being denigrated and obliterated. To quote the wisdom of our Founding Fathers today, or to cite the U.S. Constitution in a court of law, in a public forum, or in the media, is to be laughed at, scorned, or looked down upon in derision.

Remember in George Orwell's *1984,* Big Brother erased the old history and heritage and fabricated a brand-new socialist history. The communists did the same thing in Russia and China. The same was done in Nazi Germany and the same thing is being done in America today through revisionist history and multiculturalism.

7. Gun Control Laws

The Nazis passed Draconian gun control laws to disarm the German people so that they could control them and set up their dictatorship. (The communists in Russia, China, and Cuba also disarmed their people.) Hitler bragged that: "1935 will go down in history! For the first time a civilized nation has full gun registration! Our streets will be safer, our police more efficient, and the world will follow our lead in the future." And the Nazi dictatorship was ushered in!

America is following Hitler's lead as the political left today are pushing Nazi-style gun control laws and talk openly about disarming the American people. Aaron Zelman, head of Jews for the Preservation of Firearms Ownership, did a comparison of the Nazi's 1928 and 1938 gun control laws, and those passed in the U.S. in 1968 and since, and found them to be almost identical—as if they had been copied. There will be a big push to disarm Americans over the next five years. It is a major element in the New World Order agenda and has recently been accomplished in Australia and England.

8. Hitler Used Homosexuals, Drug Addicts, and Criminal Elements to Destabilize the Country and Advance the Nazi Political Machine

Hitler organized these groups into the S.A. (the Brown Shirts) and from early 1933 to June 30, 1934, they did his dirty work—breaking up opponents' political meetings, beating up or killing the opposition, and intimidating the people.

Then in 1934 the German military came to Hitler and told him to eliminate the Brown Shirts or he would lose their support. So Hitler unleashed the S.S. on the Brown Shirts to exterminate them. Over 1,000 S.A. leaders were killed on June 30, 1934, (it was called "the night of the long knives") and that was the beginning of the end for the S.A. It is very significant that in Hitler's first eighteen months in power, he recruited thousands of homosexuals to help lead his Brown Shirt storm troopers.

Even after many of the Brown Shirts' homosexuals were murdered, there remained many homosexuals in the upper echelons of the Third Reich—a number of them very close to Hitler. The powerful homosexual influence in the Nazi leadership is documented in the excellent book *The Pink Swastika* by Scott Lively.

Compare this to the thirty or more open homosexuals in the upper echelon of the Clinton Administration, and the open pushing by the Administration of the homosexual agenda (including the president's use of an Executive Order on day number three of his first Administration ordering gays to be admitted to the military). Consider the drug and other criminal activity in the upper levels of the U.S. government. Ominous parallels with Nazi Germany!

Lessons for Today from the Rise of Nazi Germany

The parallels with how the Nazis rose to power in the 1930s and present developments in America are ominous. If one studies the Nazi press, the electronic media, the pushing of Germany to the brink of dictatorship, and the role of the Reichstag fire, and looks at America over the past decade, one will get a sense of *deja vu*.

The Media in Nazi Germany

William Shirer, in his epic book *The Rise and Fall of the Third Reich*, wrote regarding the Nazi control of press, radio, and film:

Every morning the editors of the Berlin daily newspapers and the correspondents of those published elsewhere in the Reich gathered at the Propaganda Ministry to be told by Dr. Goebbels or by one of his aides what news to print and suppress, how to write the news and headline it, what campaigns to call off or institute, and what editorials were desired for the day. In case of any misunderstanding, a daily written directive was furnished along with the oral instructions. For the smaller out-of-town papers and the periodicals the directives were dispatched by telegram or by mail. . . .

With all newspapers in Germany being told what to publish and how to write the news and editorials, it was inevitable that a deadly conformity would come over the nation's press. Even a people so regimented and so given to accepting authority became bored by the daily newspapers. Circulation declined even for the leading Nazi daily newspapers such as the morning *Voelkischer Beobachter* and the evening *Der Angriff.* And the total circulation of all journals fell off steeply as one paper after another went under or was taken over by Nazi publishers. In the first four years of the Third Reich the number of daily newspapers declined from 3,607 to 2,671.

It is a true statement to say that the basic purpose of the Nazi press program was to eliminate all the press which was in opposition to the party. [*Note:* Just as the Establishment (which similarly controls and orchestrates the media in the U.S. in our day) would like to suppress and stamp out the alternate media in America today.]

Radio and Motion Pictures: The radio and the motion pictures were also quickly harnessed to serve the propaganda of the Nazi state. Goebbels (the Minister of Propaganda) had always seen in radio (television had not yet come in) the chief instrument of propaganda in modern society and through the Radio Department of his ministry and the Chamber of Radio he gained complete control of broadcasting and shaped it to his own ends. His task was made easier because in Germany, as in the other countries of Europe, broadcasting was a monopoly owned and operated by the state. In 1933 the Nazi government automatically found itself in possession of the Reich Broadcasting Corporation. . . .

Dr. Goebbels proved himself right, in that the radio became by far the regime's most effective means of propaganda, doing more than any other single instrument of communication to shape the German people to Hitler's ends. [*Note:* In America today, it would, of course, be television, which is used by the Establishment and the political left in almost exactly the same way.]

Manipulating the Thinking of the People: I myself [Shirer] was to experience how easily one is taken in by a lying and censored press and radio in a totalitarian state. A steady diet over the years of falsifications and distortions made a certain impression on one's mind and often misled it. No one who has not lived for years in a totalitarian land can possibly conceive how difficult it is to escape the dreaded consequences of a regime's calculated and incessant propaganda. [*Note:* Television news, such as CNN, in America today has much the same effect on the collective American psyche.]

Often in a German home or office or sometimes in a casual conversation with a stranger in a restaurant, a beer hall, a cafe, I would meet with the most outlandish assertions from seemingly educated and intelligent persons. It was obvious that they were parroting some piece of nonsense they had heard on the radio or read in the newspaper.

Sometimes one was tempted to say as much, but on such occasions one was met with such a stare of incredulity, such a shock of silence, as if one had blasphemed the Almighty, that one realized how useless it was even to try to make contact with a mind which had become warped and for whom the facts of life had become what Hitler and Goebbels, with their cynical disregard for truth, said they were.

Shirer wrote the following about Germany's last free election in 1938:

New elections were set for March 5. For the first time (in the last relatively free election Germany was to have) the Nazi Party now could employ all the vast resources of the government to win votes. Goebbels was jubilant. "Now it will be easy," he wrote in his diary on February 3, "to carry on the fight, for we can call on all the resources of the State. Radio and press are at our disposal. We shall stage a masterpiece of propaganda. And this time, naturally, there is no lack of money."

Does this sound like recent national elections in America?

[*Note:* Television in America today is the rough equivalent of the Nazi brainwashing by radio in the 1930s and in time of crisis (such as the weeks following the 1995 Oklahoma City bombing) becomes even more important in giving the coordinated, orchestrated Establishment party line. Note the uniformity of reporting and attacking the political right in the mainline newspapers, news magazines, and on television following the Oklahoma City bombing—the same scare phrases, epithets, and party line—the uniformity of the spiking of the information on the second bomb, etc. Consider the media programming of the American public during the Clinton impeachment trial, so that the reaction of the public to the Clinton crimes was almost completely muted. Surely Goebbels' Propaganda Ministry must be alive and well somewhere in America today under the watchful care of the Establishment with a very skilled orchestra leader wielding his (or its) baton.]

Pushing Germany to the Brink of Dictatorship

Shirer and many others have written extensively about the incredible support Hitler and the Nazis received from Germany's industrial giants and corporate leaders during Hitler's rise to power and throughout his reign of terror. Tony Sutton has also written in his excellent book *Wall Street and the Rise of Hitler* how a number of American industrial giants supported Hitler financially before and during the War. Nazi Germany was in fact a fascist regime with an unholy alliance between big business and the socialist government. That is significant because that is exactly what we have in America today—big business and the government are collaborating to move America into the New World Order.

Hitler in 1933 had to have a "strawman," an enemy or scapegoat to rally the people against. The strawmen were the communists (and the Jews). (In America today the strawmen are the right wing, the militia movement, gun owners, and ultimately it will be the Christian or religious right.) In February 1933 Herman Goering (the Minister of Police—the German equivalent to the American Attorney General) unleashed the government police against the Nazi opposition.

As Shirer wrote:

He urged the police "to make use of firearms" and warned that those who didn't would be punished. This was an outright call for the shooting down of all who opposed Hitler by the police of a state (Prussia) which controlled two-thirds of Germany. Just to make sure that the job would be ruthlessly done, Goering on February 22 established an auxiliary police force of 50,000 men, of whom 40,000 were drawn from the ranks of the S.A. and the S.S. and the rest from the Stahlhelm. Police power in Prussia was thus largely carried out by Nazi thugs.

And yet despite all the terror, the "Bolshevik revolution" which Goebbels, Hitler, and Goering were looking for, failed to "burst into flames." If it could not be provoked, might it not have to be invented?

On February 24, Goering's police raided the Karl Liebknecht Haus, the communist headquarters in Berlin. It had been abandoned some weeks before by the communist leaders, a number of whom had already gone underground or quietly slipped off to Russia. But piles of propaganda pamphlets had been left in the cellar and these were enough to enable Goering to announce in an official communique that the seized "documents" proved that the communists were about to launch the revolution. The reaction of the public and even of some of the conservatives in the government was one of skepticism. It was obvious that something more sensational must be found to stampede the public before the election took place on March 5.

Lessons from the Reichstag Fire:
The Beginning of the Nazi Dictatorship

At 10 p.m. on the night of February 27, 1933, the huge German parliament building in Berlin caught fire and was subsequently gutted. Herman Goering's *"somethimg more sensational to stampede the Germany people"* had been ignited. Virtually all historians of the period (including William Shirer) agree that the burning of the Reichstag (blamed on the communists) by the Nazis was the event which signaled the beginning of the Nazi dictatorship.

The public were panicked by the Nazi propaganda machine and stampeded into handing dictatorial power to Hitler and the Nazis. There could be very important lessons in the Reichstag fire for Americans in the wake of the Oklahoma City bombing and other terrorist attacks. If Congress (supported by the public) are stampeded by some crisis or catastrophe (real or staged) into passing a host of counterterrorism, gun control, people-control initiatives, America could become a Nazi-style police state (with most of our Bill of Rights' freedoms canceled) all in the name of fighting terrorism.

Is it possible that the political right in America was being used as a scapegoat in the Oklahoma City bombing and other terrorist attacks, as the communists were in the Reichstag fire? Does history repeat itself? Hegel said "We learn from history, we learn nothing from history." And Santayana said: "Those who do not learn the lessons of history are doomed to repeat the mistakes of history."

The following is what historian William Shirer (incidently, a liberal) had to say about the Reichstag fire:

> On the evening of February 27, four of the most powerful men in Germany were gathered at two separate dinners in Berlin. In the exclusive Herrenklub in the Vosstrasse, Vice-Chancellor von Papen was entertaining President von Hindenburg. Out at Goebbels' home, Chancellor Hitler had arrived to dine *en famille*. According to Goebbels, they were relaxing, playing music on the gramophone, and telling stories. "Suddenly," he recounted later in his diary, "a telephone call from Dr. Hanfstoengl: The Reichstag is on fire!" Within a few seconds Goebbels (the Propaganda Minister) and his Fuehrer were racing "at sixty miles an hour down the Charlottenburger Chaussee toward the scene of the crime."
>
> That it was a crime, a communist crime, they proclaimed at once on arrival at the fire. Goering, sweating and puffing and quite beside himself with excitement, was already there ahead of them declaiming to heaven, as Papen later recalled, that "this is a communist crime against the new government." To the new Gestapo chief Rudolf Diels, Goering shouted, "This is the beginning of the communist revolution! We must not wait a minute. We will show no mercy. Every communist official must be shot, where he is found. Every communist deputy must this very night be strung up." [*Note:* Was that similar to blaming the American right wing for the Oklahoma City bombing?]

The whole truth about the Reichstag fire [or the Oklahoma City bombing] will probably never be known. Nearly all those who knew it are now dead, most of them slain by Hitler in the months that followed. But there is enough evidence to establish beyond a reasonable doubt that it was the Nazis who planned the arson and carried it out for their own political ends.

From Goering's Reichstag President's Palace an underground passage, built to carry the central heating system, ran to the Reichstag building. Through this tunnel Karl Ernst, a former hotel bellhop who had become the Berlin S.A. leader, led a small detachment of storm troopers on the night of February 27 to the Reichstag where they scattered gasoline and self-igniting chemicals and then made their way quickly back to the palace the way they had come.

At the same time a half-witted Dutch communist with a passion for arson, Marinus van der Lubbe, had made his way into the huge, darkened, and to him unfamiliar building, and set some small fires of his own. This feeble-minded pyromaniac was a godsend to the Nazis. He had been picked up by the S.A. a few days before after having been overheard in a bar boasting that he had attempted to set fire to several public buildings and that he was going to try the Reichstag next. . . . [*Note:* Could Marinus van der Lubbe have been the Timothy McVeigh of the 1930s, or vice-versa?]

The idea for the fire almost certainly originated with Goebbels and Goering. Hans Gisevius, an official in the Prussian Ministry of the Interior at the time, testified at Nuremberg that "it was Goebbels who first thought of setting the Reichstag on fire," and Rudolf Diels, the Gestapo chief, added in an affidavit that "Goering knew exactly how the fire was to be started" and had ordered him **"to prepare, prior to the fire, a list of people who were to be arrested immediately after it."** General Franz Halder, Chief of the German General Staff during the early part of World War II, recalled at Nuremberg how on one occasion Goering had boasted of his deed. . . .

Van der Lubbe, it seems clear, was a dupe of the Nazis. He was encouraged to try to set the Reichstag on fire. But the main job was to be done—without his knowledge, of course—by the storm troopers.

Indeed, it was established at the subsequent trial at Leipzig that the Dutch half-wit did not possess the means to set so vast a building on fire so quickly. Two and a half minutes after he entered, the great central hall was fiercely burning. He had only his shirt for tinder.

Over a hundred top communists were arrested, along with thousands of pacifists, liberals, and democrats. A hasty trial was arranged for Van der Lubbe and four top communists (who were all acquitted). Van der Lubbe was found guilty and decapitated.

On the day following the fire, February 28, Hitler prevailed on President Hindenburg to sign a decree "for the Protection of the People and the State" suspending the seven sections of the constitution which guaranteed individual and civil liberties. [*Note:* **The equivalent of striking down, with the stroke of a pen, the American Bill of Rights.**] Described as a "defensive measure against communist acts of violence endangering the state," the decree laid down that: "Restrictions on personal liberty, on the right of free expression of opinion, including freedom of the press; on the rights of assembly and association; and violations of the privacy of postal telegraphic and telephonic communications; and warrants for house searches, orders for confiscations as well as restrictions on property, are also permissible beyond the legal limits otherwise prescribed." [*Note:* This is almost identical, in many respects, to Bill Clinton's counterterrorism legislation passed after the Oklahoma City bombing.]

Douglas Reed, a British reporter, wrote in *The Burning of the Reichstag:*

When Germany awoke, a man's home was no longer his castle. He could be seized by private individuals, could claim no protection from the police, could be indefinitely detained without preferment of charge, his property could be seized, his verbal and written communications overheard and perused; he no longer had the right to foregather with his fellow countrymen; and his newspapers might no longer freely express their opinions. The Reichstag fire produced exactly the result that Hitler had anticipated. The Germany of the Weimar Constitution went up in flames, and from the ashes [like the phoenix] rose the Third Reich.

[*Note:* Many of these things have been happening in America in the 1990s and almost all of them could become a reality under the recent avalanche of counterterrorism legislation and Clinton Executive Orders. All phone calls, faxes, mail, e-mail, and cell phones, etc. can be monitored by the FBI and other federal agencies, and America is becoming a one hundred percent surveillance society *a la* George Orwell's *1984,* or communist Russia, or Nazi Germany.]

Shirer continued:

In addition, the decree authorized the Reich government to take over complete power in the federal states when necessary and imposed the death sentence for a number of crimes, including "serious disturbanccs of the peace" by armed persons.

Thus with one stroke Hitler was able not only to legally gag his opponents and arrest them at his will, but, by making the trumped-up communist threat official, as it were, to throw millions of the middle class and the peasantry into a frenzy of fear that, unless they voted for National Socialism at the elections a week hence, the Bolsheviks might take over. Some four thousand communist officials and a great many Social Democrat and liberal leaders were arrested, including members of the Reichstag. [*Note:* Could this happen to conservative, Christian, religious right leaders and activists in America in some future "terrorist" crisis—real or fabricated?]

This was the first experience Germans had had with Nazi terror backed up by the government. Truckloads of storm troopers roared through the streets all over Germany; breaking into homes, rounding up victims, and carrying them off to S.A. barracks, where they were tortured and beaten. The communist press and political meetings were suppressed; the Social Democrat newspapers and many liberal journals were suspended and the meetings of the democratic parties either banned or broken up. Only the Nazis and their Nationalist allies were permitted to campaign unmolested.

On March 5, 1933, the day of the last democratic elections they were to know during Hitler's life, they spoke with their ballots. Despite all the terror and intimidation, the majority of them rejected Hitler.

The Nazis led the polling with 17,277,180 votes—an increase of some five and a half million, but it comprised only forty-four percent of the total vote. [*Note:* Bill Clinton was elected with forty-three percent of the total vote in 1992 and less than fifty percent in 1996.] A clear majority still eluded Hitler. Nevertheless, the Nazis assumed power, the Third Reich was off and running, and Germany fell under a total dictatorship.

In summary, Hitler, Goering, Goebbels, and the Nazi leadership stampeded and manipulated the government and German people into giving them total power after the Reichstag fire. They then won a national election (by forty-four percent). The communists were the scapegoat of the day—the excuse for the Nazis demanding and getting total power over the people.

In 1995 in America, in the wake of the tragic Oklahoma City bombing, Bill Clinton, Janet Reno, Louis Freeh, the leftist leaders in Congress, and the Establishment-controlled mainline media are blaming the American right wing in general, and the militia movement in particular (the new scapegoats), and demanding that the equivalent to police state powers be given to Clinton and the government bureaucracy to deal with the emerging "right-wing crisis of terrorism."

New acts of terrorism are likely to occur over the next year or two—real or staged. As Congress passes a host of legislative initiatives against terrorism, and Bill Clinton writes additional Executive Orders to "fight the new American crisis of right-wing terrorism," Clinton (or Gore) may assume many of the same powers that were given to Adolf Hitler in 1933. At that point, the Bill of Rights would effectively be neutered, and there would be no turning back.

This writer hopes and prays that there will be no additional bombings or attacks against any officials, or other crises (real or manufactured) which would further be used by the political left to justify attacks on the political right, on gun ownership, or the U.S. Bill of Rights, and the expansion of federal power over the people by Congress or by Executive Orders.

It is very helpful in understanding the times in which we live to study the rise and fall of the Nazi Third Reich in the 1930s and 1940s, and the great evil it perpetrated on mankind. There are many ominous parallels with today which should be pondered. And the Third Reich was one of the most fascinating periods in human history, from which many lessons can be learned today by lovers of freedom.

Chapter 10

As the Political Left Escalates Its Attacks on Christians and Traditionalists in America

America is like a healthy body and its resistance is threefold: its patriotism, its morality, and its spiritual life. If we can undermine these three areas, America will collapse from within.

—Josef Stalin

While the people are virtuous, they cannot be subdued; but when once they lose their virtue they will be ready to surrender their liberties to the first external or internal invader.

—Samuel Adams

The political left in America is beginning to attack the Christian right, secular conservatives, and traditionalists unlike any time in U.S. history, and these attacks are likely to escalate dramatically over the next few years.

The rise of the Christian right over the past decade or so (epitomized by thousands of conservative/Christian activist/pro-life/traditional values organizations, publications, and radio talk shows) has awakened millions of Americans regarding the sharp political, social, and cultural decline which America finds herself in today. This awakening helped bring about a strong conservative sweep in the November 1994 midterm congressional elections, and subsequently a strong counterattack by the political left.

D-Day for the liberal counterattack was in the immediate aftermath of the Oklahoma City bombing, when the Clinton Administration and the political left launched a blanket indictment of the entire conservative movement in America—likening anyone on the political right (i.e., talk show hosts, gun owners, Christian right activists, militia members, pro-life activists—in other words, anyone or any group who is a critic of the government or is deemed politically incorrect) as being directly or indirectly guilty, or implicated in the Oklahoma tragedy.

The entire political right in America was branded as being guilty of the rhetoric of hate, fear, paranoia, and division which caused the Oklahoma City bombing. The **short-term** goal of the media barrage against the American right wing was the passage of Bill Clinton's Counterterrorism Bill (called by some the "Government Terror Bill"). But the **long-term** strategy, which was actually launched in the spring of 1993, about the time of the Waco massacre, is the silencing and neutralizing of the political right in America. The Christian right is a primary target in this respect.

The Propaganda Attack Against
American Conservatives and Christian Activists

Today a host of books and articles are emanating from the political left in America which are denigrating and slandering pro-life, pro-Constitution, pro-traditional values leaders and organizations across America, labeling them as racist, anti-Semitic, neo-Nazi, white supremacist, homophobic, etc. and trying to link many (or most) of them (using guilt by association) with the militia movement, which has been targeted by the political left for destruction.

The tactic is to expand the definition of militia to include racists, anti-Semites, White Supremacists, the Aryan Nation, etc. and then to associate most conservatives with the militias. The false conclusion the left then broadcasts is that most conservatives are therefore racist, anti-Semitic, White Supremacist, etc.

Three of the techniques being used by the political left to discredit leaders in the conservative movement and so-called Christian right are:
1. Guilt by Association; 2. *Argumentum Ad Hominem*—attacking

the character, beliefs, and reputation of a person in order to destroy his or her credibility or reputation; and **3. Expanding the Definition of Words or Concepts**—like hate, terrorism, New World Order, racist, fundamentalist, political protest, criticism of government, etc.

1. Guilt by Association

This is a technique (which the political left has long attributed to conservatives) which they are now using in an effort to discredit certain conservatives and Christian leaders. There is no doubt that there **are** far right extremist groups in this country which **are** racist, white supremacist, neo-Nazi, and anti-Semitic.

These groups, epitomized by the Ku Klux Klan, the Aryan Nations, and a few others, are reprehensible and do by and large hate the Jews and other racial minorities, but are very small, have very little support among conservatives, Christian right activists, pro-lifers, libertarians, etc., and have very little impact or influence in America today—especially in comparison to numerous influential left-wing groups including the Communist Party U.S.A.

However, the political left is striving to vastly overstate the size, influence, and impact of these rightist fringe groups, to link all acts of terrorism in the U.S. to them, and to link these groups to legitimate pro-life, conservative, traditionalist leaders and organizations in order to discredit the latter.

By way of illustration, in a book published in 1996 entitled *American Militias: Rebellion, Racism, and Religion,* the Christian-left author sought to link this writer, Chuck Missler, Pat Robertson, Jack Van Impe, Texe Marrs, Larry Pratt, and other Christian/conservative writers and leaders (all labeled as "conspiracy nuts" or "fanatics") with the militia movement, the neo-Nazis, Aryan Nations, Ku Klux Klan, and various radical rightist groups. It's called guilt by association. The author even placed this writer's picture on the same page with several militia leaders and across the page from an anti-Semitic leader giving the Nazi salute, and quoted this writer a dozen or so times in the context of racist, neo-Nazi, Aryan Nations, anti-Semitic leaders in a blatant form of "guilt by association."

The author claimed that if a person has ever attended the same conference, appeared in the same publication, or has ever been seen in public with a person he calls radical or extremist, that he is in league with that person or his group. This **guilt by association**, of course, becomes bizarre. This writer once spoke at the same meeting on the same platform with Henry Kissinger and has attended conferences at which George Bush was speaking. Does that make this writer a member of the Establishment?

In his excellent book *The Gates of Hell Shall Not Prevail*, Dr. D. James Kennedy described how the Anti-Defamation League of B'nai B'rith, in its 1994 report *The Religious Right: The Assault on Tolerance and Pluralism in America*, had eight or so references to his name. As Kennedy wrote:

> They didn't have one single thing there that I had said. It was all guilt by association. . . . It was media McCarthyism. I was guilty because I had endorsed or had some sort of relationship to someone else, who in turn endorsed or had some relationship to someone else, who in turn endorsed someone else, who in turn, reportedly said something anti-Semitic. Yet, by putting me in the book so often, I was painted as some sort of anti-Semite.

Because a person quotes a communist publication (as this author sometimes does) or a right-wing publication or author, or a New Age publication (or is quoted by same) does that mean he is in league with that person or group? If so, then this writer is guilty as charged—he must be a communist because he has read and quoted from communist publications for years (it's called "know thy enemy") and even sneaked into a few leftist meetings. It should be obvious that guilt by association is a dangerous element of the strategy of the political left and of the emerging police state in America.

2. *Argumentum Ad Hominem*

In Latin, this is called "argument against the man." This technique, long used by the communists and the political left, involves attacking (or smearing) a person (**not** his arguments, facts or positions—**but attacking the man himself**) by labeling him with emotionally charged, negative words such as racist; white supremacist; neo-Nazi; anti-Semitic; Aryan Nations; religious weirdo; paranoid hatemonger; fearmonger; paranoid nut; right-wing fanatic; right-wing extremist; inflammatory; purveyor of fear, hate, paranoia, division; conspiracy wacko; anti-government; terrorist; or any of dozens of combinations of such labels. Politically incorrect conservatives, or Christians who are so labeled, are very likely to be accused of hate crimes or inciting of terrorism in coming months or years.

The goal is to discredit, destroy the reputation of, and neutralize the target(s) of the left (i.e., the conservative or Christian activists) in order to shut them up, or turn off their audience. This was done to Barry Goldwater in 1964 as the liberal Establishment labeled and discredited him as a right-wing extremist. Former FBI agent Matt Sevetic, who infiltrated the Communist Party USA in the 1950s, was falsely labeled as a homosexual by the political left in order to destroy his reputation and credibility.

During a radio talk show in Detroit a year or two ago, on which this writer was a guest, a *very* hostile caller accused this writer of "secret" involvement in the murder of radio talk show host Alan Berg in Denver in the 1980s, pointing out that this writer had, after all, lived in Denver. This astonishing, scurrilous, libelous, totally unfounded accusation was made in order to discredit this writer, his reputation, his credibility, and his message in the eyes of the audience—a classic example of an *ad hominem* (smear) attack.

The anti-Semitic label is one of the most feared, devastating, and frequently used smear terms utilized against conservative leaders. [*Note:* While some conservatives, with whom this writer has strong disagreement, and some Christians **are** anti-Semitic, the vast majority are not. But, the political left loves to lump together all Christian-right activists with the anti-Semitic, anti-Israel minority on the right, in order to discredit them.]

For example, Pat Robertson wrote a book entitled *The New World Order,* which discussed efforts on the part of the powerful globalist Establishment to establish a world government. This writer also wrote a book entitled *Toward The New World Order: The Countdown To Armageddon*. Both books extensively quoted leaders such as George Bush, Brent Scowcroft, Henry Kissinger, Mikhail Gorbachev, H. G. Wells, Fidel Castro, and dozens of others who have advocated a one-world government which **they** called the New World Order in hundreds of speeches, books, and papers.

Never in either book did Robertson or this writer ever hint that the New World Order is a Jewish (i.e., Zionist) conspiracy or that there is a Zionist or Jewish plot to take over the world. Neither Robertson nor this writer, both of whom have been **strongly** pro-Israel and pro-Jewish in both word and deed (for biblical reasons) for many decades, have ever hinted at anti-Semitism in speeches or writings.

Nevertheless, the political left and the liberal media have attacked Robertson as being anti-Semitic because he wrote about the New World Order and the fact that there are (among others) international bankers involved in the thrust for world government. As the author of *American Militias* wrote in his book trashing the Christian right (pages 195–96):

> It must be stressed that Robertson's book does not simply contain free-floating conspiracy theories, but promotes distinctive beliefs that are specifically associated with militias. . . . Also alarming is the fact that Robertson draws upon some of the very same sources used by racist patriots and white supremacists to legitimize their anti-Semitic conspiratorial world view. . . .
>
> The influence of Robertson's book in the patriot movement can also be seen in how often it appears in patriot and militia literature and how regularly it is recommended by patriot and racist leaders. . . .
>
> Equally troubling were Robertson's references to "international bankers" and "European bankers" as the evil manipulators of humanity. Many readers assumed that he was publishing veiled anti-Semitism. Hitler, after all, equated the "Jewish menace" with the international world Jew and the "international Jewish financiers in and outside Europe." Furthermore, contemporary racist publications often call the New World Order conspiracy either "a cabal of Jewish bankers" or "(Jewish) international bankers."

Quoting Michael Lind from the February 1995 issue of the *New York Review of Books,* the author wrote: "Although Robertson never labeled his New World Order conspirators as Jews, Lind argued that Robertson's portrayal of a worldwide conspiracy of freemasons, communists, and international bankers partook of classic anti-Semitism."

These passages (and indeed that entire book) published incidentally by a large **Christian** publishing company—InterVarsity Press, is a classic illustration of guilt by association and *argumentum adhominem* (i.e., insinuating that Robertson, one of the most pro-Israel Christian leaders in America, is anti-Semitic) in order to discredit him and his message. This author strongly urges readers of this book to buy a copy of Robertson's book *The New World Order,* read his analysis of the coming world government, and decide for yourself if he is anti-Semitic. For that matter, you may wish to purchase this writer's book on the same subject.

Is There Really a New World Order?

Neither Robertson's book, nor this author's book *Toward The New World Order: Countdown To Armageddon* are anti-Semitic in any way. However, both do discuss and analyze a long-term, evil conspiracy for world government—quoting the participants and their stated goals. Based on the writings of David Rockefeller, Henry Kissinger, and other Establishment leaders, this writer is convinced that **they are serious** when they say they plan to establish a world government over the next few years. But first they must discredit and neutralize their conservative or Christian opposition to their globalist government.

Even Pope John Paul II has been quoted by Malachi Martin in the book *The Keys of This Blood* as saying: "By the end of this decade (A.D. 2000) we will live under the first one-world government that has ever existed in the society of nations . . . a government with absolute authority to decide the basic issues of human survival. One-world government is inevitable." Though that one-world government will not be fully established by the year 2000, a growing number of people around the world wonder if that one-world government could possibly be the rising kingdom of the Antichrist.

Former West German chancellor Willy Brandt, former chairman of the Fifth-Socialist International, chaired the Brandt Commission in the late 1980s, which gave a rather concise definition of the New World Order:

> The New World Order is a world that has a supernational authority to regulate world commerce and industry; an international organization that would control the production and consumption of oil; an international currency that would replace the dollar; a World Development Fund that would make funds available to free and communist nations alike; and an international police force (probably the U.N.) to enforce the edicts of the New World Order.

Specific elements of the New World Order recommended by the Brandt Commission included a global taxation system, a world court, a world army, a world central bank, a world welfare state, centralized worldwide economic planning, abolition of private firearms, mandatory global population and environmental control, centralized control of education, and a New World police force to enforce the New World Order. These elements of the New World Order were also discussed at the Gorbachev Forum on world government, hosted by Mikhail Gorbachev in San Francisco in October 1995.

David Rockefeller, one of the leading advocates of global government, has said: "We are on the verge of a global transformation. **All we need is the right major crisis and the nations will accept the New World Order**."

David Rockefeller, speaking at the Business Council for the United Nations (9/14/94), said regarding the establishment of the New World Order:

> But this present window of opportunity, during which a truly peaceful and **interdependent world order** might be built, will not be open for long. Already there are powerful forces at work that threaten to destroy all of our hopes and efforts to erect an enduring structure of global interdependence.

Brent Scowcroft, George Bush's National Security Advisor, said on the eve of the Gulf War: "A colossal event is upon us, the birth of a New World Order." Fidel Castro, speaking at the U.N., was quoted in a headline article in the Idaho Falls, Idaho, *Post Register* (10/12/79): "Fidel Castro Demands New World Order."

On September 11, 1990, President George Bush said "The Persian Gulf crisis is a rare opportunity to forge new bonds with old enemies [i.e., the Soviet Union]. . . . Out of these troubled times a New World Order can emerge under a United Nations that performs as envisioned by its founders."

In his State of the Union Address on January 29, 1991, President Bush said: "The world can therefore seize the opportunity [the Persian Gulf crisis] to fulfill the long held promise of a New World Order where diverse nations are drawn together in common cause to achieve the universal aspirations of mankind."

And the March 19, 1994, *Time* magazine carried an article by Henry Kissinger entitled "How to Achieve the New World Order." That is the same Henry Kissinger who, when campaigning for the passage of NAFTA, said: "NAFTA is a major stepping stone to the New World Order."

QUESTION: Do those quotes mean that Rockefeller, Kissinger, Bush, Scowcroft, the pope, Fidel Castro, Gorbachev, Ted Turner, Jane Fonda, etc. are all anti-Semitic because they openly refer to and **advocate** the installation of the New World Order? That is doubtful. Then why are **opponents** of the New World Order labeled as anti-Semitic?

Attacking Conservatives as Anti-Semitic

In the book *American Militias*, the author wrote: "Like [Chuck Missler], McAlvany seems to get much of his material from anti-Semitic sources." In another quote, he wrote: "Unfortunately, some of his [Missler's] sources are directly tied to the white supremacist movement." These are blatant guilt-by-association, *ad hominem* attacks to discredit Missler and this writer. These allegations are patently false.

The truth is, Missler takes biblical tours to Israel and is one of the strongest Christian supporters of Israel in America. And this author, who has traveled to Israel on eight occasions, is a strong supporter of Israel and loves the Jewish people for biblical reasons, even while disagreeing with many Israeli government policies. Larry Patterson, in his monthly newsletter, *Criminal Politics,* even refers to this writer as a "Christian Zionist." Jesus, all the twelve apostles, and the original Christian church were all Jews, as were the Old Testament patriarchs, Abraham, Isaac, Jacob (and his twelve sons), Moses, the prophets like Jeremiah, Isaiah, Ezekiel, Daniel, and kings like David, Solomon, and Hezekiah.

It says in **Genesis 12:1–3**:

> Now the LORD had said unto Abram, Get thee out of thy country, and from thy kindred, and from thy father's house, unto a land that I will shew thee: And I will make of thee a great nation, and I will bless thee, and make thy name great; and thou shalt be a blessing: **And I will bless them that bless thee, and curse him that curseth thee:** and in thee shall all families of the earth be blessed.

It is difficult for this writer to see how a person can be a true follower of the God of the Bible and His Son Jesus Christ, and be anti-Semitic. And if one studies the present thrust for world government (i.e., the New World Order) in historical or contemporary terms, it is very difficult for this writer to see how anyone can conclude that it is a Jewish or Zionist world conspiracy headquartered out of Israel, New York, London, or wherever. It is a satanic conspiracy involving participants of all races. In this writer's view, the two groups which will ultimately be persecuted by the New World Order will be evangelical Christians (beginning with the Christian right) and Orthodox Jews, a growing number of whom are anticipating the not-too-distant coming of their Messiah.

A good friend of this writer, a conservative, biblically-oriented Orthodox Jew from the Israeli intelligence community, believes that the greatest enemy today of Orthodox religious Jews and conservative Christians (in Israel, America, and around the world) are liberal secular (i.e., non-religious) Jews and leftist Christians. He believes that both groups will be in the forefront of the coming persecution of conservatives, fundamentalists, Orthodox Jews, and Christians. Interesting food for thought! No, my Jewish friend is **not** anti-Semitic!

If one travels extensively in Israel, as this writer has done, and studies the good, the bad, and the ugly of Israel's political situation, it is laughable to think that there is a giant Zionist conspiracy to take over the world. Quite the contrary, the Bible describes a time when Israel will be isolated from the rest of the world, and attacked by armies from Russia, China, the Arab states, and Europe (i.e., the kings of the north, east, south, and west). This hardly sounds like a nation about to take over the world.

Many anti-Semites around the world quote from the *Protocols of the Learned Elders of Zion,* a document purporting to outline a Zionist takeover of the world. However, knowledgeable scholars, with whom this writer agrees, believe that the document was a forgery—perhaps emanating from the Illuminati (which is *not* a Jewish conspiracy) or from the anti-Semitic Russian government under Czar Nicholas.

The historical involvement of many Jews in the Bolshevik Revolution in Russia and the contemporary reality of many Jews on the political left in America, especially in Hollywood, have unfortunately fueled the fires of anti-Semitism and beliefs in a Zionist conspiracy. But, as a matter of fact, the political left in America is made up of Christians, Gentiles, blacks, Native Americans, Orientals, and Jews; and they hate the political right in America, which is also made up of Christians, Gentiles, blacks, Native Americans, Orientals, and Jews. In other words, the struggle for political power in America (and around the world) is not racial (as the left likes to portray it)—it is political, and on a deeper level, occultic, as it was in Nazi Germany.

The Trashing of Conservative Leaders

In 1992, when the Establishment wanted to stop Pat Buchanan in his bid to take the Republican nomination away from George Bush, they labeled him as anti-Semitic, Nazi-like, Hitler-like, etc. William F. Buckley, the Establishment's "in-house conservative," led this *ad hominem* assault on Buchanan, who does not believe in foreign aid to Israel, Russia, or any one else, but who is clearly not anti-Semitic, anti-Israel, pro-Hitler, pro-Nazi, etc.

Then in the spring of 1996, during the Republican primary campaign, when Pat Buchanan was running very strong in a large field of GOP contenders, the media began a vicious smear campaign on Buchanan and his campaign co-chairman Larry Pratt, executive director of Gun Owners of America, accusing them of being racist, anti-Semitic, etc.

Pratt, a very strong Christian, was attacked and slandered by Morris Dees, of the far-left Southern Poverty Law Center and the liberal media, and accused of being racist, anti-Semitic, and tied in with the Aryan Nations. This writer knows Pratt well, and he **is not** racist, anti-Semitic, or sympathetic to the Aryan Nations or any white supremacist group. He is the nation's leading spokesman for Second Amendment gun rights, who was also Buchanan's campaign co-chairman, and so, on both counts had to be smeared, slandered, and discredited by the left.

Ad hominem attacks are regularly directed at pro-life leaders. Randall Terry, former head of Operation Rescue and popular conservative Christian radio talk show host, was called by the *Rocky Mountain News* (8/5/93) "an ayatollah in terms of crusading intolerance," a "fanatic," and "a crackpot." And Janet Reno calls pro-life leaders "terrorists." None of these attacks, of course, address the arguments of pro-life leaders in defense of the unborn—they are simply designed to discredit and demonize them in the eyes of the public and neutralize their efforts.

Using guilt by association and *ad hominem* smear tactics against Pat Robertson (the former head of the 2.5 million-member Christian Coalition), the *New York Times* carried an article (4/27/95) entitled **"New World Terror: Pat Robertson's Militias."** The *Times* tried to link Robertson to the pro-militia Mark Koernke (from Michigan) and said: "Both Mr. Koernke and Mr. Robertson **have thrown gasoline on the psychotic fires of the untethered militias running around the country.**" [*Note:* Is **that** inflammatory language? Incidentally, Robertson has had zero contact or affiliation with American militias.]

As the *Times* wrote:

> That paranoid "New World Order" rhetoric is also turning up in other
> far right groups under new scrutiny. But of all the New World Order
> fanatics, only Mr. Robertson has sown these inflammatory ideas to a

mass audience, both through his book, which sold a half million copies, and through his Christian Broadcasting Network.

In 1998, after a homosexual and abortionist were murdered in Wyoming and New York, the mainline liberal media attacked Dr. James Dobson (head of Focus on the Family) and Gary Bauer (head of the Family Research Council) accusing them of responsibility for the two murders by spreading hate against the homosexuals and abortionists. These media accusations against these two fine gentlemen are patently false, but are a preview of coming attractions. Christians, pro-life, and conservative activists will be increasingly accused of hate thought, hate speech, and hate crimes.

The name of the game for the political left from this point forward will be to attack, slander, discredit, demonize, and try to neutralize conservative Christian watchmen who are trying to warn and awaken a sleeping America.

The late James McKeever wrote in an article entitled "Why Persecution" (11/81) in a subsection titled "Strike Down the Shepherd":

> When communists have come in and taken over a country and want to abolish the church, the first thing they do is attack the pastors (or leaders). **They accuse the pastors of all sorts of things from subversion, to spying, to being traitors.** Then any of the people who fellowship with the pastor are guilty by association. First the flock begins to avoid the pastor and then eventually the pastor is arrested and removed.

This author suspects that this will be the pattern in America as we move toward persecution of Christians and traditionalists. Conservative/Christian-right leaders and watchmen will be the first to be attacked, vilified, and slandered, then isolated, and then removed. In this writer's opinion, **it has begun!**

3. Expanding the Definition of Words or Concepts

Just as National Socialist (i.e., Nazi) and fascist (traditionally seen to be on the political left) have been redefined as being on the political right;

just as "socialist" and "liberal" have been redefined as "moderate" and therefore moved semantically to the political center; and just as "anti-communist," "constitutionalist" and "belief in a limited republican form of government" have been redefined as "extreme right-wing," so the political left is expanding and changing the definition of other words as well. Note the present semantic manipulation, wherein Bill and Hillary Clinton and Al Gore (all three hard-core socialists) are now referred to as "moderates" and sometimes even as "conservatives."

Words or concepts such as terrorist, New World Order, hate, fundamentalist, racist, anti-Semitic, homophobic, child abuse, etc. are being changed and expanded to include the Christian right, anyone who disagrees with government policies, is concerned about America's social/political decline, or who believes in traditional/biblical values.

- To believe in the existence of the New World Order now is to be by leftist definition—"anti-Semitic" and a "conspiracy freak."
- To be opposed to the socialist agenda in America (political, social, or cultural) is to be a "purveyor of hate" or a "hatemonger." Also, a "purveyor of paranoia, division and fear."
- To be opposed to the unconstitutional people-control measures of the federal government, to be a gun owner/collector or a member of a militia, to be politically incorrect, to oppose the New World Order or the expansion of the powers of the United Nations is to be labeled as "anti-government" or as "a terrorist." Opposition to abortion has been redefined as "a form of terrorism." Opposition to any of the above is defined by the left as "contributing to the emotional rhetoric of hate, paranoia and division which breeds terrorism and violence."
- Criticism of the government (what ever happened to our First Amendment protection of freedom of speech?) is being redefined as "anti-government," "hate," "paranoia," or "inflammatory language."
- To be accused of anti-Semitism, white supremacy, or racism is now to be accused of a "hate crime." If "hate" is now involved in a federal crime the sentence will be extended by one-third.
- Opposition to homosexuality or citing what the Bible has to say on

the subject is now called "homophobia"—soon to be a "hate crime" (a criminal offense). Homosexuality is now redefined as an "alternate lifestyle" (see the *Newsweek* article [2/14/94] entitled "Homophobia").

- Spanking of children is being redefined as "criminal child abuse."
- To warn Americans of America's coming social, political, financial crises is to be "a paranoid purveyor of fear" or a "fearmonger."
- To believe in Bible prophecy or in the imminent Second Coming of Christ is to be "a dangerous religious cultist."
- Conservative newsletters or magazines which are critical of the direction in which our government is moving, which are pro-Constitution, or which oppose the United Nations or the New World Order, are now being redefined as "subversive." Communist publications are no longer considered subversive, nor New World Order publications, but conservative publications, especially those opposing the New World Order, are!

The political left are masters at changing the meaning of words to make their agenda and cadres look positive and their opposition look evil, wicked, dangerous, or idiotic. Hitler was also most proficient in this respect. **Isaiah 5:20** sums up the trend: "Woe unto them that call evil good, and good evil; that put darkness for light, and light for darkness; that put bitter for sweet, and sweet for bitter!"

This author has been a conservative political activist for almost forty years and an evangelical, born-again Christian for almost as long, but never in the past four decades has he seen conservatives or Christian conservatives attacked by the political left with the hatred and venom which is now spewing forth.

No longer is there honest healthy debate or disagreement between conservatives and liberals. The former are now slandered and vilified with a vengeance—with no regard to reality, in order to discredit and neutralize them. The political left is moving to silence the political right. The nature of the battle is changing. Is this the prelude to persecution of the Christian right in America? This writer believes that it may well be!

Chapter 11

The Political Left Is Setting Up the Christian Right for Persecution

There are a number of anti-Christian right political groups which have emerged on the political left in recent years which have declared war on the political right in America. No longer is the left content with debating issues or jousting over them in the political arena. It is instead moving to shut down or terminate the political right in America "with extreme prejudice."

Leftist groups such as People for the American Way, the Southern Poverty Law Center (SPLC), the Cult Awareness Network, the Conflict Analysis Group, the Northwest Coalition Against Religious Harassment, and others have launched a campaign in recent years to convince the American people and the government that the dangerous right wing and Christian conservatives want to overthrow the government and destroy America.

[*Note:* This author was under the impression that conservative/Christian Americans simply wanted to defend the Constitution and traditional, biblical, and family values, the sovereignty of the U.S., etc. Are those sentiments now to become hate, terrorist, or political crimes in America and to be equated with overthrowing the government?]

Morris Dees' Southern Poverty Law Center

The Southern Poverty Law Center is run by leftist lawyer Morris Dees. In the spring of 1996 the SPLC published *False Patriots: The Threat of Anti-Government Extremists,* a 64-page special report. The SPLC claims to have sent the report to 6,500 law enforcement agencies. Dees, a former national financial director for the George McGovern campaign, has set himself up as the "expert" on right-wing extremism and is frequently quoted in the media and consulted by law enforcement agencies.

The report says: "When 167 people were killed in the Oklahoma City explosion, it became clear that there was something more to the patriot movement than weekend war games." Joe Roy, SPLC director, added: "It is critical that media, law enforcement, and other public servants have a clear understanding of the danger these patriots represent."

The New American, an excellent conservative news magazine (which, along with many other conservative publications, is now being called "extremist" or "subversive"), wrote four excellent articles regarding the leftist attacks on the political right:

a) "No Enemies on the Left" (5/13/96); b) "SPLC's Extremist Cash Cow" (6/10/96); c) "Race and Revolution: Cultivating Conflict, Harvesting Tyranny" (8/19/96); and d) "Patriotism Under Attack—Warning: Your Love of Country May Make You a Right-Wing Extremist" (9/30/96). All four articles are highly recommended if you want to understand the coming leftist attacks on the political right in America.

The New American (in the opinion of this writer) is one of the best conservative news magazine in the world today and should be read by every person who wants to understand the times. Write to the *New American,* Box 8040, Appleton, WI 54913, 1-800-727-TRUE; annual subscription: $39.

As *The New American* (6/10/96) wrote: "It is the role of self-appointed sentinel against 'right-wing extremists' that has given the SPLC its prominence—and has made the group a potent threat to constitutional liberties." In an interview with *Soldier of Fortune* magazine (quoted in the 6/10/96 *New American*) Laird Wilcox, a frequently quoted expert on extremist groups, said:

> The SPLC tends to view their critics and the groups they hate as essentially subhuman . . . and the campaign against them acquires the character of "total warfare," where any distortion, fabrication, or sleazy legal tactic is justified in terms of the struggle.
>
> The SPLC knows that bonafide "links" between the militias and the "hate groups" are few and far between, and they know that the

[accused] perpetrators of the Oklahoma bombing have no ties what-soever to any militia organization. But in fund raising letters and media appearances, they simply lie about it because it raises money and helps to create immense mischief for those they hate.

The New American (6/10/96) continued:

The SPLC's "False Patriots" report divides the "patriot" movement into five categories: 1) Arm Chair Patriots—who discuss and debate arcane political theories on computer networks; **2)** Lifestyle Patriots—a category which includes everyone from survivalists to home school-ers; 3) Professional Patriots—which include journalists, alternative media activists, and conservative mail order entrepreneurs; 4) Outlaw Patriots—such as tax protestors and self-described "sovereign citizens"; and finally 5) Underground Patriots—who organize secret resistance cells in anticipation of urban guerilla warfare. The unstated but obvi-ous assumption here is that law abiding patriots—home schoolers for example—differ from "Outlaw Patriots" or "Underground Patriots" only in the degree of their extremism (i.e., they differ only in nuance).

The measures recommended by the SPLC to counteract the sup-posed danger presented by the patriot movement include a federal ban on militias, the imposition of policies forbidding police and military personnel to participate in militias and patriotic groups [or read al-leged subversive materials from these groups]; *aggressive federal sur-veillance of patriot organizations,* specialized training for government employees to help them in identifying extremist threats, and the adop-tion of anti-patriot editorial policies by media.

In short, the SPLC would have the government, the media, and the major opinion molding elites define the patriot movement (i.e., the en-tire conservative movement, the pro-life movement and the Christian right) as something akin to a criminal conspiracy.

The way *False Patriots* demonizes virtually all conservative Americans (i.e., the entire right wing in America) is ominous. In the glossary at the end of the report the term **"Christian patriot"** is defined as follows:

"Term used by anti-government extremists and white supremacists to identify themselves." **"Patriot"** is defined as: "Those who believe the federal government is illegitimate and is run by conspirators who seek to disarm Americans and create a world government."

So, if you believe there is a New World Order, if you believe in and own guns, if you are critical of certain government policies or individuals, you are "a dangerous right-wing extremist and potential terrorist." Fueling hatred against particular groups is a major thrust of *False Patriots*. On the cover is a child carrying a confederate flag and displaying the classic Nazi straight arm salute. *False Patriots* fans the flames of political, religious, and racial hatred in a most incredible way, and is **designed to sell the thesis that right-wing extremism is public enemy number one.**

The communists in Russia, China, and Cuba, always accused their opposition of doing what they themselves were actually doing. In like manner, the political left in America are propagating hate against conservatives while accusing the latter of fomenting hate and division.

Jihad Against the "Patriot Menace"

The September 30, 1996, *New American* article "Patriotism Under Attack" reported:

> The crusade against terrorism has become a *jihad* against the "patriot menace." What is the "patriot menace"? According to the media's pantheon of "experts," Morris Dees of the SPLC, Ken Stern of the American Jewish Committee, John Sutter of the Conflict Analysis Group and lesser known left-wing fright peddlers—the patriot movement consists of nearly everyone who stands accused of conspiratorial views.

Morris Dees' Southern Poverty Law Center, through aggressive direct mail fund raising, has a war chest to fight extremism (i.e., the political right) of about $65 million. As *The New American* wrote: "Dees is cited by both media figures and law enforcement agencies as the nation's leading expert on right wing groups. *False Patriots: The Threat of Anti-Government Extremists* is regarded as authoritative by literally thousands of law enforcement agencies across the country." [*Note:* Even though it could not be a more virulent and distorted hatchet job on the U.S. political right if it had been written by the Communist Party USA.]

The U.S. Military and the Southern Poverty Law Center

The New American continued:

> Now the SPLC is no longer content to be a "super snoop outfit" for law enforcement—**it is helping the military define America's enemies.** Eight times each year, the U.S. Air Force Special Operations School presents its "Dynamics of International Terrorism" course at Hulbert Field in Ft. Walton Beach, Florida, with representatives of all branches of the U.S. military and officials from the CIA, FBI, and Defense Intelligence Agency present.

In 1996, Joe Roy, director of the Klanwatch affiliate of the SPLC, taught for three hours in the course. A fifteen-year veteran of military intelligence, who spoke to *The New American* on condition of anonymity, said:

> Mr. Roy's presentation was focused on the Ku Klux Klan, the Aryan Nations, the Christian Identity movement, and skinheads. He also showed slides of militia groups on paramilitary training exercises. But he went on to lump together a lot of people or groups under the broad umbrella of "potential threats."
>
> He had a copy of the *False Patriots* report, and he showed how it listed "extremist groups." Roy boasted that many police chiefs and departments across the country use SPLC as a primary source of information. . . . The clear message in Roy's presentation was that if you're listed in the report, you're a "potential threat." The general tone was that these groups and organizations are preparing for war against their own government, and that later on the military will probably be involved in countering the threat.

The intelligence officer described how the course syllabus "described the nature of contemporary terrorist groups operating in the U.S., including identities, composition, operational capabilities and future potential—but all of the potential threats were called right-wing extremists; there was no mention of left wing [or Islamic] groups."

Isn't that strange? In the wake of the World Trade Center bombing by Islamic terrorists; the bombing of a U.S. barracks in Saudi Arabia by Moslem extremists; and the bombing or missile attack on TWA 800, that the SPLC only mentioned the potential for right-wing terrorism. Remember, the left always accuses their opposition of what the left is actually doing themselves.

> Another major theme of Roy's presentation, recalled the officer, was that **something would have to be done about firearms in the hands of individual citizens in this country.** He condemned the idea that the Second Amendment protects an individual's right to keep and bear arms. . . .
>
> Furthermore, the "threats" are not limited to those who own firearms. The officer recounted: "Roy seemed to suggest that people with a survivalist mentality—storing food and that sort of thing—should automatically be lumped in with those who have arsenals—whether they have weapons or not." He concluded: "I think at this stage of the game, the strategy is to garner some kind of attitudinal support within the armed services that these people are a threat to their government."

Remember a couple of years ago when a number of surveys were distributed among U.S. military troops testing their reaction to serving under the United Nations, and asking if they would turn their guns on fellow Americans if they refused to turn in their firearms. One such questionnaire was given to U.S. Marines at the Twenty-Nine Palms Marine Base in Southern California and twenty-six percent of those Marines said that they would turn their guns on their fellow Americans.

Obviously, the SPLC/Klanwatch exerts strong and growing influence on U.S. military and law enforcement officials. In light of the SPLC official lecturing at the USAF's counterterrorism school, is it possible that the U.S. military is now being prepared for use against the political right in America—calling conservatives terrorists, subversives, or a potential threat to the government?

The U.S. Justice Department and the Southern Poverty Law Center

On April 9, 1996, Morris Dees wrote a letter to U.S. Attorney General Janet Reno, according to *The New American* (9/30/96):

> . . . in which Dees declared that "the unauthorized militias" and broader so-called "patriot movement" [i.e., the conservative/Christian right in America] "are responsible for the threat of domestic terrorism that has increased sharply in the past year." Dees demanded "a coordinated governmental response to protect the public, including a joint federal and state Attorney General's task force on domestic terrorism."
>
> Reno's reply, dated June 20, 1996 said: "The Justice Department regularly reviews the publications of the Southern Poverty Law Center for information that may be of assistance to us." Reno disclosed that "the FBI is moving forward with plans to develop a federal-state-local advisory group relating to domestic terrorism" and asked Dees "to advise your local FBI office whenever you develop information that you feel may be relevant to the Department's work in the terrorism and civil rights areas."

Indoctrinating the Police

SPLC/Klanwatch is not the only left-wing group seeking to indoctrinate law enforcement agencies regarding the "patriot" menace. The Ohio-based Conflict Analysis Group, led by Dr. John Nutter, presents seminars for law enforcement agencies across the nation. . . .

Nutter—who has been presented as an "expert" on CNN, NBC, ABC, "Nightline," the "McNeil-Lehrer News Hour," and other mass media programs—describes "right-wing extremism" as a "lightning rod for the mentally disturbed." Among the warning signs for "violent or criminal activity" cited by Nutter are the display of "bumper stickers or window decals about the New World Order, Clinton, communism," [or] "I fear the government that fears my gun"—or the possession of "extremist literature" (such as this very publication). Individuals who display "excessive concern" over the Waco and Ruby Ridge incidents or the loss of American sovereignty, or an unfashionable attachment to the Second, Ninth, and Tenth Amendments, are potential terrorists as well, according to Nutter's analysis.

In early April of this year, Nutter presented a seminar entitled "Criminal Justice and Right-Wing Extremism in America" before 500 law enforcement officers in Oklahoma City. John Dirk of the Oklahoma Sheriffs and Peace Officers Association stated that Nutter was "recommended to us as an expert on right-wing organizations and how they operate."

Although Dirk did not specify from whom that recommendation came, it is safe to say that it was not offered by Mike Rafferty, a deputy sheriff from Rossville, Kansas, who suffered through a Nutter seminar in Topeka last fall. "I attended Nutter's program with about fifty other law enforcement officers and security personnel." Rafferty recalled to *The New American.* "It was a day-long affair, but there wasn't any depth to it at all. He billed himself as an authority on the subject of right-wing extremism, but most of what he had to say was just repackaged from the left-wing media—not just the mainstream liberal press, but the really left-wing variety."

Rafferty pointed out: "From Nutter's point of view, nearly anybody who expresses certain concerns about what's happening in this country are just like those really radical groups." Furthermore, Rafferty perceived that "the basic implied message in Nutter's presentation was that self-sufficiency and nonreliance on government is dangerous, and that people who display those attitudes are inclined toward antisocial and criminal behavior."

The New American article concluded with: "Outlawing the Right? Have we reached a juncture at which the mere expression of 'anti-government' or 'conspiracist' sentiments is regarded as *prima facie* evidence of intent to commit terrorist acts? Not yet, but that day may come soon."

If it is soon to be against the law to criticize the government, with our First Amendment freedom of speech rights completely brushed aside, how will we differ from communist Russia, China, Cuba, or Nazi Germany with respect to freedom of speech?

The growing attacks against the political and Christian right in America by the political left are very reminiscent of the attacks against the opposition to the Nazis in Germany in the 1930s after the Reichstag fire, set by the Nazis, and blamed on their opposition. The Nazis and the communists were (are) masters at accusing and blaming their opposition for exactly what they themselves are doing. The political left in America has begun to move into high gear to silence its Christian right opposition.

The Political Left Is Using the Y2K Crisis as an Excuse for Attacking the Political/Christian/Conservative Right

After the Oklahoma City bombing, the Clinton Administration, the liberal media, and the political left painted the political right in America with a very broad, black brush—accusing the conservatives and conservative Christians of America, radio talk show hosts, gun owners, pro-lifers, etc. of terrorism, hate crimes, and responsibility for the deaths of 168 victims in that tragedy. The truth of what really happened—the inside bombs, undetonated explosives, foreknowledge by certain government agencies—will never be fully revealed.

Now the political left has started a spin campaign that the conservatives and religious right who are talking about Y2K and urging preparations are going to use Y2K as an excuse to launch terrorist attacks across the U.S. Did you get that: they are trying to create a link between Y2K preparedness and terrorism. *FBI director Louis Freeh warned on February 4, 1999, that right-wing extremists, religious cults, or apocalyptic groups may turn to violence to fulfill their prophecies of Armageddon as the year 2000 approaches.*

The FBI is planning to set up a special unit in the northwest U.S. to monitor white supremacist groups. The FBI says that Y2K-preparedness expositions in that region are filled with people who are planning to head for the hills. *Such people are alleged to be the potential sources of terrorism in 2000.*

This concept that Christians, conservatives, survivalists, believers in the imminent return of Jesus Christ, are dangerous cultists and/or potential terrorists has been spawned by the Southern Poverty Law Center and its sister organization in the Pacific Northwest—the Northwest Coalition Against Malicious Harassment. Their theme is: "Extremists' fears and hopes surrounding Y2K have increased the dangers of domestic terrorism."

Janet Reno expanded the definition of terrorism several years ago to include pro-life demonstrators praying in front of abortion clinics. Now her subordinate, FBI director Louis Freeh, is again expanding the definition of terrorist or potential terrorist to include people who are actually preparing for Y2K.

USA Today (12/23/98) reported:

> The FBI is launching a task force on domestic terrorism in the Pacific Northwest, long considered a hotbed for white supremacist and anti-federal government activities. The action comes as anti-supremacist activists in the northwest fear an increase in terrorism coinciding with the year 2000. . . .
>
> Already, there is talk about "Doomsday" and "Armageddon" among these groups, Wassmuth (head of the Northwest Coalition Against Malicious Harassment) says, and paranoia about the possible computer collapse at the beginning of the year 2000, commonly called the Y2K problem. . . . "There are people buying two years of food and supplies and heading for the hills," Wassmuth says. His group is a coalition of organizations in six northwestern states countering white supremacists and extremist groups." [*Note:* "White supremacist" is a negative buzz phrase increasingly being used by the left to discredit large numbers of conservatives who are in no way racist and extremist, or anyone who disagrees with the government.]
>
> The FBI task force is still being assembled. It will include agents from federal, state, and local law enforcement agencies in eastern Washington, northern Idaho, and western Montana, says Burdena Pasenelli, special agent in charge of FBI division headquarters in Seattle. "Our goal is to find out ahead of time what is planned and to prevent incidents of domestic terrorism," she says. "Historically, this area has had a number of domestic terrorism incidents."
>
> Formed at a meeting this fall in Coeur d'Alene, Idaho, this is the first FBI task force to cross state lines and FBI field offices, Pasenelli says. "We call it the Inland Empire," she says, referring to the three-

state region being covered. . . . Mark Potok of the Southern Poverty Law Center in Montgomery, Ala., and editor of its quarterly *Intelligence Report* says, "The Pacific Northwest has produced some of this nation's leading domestic terrorists. The only comparable areas are certain parts of the Ozarks and rural North Carolina," he says.

On February 4, 1999, Reuters carried the following story on FBI director Louis Freeh's "Warning of Millennium Violence":

FBI director Louis Freeh warned Thursday that right-wing extremists, religious cults, or apocalyptic groups could turn to violence to fulfill their prophecies of Armageddon as the year 2000 approaches. At a congressional hearing on counterterrorism, Freeh cited "rogue terrorists" such as Saudi dissident Osama bin Laden—blamed by Washington for the bombing of two American embassies in East Africa last year—as probably the most urgent risk to U.S. interests. But he said the domestic threat could not be ignored, especially as the millennium approached.

"The possibility of an indigenous group like Aum Supreme Truth cannot be excluded," he said, referring to the cult responsible for a nerve gas attack in the Tokyo subway system in March 1995. "With the coming of the next millennium, some religious/apocalyptic groups or individuals may turn to violence as they seek to achieve dramatic effects to fulfill their prophecies," he said. Freeh expressed dismay at a "pattern of racist elements" seeping into the U.S. militia movement most of which, he said, had no racial overtones and did not espouse bigotry.

But he discussed at length "a disturbing trend" toward the pseudo-religion of Christian Identity—and other hate philosophies—that provided both a religious base for racism and anti-Semitism, as well as an ideological rationale for violence against minorities. "Many white supremacist groups adhere to the Christian Identity belief system, which holds that the world is on the verge of a final apocalyptic struggle . . . and teaches that the white race is the chosen race of God," he said. Many of those who believe in this credo are engaged in survivalist and paramilitary training, *storing foodstuffs and supplies* and caching weapons and ammunition.

[*Note:* "Christian Identity" is another broad-brush negative label the FBI and political left are beginning to apply to large groups of Christians. Note the negative connotation for people storing food reserves, supplies, or possessing firearms or ammunition. These are *not* illegal or in any way a sign of a person being a racist, a cultist, or a terrorist.]

Freeh said that as 1999 came to a close, Identity's more extreme members could prepare for Armageddon by carrying out armed robberies to finance the upcoming battle, destroying government property, and targeting Jews and non-whites. The FBI had "little credible intelligence" at this time indicating that terrorists, either domestic or international, were preparing to attack the United States, the director said. But he added that a growing number—while still small—of "lone offender" and extremist splinter elements of right-wing groups have been identified as possessing or attempting to "develop or use" chemical, biological or nuclear weapons.

Attorney General Janet Reno, who also appeared before the Senate Appropriations subcommittee, said a terrorist attack using a biological weapon might not be immediately apparent with far-reaching impact on victims and emergency personnel. "In fact, we have found recently the mere threat of the use of unconventional weapons can cause concern and panic. Threats to release harmful biological or chemical substances cannot be ignored," she said. Freeh said the FBI dealt with an "anthrax warning letter" somewhere in the country almost every day.

U.S. officials had to be able "to match wits with the bad guys," Reno said. She appealed to the Senate panel to approve funds for a National Domestic Preparedness Office to be led by the FBI to provide coordination and a single point of contact for state and local communities.

[*Note:* So, Freeh, Reno and the political left have set the stage for blaming any terrorist incidents in America (real, imagined *or staged*) on the political right, the Christian right, people preparing for Y2K, gun owners, etc. When a terrorist incident occurs, the right wing or religious right will be blamed—just as occurred after Oklahoma City.

The political left appears to be setting a giant trap which it plans to spring on the right over the next year or so, and "millennial madness" and the "Y2K fanatics" will be blamed. Watch for the growing use of the terms "cultist," "racist," "terrorist," and "hate" to be used against the religious right and those advocating preparations for Y2K.]

The End of the World As We Know It

Time magazine (1/18/99) carried a cover article by that title, with a cover featuring someone who looked remarkably like artists' portrayals of Jesus carrying a cross and a sandwich board inscribed with: "The End of the World!?! Y2K Insanity! Apocalypse Now! Will Computers Meltdown? Will Society? A Guide to Millennium Madness." Instead of analyzing the Y2K problem, the article trashed the Christian right for being concerned about Y2K, for its Y2K preparedness, and for trying to stir up a panic.

Negative, derogatory terms like "models of apocalyptic pluck," "apocalyptic fantasies," "death wish fantasies," "religious millennialists," "Y2K alarmists," "premature prophets of doom," and "apocalyptic imaginings" were used throughout the article to make Christians concerned about Y2K to appear extremist, paranoid, ridiculous, and even dangerous.

In describing Gary North (whose newsletter and web site has done an excellent job in circulating a wealth of information on Y2K) the *Time* article wrote:

> North, who declines to be interviewed, not only hopes that America will fall, he believes it's part of his duty to bring it down, to be replaced by a Bible-based Reconstructionist state that will impose the death penalty on blasphemers, heretics, adulterers, gay men and women who have had abortions or sex before marriage. So it's a fine line for him between warning against a calamity and encouraging panic. [*Note:* This writer has known Gary North for years and finds that quote false, defamatory, and totally misleading.]

This article ridiculed the Christian's concern about Y2K and is part of a growing trend toward attacking the Christian right, equating them with terrorism and dangerous religious cults, and blaming them for the coming Y2K panic. There must be a scapegoat and it seems that the political left is setting up the political right for that role. Will Clinton, Gore, Reno, Freeh, and their comrades on the political left use Y2K to defame and neutralize the political/religious right in America (what they call the "vast right-wing conspiracy")? It appears to this author that that is precisely what they are planning to do!

Chapter 12

The Rise of Anti-Christian, Anti-Traditionalist Persecution in America

> . . . they shall lay their hands on you, and persecute you, delivering you up to the synagogues, and into prisons, being brought before kings and rulers for my name's sake. . . . And ye shall be betrayed both by parents, and brethren, and kinsfolks, and friends; and some of you shall they cause to be put to death. And ye shall be hated of all men for my name's sake.
>
> **—Luke 21:12,16-17**

> If the world hate you, ye know that it hated me before it hated you.
>
> **—John 15:18**

Worldwide persecution of those who have a personal relationship with Jesus Christ has begun. Christians are the most widely hated and persecuted group of people on earth today. Marxists persecute Christians from North Korea and Vietnam to the Cuban prisons, from the Red Chinese *gulag* to the midnight disappearances in Angola and Mozambique.

Muslims persecute Christians from Saudi Arabia to Libya; from Algeria to Pakistan to the Sudan (where over two million Sudanese Christians have been killed in the 1990s alone). Animists, agitated by occult witch doctors, persecute Christians in many parts of Africa and Asia.

The *World Christian Encyclopedia* reports that Christians in two-thirds of the countries of the world are under some form of restrictions or outright persecution ranging from reduction of their freedoms to overt attempts to eradicate their faith. Up to thirty percent have no political freedom or civil liberties; twenty-five percent live under anti-Christian regimes; thirteen percent live under atheistic governments; and seventeen percent are experiencing extreme oppression for their faith—ranging from beatings, to imprisonment, from seizure of property to execution.

In America, increasingly vicious attacks against Christians are being launched by homosexual groups, the pro-abortion and radical feminist movements, the pornography industry, the film and television industries, liberal judges, government bureaucrats, and academicians, by atheist and occult groups, and by the political left. Growing pressure against Christians and Christian groups, against their freedom of speech and assembly, and against their beliefs, teachings, and practices is being exerted by an increasingly hostile, liberal, anti-Christian U.S. government and judiciary.

As Pat Robertson has said:

> Acts of Congress, signed by the president of the U.S., carry with them the full enforcement power of the FBI and the Justice Department. The time may come in America when the federal government will hunt down and prosecute any Christian who dares protest the slaughter of unborn children or the flagrant practice of homosexuality. Instead of those who break God's laws being criminals, those who uphold God's laws will be considered criminals and enemies of the state!

As stated before, traditional Bible believing, fundamental, evangelical Christians are hated by the secular humanists, by the socialists, by the homosexuals, by the abortionists and by those advocating abortion, by the women's libbers, by the liberal media, and by the global socialists. They fear and hate Christians as much as the Roman Caesars, Hitler, Lenin, Stalin, and Mao did, and see them as a great hindrance or obstacle to their secularist/socialist/people-control/globalist vision for America.

The liberal media, television, and film industries are beginning to openly trash Christians, traditionalists, pro-lifers, home schoolers, etc.;

to equate these groups with dangerous cults; and to describe them as homophobes, the dangerous religious right, religious bigots, as poor, uneducated, and easy to command, as fanatic censors of the thoughts of others, as intolerant religious warriors, as book burners, as purveyors of fear and intolerance, as rats (as a Pat Oliphant political cartoon depicted); and as dangerous as (or similar to) the Ku Klux Klan, the Nazis, or the Hezbollah Party, etc.

Today, anyone defending Christianity and biblical morality is becoming the target of malicious attacks. We see incredible hatred of those who are not politically correct from the media, the entertainment industry, academia, the government, and the judiciary. This chapter will explore this Christian bashing, the growing attacks against Christians and traditionalists in the legal and public arenas, and the growing war against Christian conservatives and their leadership.

Christian Bashing in America

It's "open season" on Christians and traditionalists in America, with the trashing of Christians and their beliefs a popular national sport. Novelist Gore Vidal has written a blasphemous book, *Live From Golgotha,* which (among other things) portrayed Paul and Timothy as homosexual lovers. The author said of Christianity that "it is the greatest disaster to ever befall the West." Recently a New York play called *Corpus Christy* depicted Jesus Christ as a homosexual kissing (opened mouth) Judas, and having homosexual relations with a number of his disciples.

In television programs and motion pictures, Christians are being portrayed as bigots, censors, intolerant, narrow-minded, hypocrites, idiots, charlatans, rapists, murderers, cannibals, as a threat to our freedom and to our very way of life. To illustrate, Showtime's movie, *Flight of the Black Angel* featured an Air Force pilot (who is a fundamentalist Christian) who goes berserk, murders his family, and shoots several fellow pilots. His ultimate objective was to nuke the world, starting with Las Vegas. The Christian villain states: "I'm doing [God's] work. Everything [on earth] must be destroyed. . . . I'm bringing 'the light of heaven [to] the diseased, the unclean, the corrupt, the liars.'"

Syndicated columnist Don Feder, a conservative Orthodox Jew, wrote in April 1993 in an article entitled "Christian Bashing Reaches New Heights":

> White Christians are about the only easy target left. . . . Christian bashing, in all of its raw ugliness is: 1) ridiculing conservative Christians as benighted and sheeplike; 2) suggesting there's something sinister about political ideas based on scriptural standards; or 3) implying that the clergy forfeit their constitutional rights when they don a clerical collar.

Because of their commitment to chastity, fidelity, and heterosexuality, Christians are commonly depicted in the media and entertainment industry as narrow-minded bigots. At abortion protests and homosexual marches, the following chant can be heard: "Racists, sexists, anti-gay—born-again bigots go away."

A few years ago liberal editorial cartoonist Pat Oliphant drew a syndicated cartoon showing a group of Christians portrayed as a pack of rats dragging the Republican elephant into a Christian mission, replete with a cross which says "Jesus Saves." Christians should recognize that such dehumanizing characterizations of Christians are very similar to the dehumanizing portrayal of Jews by the Nazi press prior to World War II. The anti-Christian hate campaign in America is looking more and more like the Nazi anti-Jewish hate campaign of the 1930s.

Newsweek magazine seems to have a special flare for Christian bashing by utilizing stereotypes, innuendos, exaggeration, and outright anti-Christian bias in various articles. In a *Newsweek* cover story (9/14/96) entitled "Gays Under Fire," the "religious right" (a derogatory epithet coined by the liberal media) was blamed for "a powerful backlash against gay America's struggle for acceptance." *Newsweek* blamed the Christians' bigotry against the downtrodden homosexuals and "their struggle for equal treatment" on the Christians' belief in the Bible.

In a March 1, 1993, *Newsweek* article entitled "Onward Muscular Christian," the writers compared the growing Christian influence in Colorado Springs as being similar to "Muslims in Mecca," and referred to the Christians' "hate campaign" against homosexuals in Colorado. The inference was clear: wherever Christians gather, hatred, bigotry and even violence are sure to follow.

The print and electronic media now regularly refer to Christians and traditionalists using terms such as: "hateful," "violent," "detrimental," "bigoted," "gay bashing," "homophobic," "the same as Ayatollah Khomeini," etc. and refer to their faith as "a contagion from the right." Ted Turner has called Christians and pro-life demonstrators "bozos" and "idiots." These terms are used in the context of fundamentalist, evangelical, conservative Catholics, and religious right.

The malignant examples of Christians in the media come in three primary flavors: **1) Catholic Christians; 2) Fundamentalist Christians; and 3) Rabid, Lunatic Pentecostals.** The **Catholic Christian** is often stereotyped as a neurotic, timid paranoid who is obsessed with superstitious practices that more closely portray witchcraft than Christian worship. The female version of the Catholic Christian is usually timid and nervous; whereas the male version is aggressive, belligerent, and emotional, and perpetrates horrible crimes while often conducting pseudo-Catholic rites.

The **Fundamentalist Christian** is the most wicked of the Christian villains on the silver screen. This stereotype is generally white, male, a racist, a bigot, a chauvinist, ignorant, hypocritical, evil, or some combination of those negative attributes. In rock music, movies and television, the fundamentalist is portrayed as the perpetrator of the most horrible crimes while maintaining his facade of piety, self-righteousness, and religiosity.

The **Pentecostal Christian** is regularly stereotyped as a crazed, homicidal maniac, who while speaking in tongues or expressing dreams or visions commits heinous crimes (i.e., murder, rape, incest, dismemberment, etc.)

Today's rock and rap musicians, stand-up comics, Hollywood screenwriters, TV talk show hosts, news commentators, journalists, and novelists have developed the bashing of these three groups of Christians almost to an art form, referring to them regularly as fools, bigots, hypocrites, and as dangerous.

A growing number of movies and TV shows portray Christian ministers, priests, nuns, and laymen committing horrible murders, dealing or using drugs, having sex or incest with children, or killing or maiming while quoting Bible verses or praying to God.

And, usually opposite this Christian reprobate is a clever, poised skeptic or non-believer who helps to expose the mendacity of the Christian, or bring him to justice. In this way, the political left in Hollywood is creating a stereotype of Christians which is loathsome, easy to hate, and easy to create negative emotion against.

Hollywood's Attack Against Christian/Traditionalists

Hollywood producers and screenwriters are propagating a vicious form of anti-Christian propaganda that characterizes practicing Christians as wicked devils who prey upon the weak, the sincere, the good people. Michael Medved, a Jewish critic of the Hollywood left, has documented this anti-Christian stereotype and trashing in his book *Hollywood vs. America.*

He points out how "clergy kills illicit lover" is a recurrent theme in a number of modern films—a theme that portrays Christian clergymen as dangerous murderers who prey upon innocents while hiding behind the mask of peaceful clerics. Medved cites a number of films which trash Christians:

- *The Runner Stumbles* (1979)—with Dick Van Dyke in a deadly serious role of a small town priest who falls in love with a young nun . . . and then stands trial for her murder.
- *Monsignor* (1982)—In this film, a priest (a cardinal) engages in every imaginable sin, seduces a glamorous nun, and is involved in her death. The corrupt and powerful cardinal is involved with the Vatican bank and the Mafia under the approving eye of the pope.
- *Agnes of God* (1985)—with Jane Fonda. A young nun gives birth to an illegitimate baby in a convent, murders the baby, and then flushes the tiny, bloody corpse down the toilet. The movie has an anti-Catholic, pro-feminist, pro-abortion theme (i.e., if the nun could have aborted, she wouldn't have been forced to murder the baby).
- *The Penitent* (1988)—Raul Julia "plays a farmer in New Mexico who joins a primitive and brutal Catholic cult which every year cru-

cifies (sacrifices) an unlikely victim—with a maximum of blood, gore, and whacked-out, quasi-religious visions." As Medved points out, the desecration of the crucifixion, the mass, worship, preaching, and baptism is thematic in much of Hollywood's anti-religious fare.

- **Crimes of Passion** (1984)—Anthony Perkins portrays "a sweaty, Bible-toting skid row evangelist" who frequents peep shows while quoting Bible verses, who is obsessed with a hooker, and who plans to "save her soul" by a grotesque sexual murder.

- **The Handmaid's Tale** (1990)—starring Robert Duval and Faye Dunaway. As Medved wrote: "This film is a pointedly political polemic about what life would be like if Christian fundamentalists came to power in America. . . . These religious zealots are considerably less loveable than Nazis. . . . Their vicious, theocratic government pursues genocidal policies against ethnic minorities, bans books with non-scriptural messages . . . assembles huge crowds to watch public hangings and torture, and uses brute force to enforce the most arcane regulations from the Bible. . . . The evil evangelists who run the country aren't even sincere in their fanaticism as they secretly operate bordellos for their pleasure."

- **The Rapture** (1991)—As Medved wrote: "An ex-swinger, addicted to group sex, suddenly becomes a Christian. Her new faith causes her to go to the desert with her six-year-old daughter to wait for the Rapture. When it doesn't come, she blows her daughter's brains out while mumbling invocations to the Almighty."

- **At Play In the Fields of the Lord** (1991)—Medved writes that "no faith is spared. In addition to the psychotic, repressed, relentlessly obnoxious and mean-spirited Protestant missionaries, the cast of characters include a foul-smelling, cynical Catholic priest and an alcoholic, whore-mongering, heavily tattooed Jewish mercenary who offers contemptuous recollections of his own Bar Mitzvah."

- **Guilty As Charged** (1992)—"Rod Steiger is a murderous maniac who just happens to be a Christian fanatic. . . . He imprisons poor souls in a homemade dungeon and one by one executes them in a huge electric chair decorated with religious motifs. . . . As the victims fry, howling in fear and pain, Steiger exalts at the top of his lungs: 'We praise the Lord for the Department of Water and Power! The Holy Spirit is electricity, and the chair is God's instrument of Justice and Salvation!'"

· *Priest* (1995)—This Walt Disney film portrayed a troubled gay priest, a self-satisfied heterosexual priest openly living with his housekeeper, an alcoholic priest, a spiteful bishop, and a teenage girl abused by her Catholic father—all warped by the Christian doctrines to which they adhere.

These are just a few of the hundreds of anti-Christian films which have emanated from Hollywood over the past decade or so. In *The Quick and the Dead* (1995) a preacher's faith and his God are shown to be irrelevant; in *Alien 3* (1992), born again Christians in a future world are rampant rapists and violent criminals; in *Star Trek V: The Final Frontier,* God is presented as an evil being and all religions as man-made—both of which will be obsolete in the future; in *Johnny Mnemonic* (1995) the evil character is a street preacher who stabs people to death with his crucifix.

In the film *Cape Fear*, Robert DeNiro plays a Pentecostal Christian (adorned with a body-sized cross tattooed on his back) who is homicidal, a rapist, and murderer. This "Pentecostal Christian" smokes pot, tries to seduce a teenage girl, brutally rapes and partially cannibalizes a woman, commits serial murder, and finally sinks to a watery grave while "speaking in tongues."

As Don Feder wrote in response to the 1988 film *The Last Temptation of Christ* produced by MCA's Universal Studios (which depicted Jesus as a homosexual, a whoremonger, and demon possessed):

> Christians are the only group Hollywood can offend with impunity, the only creed it actually goes out of its way to insult. Clerics, from fundamentalist preachers to Catholic monks, are routinely represented as hypocrites, hucksters, sadists, and lechers. The tenets of Christianity are held up to ridicule.

While Hollywood continues to depict practicing Christians (and to a lesser extent observant Jews) as hypocritical lunatics, fanatics, rapists, mass murderers, and cannibals, television is not treating believers any better. The same is now true of a number of prime time television series, on MTV and on rock and rap music. It is open season on Christianity in pop culture.

Anti-Christian diatribes and stereotypes are found throughout television programming and on thousands of music recordings. MTV ridicules Christ, Christians, priests, ministers, the Bible, and the crucifixion while mixing them in with sex (straight and gay) and making them appear sadistic. Madonna told *Spin* magazine: "Crucifixes are sexy because there is a naked man on them."

Robert and Linda Lichter of the Center for Media and Public Affairs conducted a survey of 104 of the most influential television writers, producers, and executives, which confirmed their liberal, anti-religious mindset:

- 93 percent "say they seldom or never attend religious services."
- 75 percent "describe themselves as left of center politically, compared to only 14 percent who place themselves to the right of center."
- 97 percent are pro-choice with respect to abortion.
- 80 percent "do not regard homosexual relations as wrong."
- Only 5 percent "agree strongly that homosexuality is wrong, compared to 49 percent who disagree strongly."
- 86 percent "support the rights of homosexuals to teach in public schools."
- 51 percent "do not regard adultery as wrong."
- Only 17 percent "strongly agree that extramarital affairs are wrong."

These are the people who are creating anti-Christian, anti-traditional values television programming and brainwashing 75 to 100 million American television viewers every day with the new anti-Christian consensus. Prime time television continues to portray Christians as miscreants, fun-hating puritans, sexually dysfunctional women haters, and dangerous fanatics.

It could be argued, "Well, just don't watch such movies, or television, or listen to such anti-Christian music. After all, as the children's rhyme goes: 'sticks and stones can break my bones, but words can never hurt me.'" Yes, but **what these vehicles for anti-Christian propaganda are doing is changing the way hundreds of millions of people think about Christians, and biblical and traditional values.**

They are making it socially acceptable to demean and hate Christians. And American movies and rock/rap music do not just reach an American audience. They reach billions of people all over the world, and are consequently helping to establish an anti-Christian consensus not just in America, but on a global scale as well.

Attacking Christians in the Legal Arena

For the past forty years or more, the political left in America has been quietly working to take over our legal institutions, starting with the law schools in the 1950s and 1960s and now reaching into our entire legal system—our judiciary (local, federal, and state) and even our legislatures (state and federal).

Virtually all judges and most legislators in America are lawyers. Most lawyers in America have graduated from liberal, secular humanist oriented law schools who take a liberal or socialist view of the Constitution, a big government approach to politics, and a secular humanist/Freudian/evolutionist approach to religion or Christianity.

Hence, over the past thirty years, the legal system has moved dramatically against Christians and the traditional biblical values they support and believe in—outlawing prayer in schools and God or any manifestation of Christianity in public life; legalizing the murder of unborn children (now totaling close to 40 million since 1973); expanding the definition of child abuse to include biblically-ordained spanking; creating special rights and legal protections for homosexuals; expanding the definition of sexual harassment; undermining parental authority; legalizing pornography; forcing the teaching of alternate lifestyles (i.e., homosexuality) to students in public schools; and much more.

New legal initiatives which are now being pushed throughout our leftist-dominated legal system and which will put Christians and traditionalists on a collision course with the government and the new anti-Christian consensus include: 1) euthanasia; 2) homosexual marriage; 3) greater government involvement in childraising and decisions regarding children's education and careers (as per Hillary Clinton's *It Takes a Village*; 4) government registration and tracking of all children from day one to death; 5) new "hate crime" legislation which will make it a federal crime to criticize a homosexual or their lifestyle or to oppose abortionists; 6) new anti-discrimination legislation which will make it a federal crime not to hire a homosexual or have up to a ten percent quota of homosexuals working for a business or ministry; new anti-terrorist legislation which will make it illegal to criticize the government, to pray or demonstrate in front of an abortion clinic, and much more.

Many practicing Christians (fundamentalist, Catholic, and Pentecostals) will have a major problem with many of these initiatives—the ones already in place and the ones which will be adopted over the next few years. So the liberal U.S. legal system and the Christian traditionalists are on an unavoidable collision course. The more the Christian traditionalists oppose these unbiblical (and unconstitutional) measures, the more they will be isolated, slandered, ostracized, marginalized, and ultimately targeted for persecution by the liberal power structure and the new anti-Christian consensus. This is the way the pressure began to build against the Jews in Nazi Germany in the 1930s.

The tragedy is that the liberals have been able (with very little opposition from conservatives or Christians) to co-op the courts in their drive to suppress religious ideas. From 1988 forward many judges allowed themselves to be used as patron saints of the abortion industry in America by writing restraining orders and injunctions prohibiting conscientious Christian protestors the rights of assembly, speech, religious exercise, and expression. During this period (especially from 1988 through 1992) Christians were hauled into courts, fined tens of thousands of dollars, had their assets frozen, and were imprisoned for violating court orders against kneeling in prayer, singing hymns, distributing Bibles and religious tracts, and preaching in public. This period saw the most blatant denials of civil and human rights since the civil rights struggle of the previous generation.

Legal Attacks on Christians' Freedom of Speech

Over the past decade dozens of liberal, anti-Christian judges have handed down orders, edicts, and injunctions prohibiting Christians from their exercise of free speech and religious freedoms (i.e., praying, carrying a Bible, or mentioning God on public property, in or around a courtroom, etc.). Paul Schenck, author of the excellent book *The Extermination of Christianity,* was sentenced to thirty days in jail in 1992 by a New York judge for praying in the courtroom.

During the course of the trial of pro-life demonstrators who had been arrested in the "Spring of Life" rescue campaign in Buffalo, the judge, Sherwood L. Bestry, ordered that any prayers anywhere in or near the courthouse would be punishable by thirty days in the county prison. Judge Bestry considered public prayers "disgusting and would not tolerate any religious ceremonies" that included clergy vestments in or around the courthouse.

As Schenck wrote:

Judge Bestry's ban on prayer is an example of the same kind of bias that shows up in scores of judicial decrees in the form of restraining orders, injunctions, and decisions that have intruded upon that form of speech once considered sacrosanct (religious exercise). In fact, utilizing their enormously broad powers, "politically correct" judges have seriously curtailed the first amendment rights of Christians and other religionists.

There is a growing trend throughout the country for secularist organizations, groups, and individuals to petition the courts to restrict religious expressions in public. For instance, a state court judge in Houston, Texas, granted relief to abortion groups by issuing an injunction barring preaching, hymn singing, witnessing, and Bible and tract distribution on public sidewalks around abortion clinics. Similar injunctions were issued in Atlanta, Wichita, and Buffalo.

So, courts are now moving to deny Christians their basic, constitutional rights, with judges prohibiting the possession and distribution of Bibles and religious tracts, witnessing, and prayer in public buildings, parks, and on street corners, with huge fines and imprisonment for violation thereof. And these violations of Christians' constitutional rights of free speech and freedom of religion are growing and expanding each year, even as the media and the vast majority of Americans, including most Christians, barely take note. No other groups in America (i.e., homosexuals, feminists, African-Americans, Hispanics, Islamics, Jews, atheists, witches, Satanists, etc.) are being restricted in this manner—only Christians!

According to Keith Fournier, executive director of the American Center for Law and Justice:

> Under the banner of . . . liberty . . . as redefined in our secularized state, unpopular speech and, in a particular way, Christian speech is being censored from the public arena. Rather than free speech, we now have a growing effort to enforce "speech free" zones throughout the country. The "political correctness" movement is but one example of a growing intolerance toward religious speech.

Dr. D. James Kennedy wrote in his book, *The Gates of Hell Shall Not Prevail: The Attack on Christianity and What You Need to Know to Combat It:*

> The attack on Christ in America in the public arena stems from a misreading of the religion clause of the First Amendment: "Congress shall make no law respecting an establishment of religion or prohibiting the free exercise thereof."
>
> Although the First Amendment has historically given Americans unprecedented religious freedom, today the Amendment's interpretation has been so twisted that it has become a hammer of oppression. Traditionally it has been understood that the Establishment Clause of the First Amendment meant that in America there would be no national church like they had in England. The framers wanted a separation of the function of the church from the function of the national government. But they did not want a separation of God or Christianity from the state, which we find in our country today.

Our Founding Fathers never expected or intended our liberal/secular humanist leaders of today to take this establishment clause of the First Amendment and interpret it as the separation of church and state, and twist and distort it, so as to ban all religious free speech or expression in public, in schools, on public property, in the courts, in government, etc. The First Amendment, written to guarantee religious freedom, is now being used by the political left to take it away.

This liberal distortion of the First Amendment is resulting in the following twisted decisions: A guilty verdict in a murder trial was thrown out of court because the prosecution quoted from the Bible; the Supreme Court has ruled that the Ten Commandments cannot be posted in public school classrooms; Christian pro-life activists are now being prosecuted for public prayer under RICO (racketeering) statutes designed for use against organized crime.

There is an interesting parallel here with the former Soviet Union. Throughout the communist history of the Soviet Union, the Soviets prided themselves on having separation of church and state. It was even written into their Soviet Constitution (Article 52). But, the church-state view of the Soviets was used to muzzle the freedom of the church and virtually all religious free speech in the former Soviet Union. This was a major factor in forcing the persecuted Russian church underground.

In theory, religion was free to do anything that the government was not involved in, but the government was involved in everything. So, religion, the Bible, witnessing, etc. was banned from virtually every aspect of Soviet life. The same thing is happening in America today, where the doctrine of separation of church and state is being used to ban religion and the Christian church from almost every aspect of American life (i.e., no public prayers, Bible readings, prayer in school or at graduation commencements, football games, etc.) After all, the government in America (like its former Soviet counterpart) is involved in almost everything, including the running of the public schools. The parallels with the restriction of religion in Russia and in America, using separation of church and state is ominous. It has turned the First Amendment into a hammer that pounds away at the church and any public expression of Christianity. It could one day result in Christians being thrown off the airwaves, revocation of the tax exempt status of all churches and para-church groups, and possibly one day the illegality of Christianity as we have known it in America.

The ACLU Attack on Religious Freedom in America

The American Civil Liberties Union (ACLU), founded in 1920, the legal arm of the political left in America, has pursued a relentless campaign of legal harassment against Christians, Christian symbols, Christian practices, and traditional Judeo-Christian values for many decades, but especially over the past ten years. The ACLU was actually founded as the Bureau for Conscientious Objectors in 1918 by Roger Baldwin, who served one year in federal prison for sedition. He renamed the group the American Civil Liberties Union upon his release from prison. According to an investigative committee of the U.S. Congress, "The ACLU claims to stand for free speech, free press, and free assembly, but it is quite apparent that the main function of the ACLU is to attempt to protect communists in their advocacy of force and violence to overthrow the U.S. government."

Several of the original board members, besides Baldwin, including William Foster, Elizabeth Gurley Flynn, and Louis Budenz, were later prominent members of the Communist Party USA. (Foster became head of the Communist Party USA.) As of 1993, the national board read like a "Who's Who of the American Left": George McGovern, Norman Lear, Ed Asner, Carl Sagan, Patricia Schroeder, Norman Cousins, Birch Bayh, Ramsey Clark, Arthur Schlessinger, Lowell Weiker, Morton Halperin, etc. The ACLU presently maintains a membership of 250,000, 70 staff lawyers, and 5,000 volunteer attorneys, **handling an average of 6,000 cases at any one time,** with an annual budget of $14 million. According to Coral Ridge Ministries, the ACLU has sought to:

- Halt the singing of Christian carols like *Silent Night* and *Away in a Manger* in public facilities;
- Deny the tax-exempt status of all churches;
- Disallow prayer—not just in public classrooms—but in locker rooms, sports arenas, graduation exercises, and legislative assemblies;

- Terminate all military and prison chaplains;
- Deny Christian school children access to publicly-funded services;
- Eliminate nativity scenes, crosses, and all other Christian symbols from all public property;
- Repeal of "blue (Sunday) law" statutes;
- Prohibit voluntary Bible reading in public schools—even during free time or after classes;
- Remove "In God We Trust" from our coins;
- Deny accreditation to science departments at Bible-believing Christian universities;
- Prevent the posting of the Ten Commandments in classrooms;
- Terminate all voucher programs and tuition tax credits;
- Purge the words "under God" from the Pledge of Allegiance.

In an incredible twisting of the principles of freedom of speech, freedom of religion, and separation of church and state, the ACLU has pursued efforts to legalize all forms of pornography (including child porn), legalize and legitimize all kinds of deviant sexual behavior as "victimless crimes," and eradicate all vestiges of religious faith from public life.

Churches, Christian schools, and other Christian structures have been the targets of lawsuits by the ACLU all over the country. Most of its lawyers and representatives are rabidly anti-Christian. Its lawsuits are designed to cripple and then eliminate Christian structures and institutions, to undermine America's few remaining traditional values (especially the family), and to advance the agenda of the political left. This should not be surprising when one considers that the ACLU's founder said in 1935 (at the height of Stalinism), "Communism is the goal."

In 1988, the ACLU sent a letter to the California Assembly Education Committee opposing a proposed sex education bill. The letter stated:

> It is our position that teaching that monogamous, heterosexual intercourse within marriage as a traditional American value **is an unconstitutional establishment of a religious doctrine in public schools.** There are various religions which hold contrary beliefs with respect to marriage and monogamy.

A Gadsden, Alabama, state judge, Roy S. Moore, was sued by the ACLU for having a hand-carved copy of the Ten Commandments hanging on his courtroom wall, and for allowing a guest clergyman to pray at the opening general sessions of his court (i.e., once a month). In Bloomingdale, Michigan, a painting of Jesus had been hanging in the public high school since 1962. One agnostic student claimed he received "psychological damage" from seeing the portrait. The ACLU sued on his behalf and won—and the portrait came down.

The ACLU is very active during the Christmas season to make sure there are no manger scenes or other remnants of religion on public property. In the late 1970s the ACLU tried to stop Congressman Henry Hyde's (R-IL) Hyde Amendment, which prohibited federal funding for abortion. The ACLU opposed the Hyde Amendment on the basis that "it violated separation of church and state," because Hyde was a Catholic, his religion was opposed to abortion, and therefore the legislation should be opposed. The ACLU even followed Hyde to church to overhear him read from the Bible at a special service, illegally intercepted his mail looking for "religious communications," and tried to use this as "a separation of church and state" argument against the legislation. Such mendacity is not new to the ACLU.

In 1925, during the Scopes "Monkey Trial," which the ACLU initiated, their attorney, Clarence Darrow, belittled biblical fundamentalism as personified in William Jennings Bryant, and created "scientific" evidence that was later proven to be false.

Two excellent books have been written exposing the nefarious agenda of the ACLU by Dr. William Donohue (founder of the Catholic League): *The Politics of the American Civil Liberties Union* and *Twilight of Liberty: The Legacy of the ACLU*.

The ACLU is not the only legal group leading the charge against Christian America. The American Bar Association held a seminar in San Francisco in May 1989 to train attorneys on how to use tort law to sue religious organizations and churches. The seminar was advertized as being for "attorneys who want to be on the leading edge of an explosive new area of law." The selling point of the seminar was that attorneys could make money using this ideological weapon against churches and religious organizations.

Subjects presented at the seminar included: "Expanding the Use of Tort Law Against Religions"; "Tort as an Ideological Weapon"; "Tort Law as Essential Restraint on Religious Abuses;" "Tort Liability for Brainwashing"; etc. Brainwashing was described as emotionally traumatizing a person by telling them they will go to hell if they do not accept Christ, or that they are sinners in need of a Savior. Goodbye Christian witnessing! Goodbye Billy Graham crusades!

Clearly war has been declared and Christianity is in a fight for its life. Incidentally, churches are being sued in America (a decade after this seminar) like never before. One conservative Christian attorney who attended that seminar (Shelby Sharpe) described it as "a nuclear attack against Christianity."

Chapter 13

The "Legal" Isolation
of Christians in America

On May 21, 1993, the Clinton Administration petitioned the Supreme Court to allow the National Organization for Women (NOW) and the government to use the federal racketeering (RICO) statutes against abortion protestors. RICO punishes people and organizations which operate through a pattern of criminal activity (i.e., two or more repetitions of the "misdeed"). The government's appeal claimed that anti-abortion groups (which consist largely of evangelical and Catholic Christians) comprise "a nationwide criminal conspiracy of extremists" bent on "unlawful and violent methods" to drive abortion clinics out of business.

U.S. district courts in New York and Philadelphia had hit abortion protestors with huge fines for RICO violations. But the 7th Circuit Court of Appeals reversed the fines, ruling that RICO requires proof that alleged racketeering acts were motivated by an economic purpose.

On January 25, 1994, the U.S. Supreme Court ruled in favor of the Clinton Administration, NOW, and the abortionists, that criminal racketeering statutes could be used to prosecute pro-life demonstrators who are demonstrating or praying in front of abortion clinics with treble damages to be awarded. This ruling means that any government agency (or private group) can file a RICO suit against any group, or its members, who commit any act that the agency (or private group) claims constitutes a criminal conspiracy and that uses unlawful and violent methods.

There would be no need to demonstrate that economic gain was a consideration. Potential targets could be any politically incorrect group of Christians, conservatives, or traditionalists. RICO can therefore be used against any organization or its members which do their "misdeed" twice (i.e., hold an anti-government, anti-abortion, anti-war demonstration or any other politically incorrect activity targeted by the government). If public prayer in front of an abortion clinic can be a punishable offense under RICO, dozens of other politically incorrect offenses will eventually be included as well.

A New Legal Structure to Protect Homosexuals and Abortionists

There is a strong push by the political left to have homosexuals and women seeking abortions classified as "protected minorities" and certain forms of speech defined as "hate crimes." The government can then protect such groups under the guise of "compelling interest." If a Christian or traditionalist refers to homosexuality or abortion as a sin, or quotes Scripture regarding same, he (or she) will be guilty of a hate crime.

The political left is also pushing to have abortion legislatively guaranteed as a constitutional right (i.e., a "civil right") under the Freedom of Choice Act. Under that act, any effort to persuade a young mother to put up for adoption or keep her baby instead of aborting will be an "obstruction of that unfettered right." People causing that obstruction will be guilty of violation of federal law and prosecuted accordingly. Pro-life (i.e., pro-adoption) crisis pregnancy centers and their representatives will be targeted. Incredible! It may soon be against the law to suggest to a pregnant girl to put her baby up for adoption rather than to kill it!

Special protection for homosexuals has some frightening implications. When homosexuals become a protected class of citizens, they will be entitled not only to special treatment, but also to extraordinary rights—one of which will be a government guarantee of legal (same-sex) marriage. The ramifications for Christian churches and organizations are ominous.

For a clergyman to refuse to marry a homosexual couple will be a civil rights (i.e., criminal) violation punishable by fines, imprisonment, or a court-ordered ban from the ministry. Clergy who refuse to officiate such unions (believing it violates Scripture) will be denounced as hateful, bigoted, or even guilty of a hate crime. Many clergymen in the former Soviet Union, in Red China, Cuba, and other communist countries have been officially banned from the ministry, have suffered civil penalties, imprisonment, exile, or execution for refusing to obey such compulsory (anti-biblical) measures.

Under the coming special protection for homosexuals, a church, ministry, or business which refuses to hire homosexuals or to hire them in the ratio they say they represent in the general population (i.e., ten percent) will be guilty of a civil and criminal civil rights violation.

So, Christians and traditionalists in America who oppose abortion and the practice of homosexuality, who speak or write of that opposition, who take overt action to stop these practices, or who teach their children that they are wrong, **could soon be declared to be criminals.** Shades of Nazi Germany and communist Russia and China!

In 1993, Dr. Robert Isay, chairman of an American Psychiatric Association committee formed to legitimize homosexuality, was quoted in the *New York Times* as calling for strong measures to be brought against anyone who considers homosexuality to be a perversion. Psychiatrist Isay said that an "irrational fear and hatred of homosexuals is a psychological abnormality that interferes with the judgment and reliability of those afflicted." In other words, straight Christians, who believe in the Bible prohibition of homosexuality are the "sick ones" (now called "homophobes").

Banning Christians from the Public Arena

The political left in America, after several decades of carefully laying the groundwork, has almost totally banned religion, religious personalities, and moral issues based on biblical consideration from the public sector.

This includes banning from courthouses, public buildings, sports arenas, libraries, schools, colleges, universities, public broadcasting, and publishing all references to God, Jesus Christ, the Gospel, the crucifixion, prayer, and hymn singing. Thousands of lawsuits have been launched in recent years by the ACLU and other leftist or atheist groups to remove the last vestiges of Christianity from the public square.

In 1994 the Clinton Equal Employment Opportunity Commission, through a series of regulations, almost succeeded in banning all mention of God, the Bible, religion, etc. in the American workplace. The ban would have included all Bibles or religious books in the office or factory, on a desk, in a bookcase, etc. No crosses, Stars of David, or yarmulkes could be worn. No Christmas or Thanksgiving parties, prayers, witnessing, singing of hymns, or any activity even remotely related to God, Jesus Christ, or any religion would have been tolerated. No prayer meetings, Bible classes, religious pictures, or quotations on the wall could have been allowed in the work place.

These regulations would have been quietly implemented had not over a million Christians loudly protested to Congress, which pressured the Clinton Administration to back off. When the time seems right, and the Christians and traditionalists are not paying attention, the Clintons will again try to put this EEOC religious ban into place.

Today, most public or school libraries carry very few (if any) religious books or Bibles. They have never been stocked, have been officially removed, or stolen and not replaced. In most instances churches or religious groups are precluded from renting auditoriums at public schools or universities using "separation of church and state" as the justification. On a practical level, however, it is usually only **Christian** churches or groups which are denied access.

Time magazine (12/9/91), in an article entitled "Has the Separation of Church and State Gone Too Far," wrote:

> In this nation of spiritual paradoxes, **it is legal** to hang a picture in a public exhibit of a crucifix submerged in urine, or to utter virtually any conceivable blasphemy in a public place; **it is not legal,** the federal courts have ruled, to mention God reverently in a classroom, on a football field or at a commencement ceremony as part of a public prayer.

Rush Limbaugh said on his television program on June 9, 1996, "There is an all-out assault on the Christian community in this country." Indeed there is! The political left has changed the rules so that the ideal of freedom **of** religion has now become freedom **from** religion. As Nathan A. Forrester of the Bechett Fund for Religious Liberty commented: "The perception now is that the Constitution requires that we purge all religion from the public square."

It is an interesting paradox how the U.S. government funds anti-

Christian activities (i.e., abortion, homosexuality, and pornographic art) while at the same time banning and opposing all public manifestations of Christianity. The government (via the U.S. taxpayer) has been funding the National Endowment for the Arts.

As Dr. D. James Kennedy wrote in his book on persecution:

> Some of these "works of art" have been directly blasphemous against Jesus of Nazareth—such as the bust of Jesus as a transvestite, the picture of Christ as a heroin junkie, the photo of the crucifix submerged in the artist's urine, or the sketches of Christ engaged in homosexual acts. . . . Think about the implication of **state-sponsored blasphemy:** on the one hand, the government, in all its various branches, prohibits the public expression of **pro-**Christian symbols (even if paid for privately). On the other hand, that same government sanctions **anti-**Christian expressions (and even sponsors them). Wow! The NEA's funding of anti-Christian art has clearly put the **official** government approval on the attack on Christ in America.

The U.S. courts have played a major role in censoring Christianity (and even Orthodox Judaism) from public life in America. The U.S. Supreme Court has called it unconstitutional for a rabbi to deliver a non-sectarian, general prayer at a high school graduation. A U.S. district court judge declared a prayer before a school football game to be illegal. A federal judge in Michigan ordered a portrait of Jesus that had hung in a high school for twenty years next to one of Martin Luther King, Jr. to be a violation of the separation of church and state, and forced the school to take it down. The courts across America seem to be totally consistent on one thing: the concept that religion in America can be incredibly dangerous!

Examples of Government Censorship of Christians in the Public Arena

- One June 24, 1991, the Supreme Court ruled that it is illegal for clergy to offer prayers as part of an official public school graduation ceremony.

- A federal appeals court in Zion, Illinois ruled that a 100-year old city seal, which incorporated a cross and the motto "God reigns" are unconstitutional. The seal, which was supported by ninety percent of the townspeople, was removed.
- In December 1991 a county court in San Diego ruled that a monument, which was designated as an historic landmark, must be removed because it contained a cross. The monument, located on Mt. Solidad, was originally on private property which was given to the state of California with the agreement that the cross would remain. The court reneged the contract and gave the county ninety days to remove the cross.
- In Orange County (Orlando), Florida, a fourth grader brought his Bible with him to school to read in his spare time. His teacher took it away and chastised him, telling him to never bring it back. As punishment he was forced to sit in a corner facing the wall and was later questioned by the principal and detained in her office all day for his wrongful "violation of church and state."
- In Tulsa, Oklahoma, a fourth grader attempted to pray before a math test. He was sent to the principal's office and made to write 100 times "I will not pray in class."
- In San Jose, California, the city ruled that a manger with the baby Jesus in it was illegal, but went on to build a half-million dollar, taxpayer-funded statue of the Aztec god Quetzalcoatl, to whom tens of thousands of human victims were sacrificed in centuries past. The mayor said the Aztec religion possessed "those elements that seek to elevate the human consciousness to a higher plane."
- In Chicago, Illinois, the city, over a four-year period, shut down thirty South Side storefront churches (mostly African-American) and denied building permits to over a dozen more churches—utilizing special stringent zoning requirements.

The American Center for Law and Justice cited a few (of hundreds) such religious censorship and harassment cases:

- An elderly man was arrested and handcuffed for distributing religious literature outside an office complex. The charges were later dropped.

- Two New York street preachers (who had ministered on the same streets for ten years) were arrested for preaching without a permit and charged with disorderly conduct. The charges were later dropped.
- A school district in the Midwest was sued for allowing the Gideons to distribute Bibles to students who requested them—a practice they had been doing for forty-one years.
- A pastor from North Carolina was denied use of a public building because he wanted to use it to perform a Christmas play.
- Christian students were denied by their school board the right to announce after school meetings in their school newspaper.

There are thousands of such examples across America every month whereby Christians are being censored, harassed, and denied public access, and the incidents (backed by the courts and the legal system) are growing geometrically. **We are seeing the onset of official government censorship of Christianity in America.** This is how it happened to Christians in Russia, China, and Cuba. This is how it happened to Jews in Nazi Germany in the mid-1930s. First they were stereotyped, then vilified, then marginalized, then ostracized, and finally persecuted, jailed, and exterminated.

The Intellectual Assault Against Christianity

Over two generations of Americans have been educated in a public school system (i.e., from grade school through the university) which disdains Christianity and almost all forms of traditional religion. In Nazi Germany, Hitler recognized the importance of controlling education. As William Shirer wrote in *The Rise and Fall of the Third Reich:*

The German schools from the first grade through the universities were quickly Nazified.

In a speech on November 6, 1933, Hitler said: "When an opponent declares, I will not come over to your side," I calmly say, "Your child belongs to us already. Where are you? You will pass on. Your descendants, however, stand in the new camp. In a short time they will know nothing else but this community.'

As Shirer wrote, quoting a speech by Hitler on May 1, 1937: "This new Reich will give its youth to no one, but it will take youth and give to youth its own education and upbringing." So we can learn an important lesson from the Third Reich—those who control the classroom will control the next generation.

Today, trashing Christ, Christians, and Christianity is a major endeavor at many (if not most) large universities and many high schools across America. Dr. D. James Kennedy, in his book *The Gates of Hell Shall Not Prevail,* quoted a Campus Crusade for Christ staff member who headed a campus ministry at a state university in the Bible Belt, wherein a professor taught: "Jesus was a homosexual," "Jesus had sex with Mary Magdalene," "Both Jesus and Moses were legends," and "Jesus had a twin brother." Across America, Christ and Christianity are denigrated in the college classroom, funded with our tax dollars in state schools.

Don Feder, the Jewish columnist who often speaks out against anti-Christian bigotry, wrote in his book *A Jewish Conservative Looks at Pagan America:*

> It has reached the point where public school students can experience anything—things the average sailor on shore leave doesn't encounter—except God. Sex education, suicide studies, life boat ethics, condom distribution, abortion pleading, which when taken together constitute the propagation of the humanist creed—all are essential aspects of the public school experience in the 1990s. It is only prayers, Bibles, and references to a supreme being which offend the sensibilities of secularist puritans.
>
> We may fail to teach our students the rudiments of literature, science, and history. Twenty percent of high school graduates may be functional illiterates, or semi-literate. We may be unable to maintain even a semblance of order in our urban schools, which increasingly resemble happy hour in Beirut. But, hallelujah, we sure know how to protect kids from God.

The anti-Christian consensus in American education didn't just start in the 1990s. It started in the 1960s (and probably much earlier) when the political left began to take over American education—especially at the university level. The theories of Marx; Sigmund Freud, and Darwin (all three hard-core atheists) began to really take root in academia in the 1960s and 1970s.

Freud's writings were extremely anti-religion (both Christianity and Judaism). Freud even taught that religious faith was a manifestation of mental illness—a sickness which is a severe danger to normal human development. This helps explain why so many college-educated people over the past thirty years have emerged from academia so hostile (or at best neutral) to the Christian faith. They have been taught that religious people are mentally and emotionally ill, and that Christianity must be treated, eradicated, or at least managed and closely controlled.

The theories of Darwinian evolution have also been a major element of American education since the 1960s. Now accepted in academia as a fact (not theory) this altruistic, unproven, and unscientific theory has replaced the biblical account of God's creation in the minds of tens of millions of high school and college-educated Americans in recent decades and set the stage for wholesale rejection of God, the Bible, Jesus Christ, and Christianity. Anyone who would deny the accidental advent of biological life, in the face of "overwhelming evidence," we are told is an idiot, a fool, a charlatan—in other words, a mentally unstable, irresponsible Christian.

As tens of millions of Americans have come through America's higher education system in recent decades, this helps to explain the growing hostility toward, and ostracism and isolation of Christians in America. In Russia and other communist countries, Christians and other "reactionary" traditionalists have been locked up in mental institutions and subjected to imprisonment, brainwashing, shock treatment, and drug reprogramming "therapies." Could this be the growing anti-Christian consensus in America as well?

In addition to the now widely accepted theories of Marx, Freud, and Darwin, the pervasiveness of atheism, agnosticism, and skepticism in American education have led to a growing hatred of religious faith in general and Christianity in particular. Had these theories and ideologies remained isolated in the universities, the damage to America, its culture, and foundations would have been minimal, or at least contained. But unfortunately, that has not been the case.

Since the early 1960s the political left and those espousing these theories and ideologies have systematically taken over the law schools, journalism schools, teachers colleges, schools of psychology, philosophy, sociology, etc., and have produced millions of lawyers, journalists, teachers, psychologists, and Americans in every walk of life who are hostile to Christianity, traditional values, the U.S. Constitution, etc.

For over thirty years the great majority of teachers emerging from American colleges and universities have been educated (or brainwashed) in the theories or ideologies of Marx, Darwin, Freud, atheism, agnosticism, and secular humanism. These teachers went into America's elementary, middle, and high school classrooms with these philosophies, helped write textbooks espousing same, and have redirected tens of millions of students away from, or against, Christianity and traditional American values. [*Note:* There are teachers who are notable exceptions, but they are a small minority.]

These essentially anti-Christian philosophies have also been spread over the past four decades by journalists, reporters and writers, who were turned away from God, religion, and Christianity in their colleges or universities in the sixties and seventies, and who now propagate the political left's ideology through the entertainment/news media to hundreds of millions of Americans who have been gradually influenced by their anti-Christian, anti-traditionalist, liberal philosophy. The same process has happened to a whole generation of lawyers, who were educated for over thirty years in American law schools dominated by the political left and who now are writing and interpreting laws as attorneys, legislators, and judges that are neutralizing and undermining our Christian, biblical, traditional values and traditions in America.

The turning of America's educational system, legal system, and media/entertainment industries to the political left and against Christianity and traditional American values did not happen by accident. It all began with the political left's takeover of the education system in the 1960s and

1970s and has now infected the thinking and actions of the great majority of Americans.

As the political left moved into a dominant position in education, entertainment and the media, the legal establishment, and government over the past thirty years, evangelical/fundamental Christians, who were being taught not "to concern themselves with the affairs of this world," increasingly avoided participation in these arenas—leaving them almost exclusively, by default, to the political left. So today, even though the political left (like the Nazis in Germany and the communists in Russia) is still just a minority, they have carefully and successfully strategized the takeover of these critical and influential bastions of cultural influence.

Political Correctness and the Growing Anti-Christian Consensus

Political correctness has swept the university and college campuses in recent years and is now emerging in high schools as well. One major element of political correctness is the total elimination of religion from education in America. Speech codes have sanctioned students for opposing homosexuality or abortion and for taking a stand for, or even mentioning God, Christ, the Bible, or traditional values. For a practicing Christian today, the American campus is a very hostile environment.

Now intimidation and punishment of Christian students who are not politically correct has begun to spread in U.S. high schools. Anti-Christian decrees are now regularly announced by teachers, school boards, and administrators which attack students' First Amendment rights and individual civil liberties. Students regularly receive a low grade, or no grade, or are failed because they have written a paper on a Christian or politically incorrect topic. They have been disqualified from school assemblies or special programs for choosing a piece of religious music to perform. They have been arrested and/or removed from the campus by police (like drug dealers) for simply gathering in prayer around the flag pole.

Paranoia over separation of church and state in education has caused a growing number of educators and educational institutions to become extremely hostile toward religion and religious persons. A whole generation of students has now been educated in America's public school system to believe that religious faith (and its values) is incompatible with intelligence and the honest pursuit of knowledge.

Many liberal educators are actively fostering hostility toward religious students, treating them with condescension and contempt. This is the way it began against the Jews in Nazi Germany and the Christians in Russia and China.

The EEOC Guidelines Outlawing Religion in the Workplace

In 1994 the Clinton Equal Employment Opportunity Commission tried to implement regulations which would have banned all mention of God, Christianity, the Bible, or any religion in the American workplace. The Clinton Administration backed off after over a million irate phone calls, faxes, and letters from Christians opposing this banning of religious free speech swamped the Congress.

Twenty-five actions on the job that, according to retired Senator Hank Brown (R-CO), would have been prohibited by the EEOC:

1. Wearing a cross around the neck, wrist, or any openly visible part of the body.
2. Wearing a yarmulke (yarmulkeh)—a century-old tradition of Jews wearing a head covering while they are attending synagogue. Orthodox Jews, however, wear the head covering seven days a week.
3. Displaying a picture of Christ on an office desk or wall.
4. Wearing a T-shirt, hat, or other clothing that has any religious emblem or phrasing on its face.
5. Displaying a Bible or other religious book on a desk, or otherwise making the same openly visible in an office or lounge area.
6. Hosting Christmas, Hanukkah, Thanksgiving, or Easter celebrations, parties or events in any form that have any focus on Christ, God, or other religious connotations.
7. Celebrations or parties in any form which have any religious focus or reference.
8. Opening or closing prayer or invocation at a company program, banquet, celebration, or event.
9. Witnessing the Gospel, sharing your faith, and generally speaking to other employees about religion.

10. Nativity displays or scenes.
11. Inviting a fellow employee to a synagogue, church, temple, or other place of worship.
12. Conversations about religion or religious groups, functions, and events.
13. Prayer breakfasts.
14. Singing or humming a religious song while at a copy machine.
15. Serving only pork or beef at a company Fourth of July picnic.
16. Having a local church choir or school choir come in for a Christmas celebration and sing any songs which make reference to Christ, God, or any religion or religious principle. (Christmas carols would be out!)
17. Telling any joke (regardless of the innocence of the subject matter or intent) that refers to any religion or religious group whatsoever.
18. Giving a fellow employee a holiday card, birthday card, get-well card, greeting card, or plaque which includes any religious reference.
19. Making reference to Christ, God, or any religious figure or subject matter in a company mission, plan, or goal statement.
20. Praying while in the workplace.
21. The display of calendars or "thoughts of the day" books which make reference to Scripture or religious sayings.
22. Displaying any religious artwork, book, devotional, figure, symbol, or trinket in an openly visible area.
23. Hosting a Bible study or other religious gathering.
24. Company uniform and work apparel requirements.
25. Almost any form of religious expression in the workplace.

[*Note:* Do you get the idea? The political left is serious about shutting down Christians and their free speech!]

Columnist Don Feder put the matter into historical perspective:

> Coming soon to your office—courtesy of Bill Clinton and the Equal Employment Opportunity Commission—the religion-free workplace. The areas in which religion is tolerated in our society are constantly contracting. In the 1960s, school prayer was eliminated. Since then,

invocations at graduation have been banned, Christmas decorations and caroling are out, and even voluntary, student-initiated activities (Bible study groups, etc.) are suspect.

The Clinton/Gore Administration is likely to push this EEOC ban on religious free speech again when the time seems right (i.e., when the growing anti-Christian sentiment is deemed to be high enough).

Chapter 14

The New Left and the Isolation of American Christians

There are a number of interesting and ominous parallels between the Nazi persecution of Jews and the communist persecution of Christians which can now be seen emerging in the U.S., South Africa, and a number of other Western countries.

As these elements of persecution were implemented, millions of Jews were ultimately killed by the Nazis and millions of Christians were slaughtered by the communists. While the ideological/philosophical reasons behind these persecutions were quite different, the elements of isolating, ostracizing, and targeting the two groups for persecution and elimination were quite similar. These elements were utilized in most of the persecutions from Nero in Rome to the communists in China in our day.

Hitler blamed the Jews for all of Germany's problems—economic, social, moral, and spiritual—accusing them of controlling and manipulating the European economic world and undermining Aryan ingenuity and superiority. The Nazis believed that if the Jews were eliminated from the world, it would pave the way for the ascent of the Aryan race, which would ultimately save the world. Hitler and the Nazis would head this superrace, but first, the major obstacle to their plans, the Jews, had to be eradicated.

The reasons behind the communist persecution of Christians were far more complex. Marxist philosophy is materialistic, atheistic, and as such, opposed to all forms of religion. But Christianity, and especially evangelical/fundamentalist Christians, posed a great problem for the Marxists in that (just as during the Roman Empire) they refused to worship the state. Christians were not afraid of the state, nor were they intimidated by the threat of persecution, imprisonment or even death. Thus, they were more difficult to control, and had to be neutralized in order to complete the revolution.

From 1917 through 1945, Baptists, evangelicals, Pentecostals, Adventists, and Catholics were targeted by the communists. Orthodox Christians and especially the priests resisted the purging of Christianity from Soviet life and the installation of atheism as the new religion. During this period, millions of Christians were fined, had their property seized, faced internal exile, imprisonment in mental hospitals or forced labor camps, or were killed for resisting atheism and the abolition of Christianity.

Of the 60 million or so people killed by the communists in the Soviet Union, an estimated ten to twenty percent were Christians who were killed because of their faith. These are numbers which are incomprehensible to most Westerners. The Christian church was driven underground, where it remained until the late 1980s. The persecution of Christians in communist China followed a similar pattern and continues (and in fact is accelerating) right up through the present.

After World War II, the communist persecution of Christians became more subtle and sophisticated, but was just as ruthless as during the Stalin era. Educators and scientists, bolstered by the Communist Party, began a massive propaganda campaign for atheism and against religion in general and Christianity in particular. The ideas of Marx, Darwin, and Freud were used to eradicate the roots of religious belief (just as they have been used in American and other Western universities since the 1960s).

To be a Christian in the Soviet Union from 1945 to 1985 was to be isolated, maligned, slandered, denied access to universities, relegated to menial jobs or no jobs at all, and if you were a Christian activist, to be beaten, jailed, tortured, or killed. Richard Wurmbrand, a Romanian pastor and a leader in the underground Christian church, has documented the communist persecution of Christians and the Christian church in a number of excellent books: *Tortured for Christ, In God's Underground, My Correspondence with Jesus,* etc.

Wurmbrand, who was imprisoned and tortured by the communists for fourteen years, and who now heads a Christian ministry called Voice of the Martyrs (located in Tulsa, Oklahoma) believes that similar persecution against Christians will break out in America in the not-too-distant future. He has accordingly written a booklet **to American Christians** entitled: *Preparing for the Underground Church.*

The Rise of the New Left in America

Over the past four decades the political left (or the "old political left"), made up of communists, socialists, and old-line liberals, has been, for the most part, supplanted by the New Left. While the New Left does not reject communism or any of the tenets of the old left, it has also embraced and advanced the values of the sixties—the sexual revolution, radical feminism, homosexuality, abortion, and socialistic structures such as government domination of education and the environment. The New Left espouses atheism as a national dogma. [*Note:* A large portion of the Clinton/Gore Administration is made up of New Left activists.]

The New Left is a blend of the old Marxist and Freudian ideology and the cultural and moral relativism of the 1960s which had its roots in existentialism and nihilism. The New Left, which has dominated our college and university campuses since the 1960s, has been successfully advancing an agenda for the past three and a half decades which is Marxist, socialistic, materialistic, hedonistic, atheistic, which has redefined morality, and which is rabidly opposed to religious (especially Christian) beliefs.

The New Left has adopted and is employing the strategy of Antonio Gramsci, founder of the Italian Communist Party. Gramsci visited with Lenin and Stalin in Russia in the 1930s, and concluded that they were not pursuing the communist revolution correctly. Gramsci believed that before a capitalist nation could be converted to communism it first had to have its heritage, its culture, its ideology, its morality, and its spiritual life undermined. Even Stalin recognized that America's strength was in its morality, its patriotism, and its spiritual life, and that if those three areas could be subverted, that it would collapse from within. Consequently, the Gramsci strategy has been used by the communists and the New Left against targeted countries in recent decades—South Africa being a notable example.

In America, the New Left is pushing hedonism, the drug culture, immorality, pornography, homosexuality, radical feminism, abortion, and attacking traditional values, religion (especially Christianity), patriotism and our historical heritage—all as a part of the Gramsci strategy to weaken America and set her up for the fall. So successful were the communists and the political left in employing the Gramsci strategy against the people of South Africa over a fifteen-year period, that the South Africans actually voted the communists into power in April 1994.

In its thrust to control the American middle class, the New Left has initiated a policy of intimidation, censorship, and slander against anyone opposing their agenda for America. They have harnessed the universities, the media, the entertainment industry, and the courts (which have all been dominated by the New Left since the 1960s) to intimidate, harass, threaten, and punish the political right and especially the Christian right.

The entire agenda of the New Left, including its growing attacks against the Christian right, conservatives, and traditionalists has accelerated dramatically since Bill and Hillary Clinton, Al Gore and their New Left comrades came to power in 1993, and has accelerated dramatically since Bill Clinton's impeachment, Senate trial, and acquittal. The Clinton Administration is comprised almost totally of New Left activists who wish to change America into a Marxist/socialist state. A major part of that agenda is the banning of religion, biblical values and standards, and Christians from all public life—indeed from all areas of influence in American life.

The New Left has been very successful in using the media (especially television and movies) to ridicule biblical beliefs about morality, marriage, family, and religions. They have also been very successful in using the courts to ban religion from public education and all of public life, and with it the traditional values which kept America strong, stable, and invincible for over two centuries.

Over the past thirty years, using its power and leverage in the media, academia, and the legal system, the New Left has successfully created the perception of an overwhelming majority of Americans, a consensus, which support the agenda of the New Left (i.e., the sexual revolution, homosexuality, abortion, big government, cradle-to-the-grave control over people, etc.). If a person or group dares to challenge this "consensus," they are subjected to ridicule, scorn, censorship, and perhaps even legal action—as the pro-life movement is now experiencing.

One of the primary targets of the New Left is the American family. The promotion through the media and public education system of homosexuality, cohabitation without marriage, divorce, coerced sexual education programs, condom distribution programs in schools, effective parenting seminars, anti-spanking laws, expansion of the definition of child abuse, and anti-parent legislation, are all part of the New Left's attack on the family. A nation is only as strong as its family units. The communists in Russia, China, Cuba, etc. knew that they had to attack and break down the family if they were to conquer and subjugate the people, and they did so with a vengeance.

The other primary target of the New Left is religion. Like all Marxists, the New Left believes that religion (especially evangelical Christianity, which is the religion they fear the most) must be abolished. As Christian writers Josh McDowell and Don Stewart wrote in *Understanding Secular Religions: Handbook of Today's Religions:*

> Marx saw two compelling reasons to abolish religion and promote atheism: first his materialism denied the existence of the supernatural; and second, the very structure of organized religion had, through the ages, condoned and supported the bourgeois suppression of the proletariat.
> . . . **We must make this clear: abolition of religion was an integral part of Marx's dialectical materialism.**

A large number of today's high school teachers, college and university professors, lawyers, judges and legislators who obtained their positions in the 1970s and 1980s were heavily influenced by atheism, agnosticism, Marxism, and the New Left in the 1960s at the various universities or law schools across America. This leftist influence explains their hatred for Christianity and traditional values and their growing efforts to silence, censor, intimidate, and even jail activists from the conservative, Christian right.

The Isolation of Christians in America

The isolation of practicing, serious Christians from mainstream America is one of the key elements in the coming persecution. The three great molders of our culture, **the entertainment/news media, academia, and the liberal law establishment** have dictated what America's standards are to be: homosexuality is in; same-sex marriage is in; promiscuity and sex outside marriage are in; abortion is in; government interference with the family is in; biblical morality is out; biblical discipline (i.e., spanking) is out, etc.

These three institutions have created a new moral/cultural consensus which is deliberately hostile to Bible-believing Christians, which they cannot follow or accept and remain true to their faith, and which is forcing conscientious Christians into cultural isolation.

As Paul Schenck wrote in his excellent book *The Extermination of Christianity—The Tyranny of the Consensus:*

> As conscientious Christians are increasingly treated as undesirables, and are forced out of mainstream America through the effective use of stereotypes, hyperbole, and misrepresentation, the consequence for millions of citizens who hold to traditional beliefs and practices will be defamation, discrimination, and ostracism. . . . Over the last thirty years, the ivory towers of academia have specialized in desecrating the Judeo-Christian philosophy and replacing it with varied strains of Marxist, Darwinist, and Freudian determinism. The result is that Christians are presented in the classroom as bourgeois oppressors, superstitious primitives, and sexually frustrated neurotics.

There are certain traditional beliefs and standards that are very important to Christians which are based on biblical teachings: marriage, monogamous sex within marriage, the sanctity of human life, public prayer, and opposition to suicide, abortion, euthanasia, homosexuality, promiscuity, etc. Now the institutions of the New Left are attacking Christians and traditionalists for their beliefs—insulting, maligning, ridiculing, and defaming them for standing for what Americans have always stood for, but have now abandoned.

The media, academia, and legal system have portrayed people who still support these traditional beliefs as weird, hateful, divisive, mean-spirited, bigots, emotionally unstable, hysterical, anti-social, a threat to society, and the cause of most of America's social and political problems. These "dangerous" Christians and traditionalists are accused of being responsible for poverty, gang warfare, violence, the arms race, child abuse, the spread of AIDS (i.e., because they oppose homosexual marriage), racial and sexual discrimination and harassment, homophobia, hate, the rise of the "dangerous religious cults," and for creating the environment of hate, paranoia, and fear which breed terrorism.

Christians, because of their traditional beliefs, are being systematically pushed out of the mainstream of American life (i.e., they are being marginalized), are being made to appear weird, radical, extremist, and dangerous to society, and are being vilified in every way. This attack on Christians, biblical beliefs, and traditional values is not happening spontaneously or by accident. It has been carefully orchestrated by the New Left for several decades, but especially since 1992 when the Clintons and their "comrades" came to power, in order to discredit, stereotype, isolate, muzzle, and neutralize the political left's primary opposition—the Christian right.

Is the political left's program of isolating conservative, traditionalist Christians working? Apparently so! The public has been programmed by the political left to dislike, distrust and fear fundamentalist Christians—who are being stereotyped by the media and entertainment industry as dangerous trouble makers and weird wackos. One of the prerequisites for persecution, as the Jews in Germany learned, was to be viewed by the general population as "undesirable."

Is U.S. Law Enforcement Turning Against Christians?

Even law enforcement people have fallen for the anti-Christian propaganda and stereotyping. They are bombarded by anti-Christian laws, rules, regulation, and court decision and constant media portrayals which demonize Christian activists. Hence in recent years many federal agents and local law enforcement personnel have become increasingly hostile and brutal toward pro-life demonstrators and those portrayed by the political left as dangerous religious cults, right-wing radicals, gun-toting religious freaks, etc.

Law enforcement overreaction in Waco against the Branch Davidian religious sect (leaving eighty-six men, women, children, and babies dead) and against the Weaver family in Idaho (leaving a nursing mother and her fourteen-year old son dead) are but a few of many examples of over-zealous law enforcement actions against a perceived threat from conservative religious or political non-conformists. It is noteworthy that in the wake of the ten-day government siege at Ruby Ridge, that the Justice Department, while admitting to no wrongdoing, paid the survivors of the Weaver family $3.1 million for the wrongful deaths of the mother and son.

Larry Poland, in his excellent book *How To Prepare for the Coming Persecution*, described two incidents of police brutality and challenged the reader to determine where and when these incidents had occurred:

Incident 1

The police troops arrived in two vans late in the afternoon. Their orders were to locate . . . sympathizers. . . . The police hauled hundreds of suspects into Market Square where the scene turned violent. Before arresting anyone, the authorities forced men and women to run a gauntlet of jeering, kicking, spitting troopers.

Their thirst for pain seemingly could not be quenched. They turned on women and children. A frail woman of sixty-six hid her sons from the attackers, and the police set upon her. "Where are your sons?" they demanded. Grabbing her by the hair, they dragged the sickly woman down the street. They hoped to wrench a confession either through her torment or humiliation before watching neighbors. But many neighbors, fearing for themselves, turned away. The woman was pulled to Market Square, her face bloodied as it scraped along the street. In the end her noble effort to spare her boys seemed foolish, as they were found and herded into the town square.

Incident 2

The police . . . brought in a double-decker bus, complete with tinted windows (thus it was impossible to see what was going on inside the bus . . .). Brutality started on the bus. Angela was dragged onto the bus by her hair. People were billy-clubbed, kicked, and punched. Police dragged women in the bus by pulling up skirts and bras over their heads, exposing them in so doing. . . . The men were denied food for thirty hours. . . . Upon arrival at the . . . jail there were over thirty police . . . lined up along five or six flights of stairs. . . . Women were then dragged up the steps, some by the hair and others by the neck. You could hear the sound of heads smacking against the steps. The warden was at the bottom of the first flight of stairs, and he kicked [the people] as they were dragged by him.

During this entire procedure there was foul language, obscenities, and threats of putting women . . . in rooms with male prisoners to be sodomized and raped. . . . They were asked to strip in front of male guards and male prisoners. All refused. They were then forcibly stripped by both male and female guards, dragged, kicked, and punched. Women . . . were fondled, verbally abused, and threatened.

Incident 1 is the description of troopers brutalizing Jews in a community in World War II Nazi Germany.

Incident 2 is the description of the police brutalizing Christians who were passively protesting outside an abortion clinic in Pittsburgh, Pennsylvania, on March 11, 1989.

Poland concluded:

The screws are tightening! The mood is getting increasingly ugly for Christians. Soon, I predict, overt persecution of believers will be commonplace. Our kids will be beat up and sexually molested at school, forced to perform perverse acts by the youthful agents of the dark side. Our churches will be desecrated and worship services disrupted. Our homes will be vandalized and our lives threatened. Our cars will be damaged and our tires slashed.

Chapter 15

The Five-Step Pattern of Persecution

> The basic problem of the Christians in this country in the last eighty
> years or so, in regard to society and in regard to government, is that
> they have seen things in bits and pieces instead of totals.
> —Francis Schaeffer, *A Christian Manifesto*

Isolation of, and discrimination against Christians is growing almost
geometrically with increasing incidents of intimidation, ostracism, fir-
ings, exaggerated and false accusations of criminal and quasicriminal
activities, false arrests, and imprisonments. This is the way it started in
Germany against the Jews. As they became more isolated and marginalized by the Nazi propaganda machine, as popular hatred and prejudice
against the Jews increased among the German people, wholesale persecution and *pogroms* followed. Could this be where the growing anti-
Christian consensus in America is taking us?

Paul and Robert Schenck wrote in their book *The Extermination of
Christianity—A Tyranny of Consensus* about a five-step pattern which
was evident in the persecutions of the Jews by the Nazis and of Christians by the communists. This escalating pattern of persecution can be
seen in the persecution of most groups going back to the persecution of
Christians by the Roman emperor Nero up through the Middle Ages
right through the present persecution of Christians in China, Sudan,
and various communist and Islamic countries around the world.

Persecution arises out of a struggle for power—to achieve it, maintain it, or expand it. Those seeking total power, whether a Roman caesar, a Nazi führer, or a communist dictator will seek to suppress their
opposition (often ruthlessly) or any group or movement (i.e., ethical,
religious, or ideological) which they believe threatens their power base.

Early on, powerful dictators have feared and hated Christians—whom they believed would not pay total allegiance to their monarchy, dictatorship, or ideology. The communists know that practicing Christians will not be easily converted to atheism (the foundational element of Marxism/Leninism), nor will they pay homage to the communist dictatorship. Christians, because of their eternal perspective and biblical belief system, are more difficult to intimidate, coerce, control, and turn into obedient servants of the state. Hence, communism from its inception has attempted to stamp out the Christian church.

The five steps or stages leading to the eventual persecution of a group are:

1. Identifying and stereotyping the group;
2. Marginalizing the group—pushing it out of the mainstream to the margins of society;
3. Vilification, slandering, and trashing of the group;
4. Passing discriminatory legal restrictions and eventually criminalizing the activities of the group;
5. Outright persecution of the group.

The word persecute is defined by *Webster's Collegiate Dictionary* as "to harass in a manner designed to injure, grieve, or afflict; specifically to cause to suffer because of a belief." Persecution is defined as "the act or practice of persecuting, especially those who differ in origin, religion, or social outlook."

Persecution consists of malicious acts perpetrated against people who are of a different belief, religion, social, or political persuasion from the vast majority, and especially from those in power who are the persecutors. Certain characteristics of the targeted group are exaggerated and attacked by the persecutors—such as Christians' distaste for homosexuality, their moral opposition to promiscuity, their belief in spanking children, or their belief in the Second Coming/end times/Armageddon scenario of history.

Stage One: Stereotyping

A stereotype is defined by the *Dictionary of Modern Sociology* as a preconceived (not based on experience), standardized, group shared idea about the alleged essential nature of those making up a whole category of persons, the most significant of such group shared ideals being without regard to individual differences among those making up the category and being an emotion charged negative evaluation.

Stereotypes often represent institutionalized misinformation, distorted information, and caricatured ideas of places, people and things; and stereotypes have profound influence on the formation of attitudes [toward the targeted groups.]

The stereotyped group or individual becomes an easy target of bigotry, slander, and abuse. The image which is created of the stereotype is not real world or accurate—it is based on extreme characteristics. The *Baker Encyclopedia of Psychology* says regarding stereotypes:

> Even though stereotypes may have a kernel of truth . . . they result in an overestimation of differences between groups. Although the beliefs, values, and other characteristics of groups may be similar, stereotypes may result in those groups being viewed as vastly different.
>
> Individuals are prejudged on the basis of their category . . . and a large number of distinguishable persons may be treated as equivalent.
>
> . . . . **As negative generalizations, stereotypes may be used as justification for hostility and oppression,** thereby providing a major mechanism by which prejudice is sustained.

The use of stereotypes increase during times of national crisis or upheaval (such as depression, war, or social upheaval) providing ready scapegoats to blame the country's ills on. Nero used the Christians as scapegoats when he burned Rome, and the Nazis used the Jews as scapegoats for all of the economic and social ills which rose out of the post-World War I Weimar Republic. The targeted group becomes labeled with exaggerated images and gross misrepresentations.

With respect to Christians, their moral and spiritual standards, beliefs, and practices stand out in stark contrast to the non-religious, secular or atheistic/agnostic majority—setting them up as targets for stereotyping. Christian morality such as sexual restraint; opposition to homosexuality; opposition to divorce, abortion, drinking, alcohol, smoking, to some forms of birth control, profanity; the propensity toward large families; etc. are exaggerated and distorted by the political left and other enemies of Christianity to make Christians look ridiculous, extreme, unbalanced, or repressive.

Biblical practices of marriage, family, and childrearing are distorted and twisted by the liberal stereotypers into bondage, child abuse, obstruction of children's rights, sexual abuse, etc. Christians and their beliefs are now being accused of creating the environment that has caused overpopulation, discrimination, violence, crime, gang warfare, pollution of the planet, oppression, and dozens of forms of evil now plaguing the world.

Christian beliefs such as biblical creation (versus Darwinian evolution), and opposition to the Marxist and Freudian view of man have left them isolated, ridiculed, and stereotyped by the political left in Hollywood, in academia, and in our legal system as ignorant, uneducated, superstitious, and unscientific (i.e., throwbacks to the unenlightened Dark Ages). The evangelistic activities of Christians (i.e., spreading the Gospel, witnessing, etc.) are now stereotyped as offensive, exclusivistic, anti-diversity, discriminatory, of spreading hate and division, and of smacking of the extremism of the fundamentalist Islamic Ayatollah.

Much of the negative stereotyping of Christians has been deliberately fostered by the entertainment/communications industry (i.e., music, television, films) which is leftist in persuasion and vocally anti-Christian. As Michael Medved has written: "In the ongoing war on traditional values, the assault on organized faith represents the front to which the entertainment industry has most clearly committed itself."

The entertainment industry (bolstered by America's leftist dominated educational system) has created a negative stereotype of committed Christians as intellectually deficient, mentally impaired, abnormal, dangerous to society, an impediment to social progress, responsible for the spread of sexually transmitted diseases (because of their opposition to sex education, condom distribution to children, and homosexual marriage) and are the root cause of millions of unwanted pregnancies.

These "small minded, antiquated, repressive Christians," stand in the way of allowing terminally ill patients to *die with dignity* (i.e., euthanasia); they wish to control "a woman's most private decisions about her body and reproduction"; they oppose medical science's quest for new cures for disease by standing in the way of partial-birth abortion and fetal research on the unborn; they would "enslave" women and children on the basis of sexual orientation; and they are 'always hypocritical." In short, committed Christians are being stereotyped to represent everything which is evil in our society. The result of this massive stereotyping of Christians is that tens of millions of Americans have become suspicious, mistrustful, and hostile toward fundamental, evangelical Christians and conservative Catholics.

In a growing number of instances, they are considered undesirable, untrustworthy, unreliable as a friend, neighbor, or in the workplace. A popular opinion poll asked the question a couple of years ago: "What kind of people would you **least** like having as a next door neighbor?" "**Fundamentalist Christian**" was named as the fourth **least** desirable. The negative stereotyping of Christians and traditionalists by the political left is working!

Stage Two: Isolation and Marginalization

Next comes **isolation and marginalization** of the stereotyped group. In Nazi Germany one of the first anti-Jewish laws was the firing of Jews from all government jobs and banning them from all civil service positions. Jews were denied membership in the Nazi Party and when the party came to total power, a person had to be a member of the party to work for or be any part of the government.

The Communists did the same thing in Russia, the Eastern bloc countries, China, and Cuba. Only Communist Party members were allowed positions in government, and only atheists were allowed to be party members—thereby excluding Christians from the party and the government. In Nazi Germany, Jews were denied positions in banks and most businesses. Those holding such positions were terminated. In Russia, China, and the other communist countries, Christians were denied higher education, all but menial jobs were precluded, and all civil service except the military was prohibited.

Today, the political left in America is systematically pushing Christians and traditionalists to the margins and out of the mainstream of American culture. It is very difficult to impossible for a committed Christian, conservative, or traditionalist to get an important job (or any job) in the entertainment industry, in Hollywood in either film or television, in the vast majority of colleges and universities, and in most large law firms. If a Christian or traditionalist should surface in one of these organizations, he or she will be told to remain silent about their beliefs or lose their position. The same is true throughout a growing segment of corporate America as well.

A Christian or traditionalist teacher in grade, middle, or high school or a college or university will be silenced quickly if their beliefs are ever mentioned and the fact that they are a Christian will in most instances limit any advancement or promotion. Christian students have also been pushed to the margins and made to appear weird, fanatical, hypocritical, or stupid. If they do speak up for their faith, pray at school, bring a Bible to school, etc., they are often disciplined, sent to the principal's office or expelled from school.

There is a concerted effort (led by the ACLU, People for the American Way, and other leftist groups) to exclude Christians (and all trappings of Christianity) from all of public life (i.e., prayers, crosses, Bibles, religious plaques, Christmas nativity scenes, etc.). They are trying to deny Christians all positions of influence in public life, just as was done to the Jews in Germany and the Christians in the various communist countries—including China at present.

If any official, politician, or civil servant takes any position which lines up with the Bible he is attacked for violating separation of church and state. Christians are not only being excluded from making or influencing public policy, but even from commenting on it.

Several years ago, a public television documentary on the Holocaust pointed out that the vast majority of the German people **did know** about the existence of over 300 Nazi concentration, slave labor, extermination camps. However, because years of anti-Jewish propaganda had isolated the Jews and pushed them to the margins of society, portraying them as evil, wicked, subhuman vermin, **the German people just didn't care.** Isolated in the margins of society, they became easy targets for slander, hate, bigotry, then outright persecution, and finally extermination. The same was (and is) true of Christians under communism and is clearly being demonstrated in the Peoples Republic of China today.

In Nazi Germany, derogatory imagery was used in cartoons and the media stigmatizing and slandering the Jews, who were depicted as vermin, vultures, thieves, and murderers. In America, the same kind of scurrilous portrayal of Christians and religious people is beginning to emerge. In a Universal Press Syndicated cartoon by liberal editorial cartoonist Pat Oliphant, Christians were portrayed as ugly sewer rats, viciously dragging the Republican elephant into a rat-infested storefront. Displayed over the door was a sign which read "Jesus Saves" and "Fundamentalist Christian Mission."

The *Chicago Tribune* published a syndicated cartoon by MacNelly with seven ugly, evil-looking vultures perched on a tree branch looking for a victim. Each vulture was labeled with the name of a religion: Christian, Islam, Hindu, Sikh, Jewish, Protestant, and Catholic, followed by the word "loonies." The vultures are all shrieking in unison: "LET US PREY."

So, whether under Naziism, communism, or in contemporary America today, the pattern is to stereotype, isolate, marginalize and next to:

Stage Three: Vilification

Vilify the targeted group. Vilification of the targeted group is the next major element in the pattern of persecution. The entire group is portrayed as evil, wicked, villainous, anti-social, dangerous miscreants who represent a very real danger for the entire society. After World War II, the Soviet press accused Christians of duplicity, hypocrisy, anti-patriotic behavior, of being reactionaries, etc. Nazi propaganda portrayed Jews as vermin, as greedy, thirsty, unscrupulous subhumans, raping the country for illegal profits.

Incredibly, recent studies of the Holocaust show that the great majority of the German people believed the anti-Semitic Nazi propaganda and hence, when the mass arrests, incarcerations, and eventually extermination of the Jews took place—they were indifferent to the plight of the Jews. Millions of Germans, who had accepted that the Jews were wicked, evil, subhumans, therefore gave their tacit (passive) approval to the mass arrests and executions.

Anti-Semitism had been growing in Germany for thirty years prior to the Nazis coming to power. In the wake of World War I and the Treaty of Versailles, massive economic, social, and political upheaval broke out in Germany during the ill-fated years of the highly flawed Weimar Republic. The Germans began to blame the ruling Social Democrats and in particular its Jewish members. Up until that time, Jews held prominent positions in the professions of law, medicine, and the arts, and held many key positions in government. But, the Jews who were being vilified by anti-Semitic propaganda as being responsible for Germany's economic, social, and political woes were labeled as subversive (a term which is presently being used to describe a growing number of Christian/conservative leaders and publications in America today).

As Paul Schenck wrote in *The Extermination of Christianity:*

> These images which in both the communist and Nazi cases led to indifference toward and prejudice against Christian and Jewish believers, were ultimately instrumental in creating a cultural context tolerant of vicious and genocidal persecution. The vilification of conscientious, practicing religionists and especially traditional Christians, threatens a similarly grave eventuality in a secularized state increasingly intolerant of religious dissent.
>
> Something ominously similar to this is beginning to shape up on the shores of secular America. As the secularist/New Left/sexual revolutionaries grasp power, they're using every available means to silence the opposition.

Today, Hollywood films, television, and popular music (the electronic industry shaping American culture) are portraying American Christians as ignorant, unscientific, superstitious, absurd, crackpots, extremists, insane, irrational, perverse, rabid, and as planning to take over America (and the government) and impose their radical views on everyone.

A New York prosecutor recently referred to two pro-life Christians, on trial for praying in front of an abortion clinic as "rabid Christians." The dictionary describes rabid as "fanatical, fierce, furious, insane, raging, rampant, virulent, violent." This is how the media, television, movies, educators, and even judges are beginning to refer to Christian traditionalists in America today. This vilification of Christians/conservatives/traditionalists as a group is setting the stage for:

Stage Four: Criminalization

The **criminalization of religious and traditionalist practices.** It is now becoming illegal to spank your children, to teach them that homosexuality is wrong, to oppose abortion by demonstrating or praying in front of an abortion clinic. The definitions of hate crimes, terrorism, sexual harassment, and child abuse are now being expanded to include many Christian practices, traditions, and beliefs.

Legal restrictions are being placed on religious ceremonies (i.e., public preaching, prayer, litany and liturgy, singing of hymns, carolling, etc.). In 1994 the Clinton Equal Employment Opportunity Commission tried to pass, by regulatory fiat, a series of regulations that would have banned all religious free speech in the work place. All Bibles, crosses, stars of David, religious plaques, mention of God, Christ or religion, Christmas parties, songs or decorations, witnessing, etc. would have been banned.

The U.N. Convention on the Rights of the Child (already ratified by 189 nations at this writing) would abolish virtually all parental rights including spanking; what you can and cannot teach your child; who your child can associate with; what materials your child can listen to, view, or read, etc. Virtually all biblical principles of childrearing would be rendered illegal if (or when) this treaty (which is strongly supported by the Clintons) is ratified in the U.S.

In recent years most of the legal restrictions on Christians and traditionalists have been imposed by bureaucrats and judges. However, as definitions of civil rights are increased to include homosexuals and abortionists, and the definition of harassment is expanded, more anti-Christian, anti-traditional values legislation can be expected to come out of Congress and the various state legislatures.

As Christians and traditionalists are stereotyped, isolated, marginalized, and vilified in the eyes of tens of millions of Americans, who have begun to believe the anti-Christian/traditionalist propaganda, the great majority will cheer new legal restrictions which are placed on these fundamentalist religious extremists, just as the German people supported such restrictions against the Jews, and the Russian people against the Christians.

Stage Five: The Onset of Persecution

Stage five is **the actual onset of persecution against Christians and traditionalists.** This persecution involves government actions employed against Christians, traditionalists (in Germany it was the Jews), or whatever the targeted group may be, and includes: harassment, the denial of civil and constitutional rights, false accusations, arrests, detentions, intimidation, imprisonment, and in some cases torture and death. Millions of Jews during the Nazi reign of terror and millions of Christians under communism have suffered such maltreatment, as have Christians dating back to the days of the Roman Caesars. Over 2 million black Christians in southern Sudan have been killed by the Islamic Sudanese government in recent years—right up through today.

Such persecution is the norm in Red China today, in the Sudan, and may soon return in the former Soviet bloc. Richard Wurmbrand, Dumitru Duduman, and numerous other victims of communist persecution of Christians and veterans of the persecuted underground Christian church, have described these persecutions in horrific, vivid detail and believe that they are coming in America. It should be remembered that about a thousand Christians a day are being martyred somewhere around the world at this writing.

Persecution does not come all at once. It comes, as described above, in stages, over time, as the targeted group becomes stereotyped and progressively more marginalized and isolated. Nowhere is the pattern of persecution more clear than in the persecution of the Jews in Germany. Up until the early 1930s, in spite of the growing anti-Semitic sentiment, the Jews, although less than one percent of the population, were prominent in all key areas of German society.

However, through the 1920s and into the 1930s, as the Nazi–inspired vilification and isolation of the Jews increased, the Nazis began enacting laws depriving Jews of citizenship and restricting their participation in the various German walks of life. When the wholesale arrests and deportation of Jews to death camps began, most Germans had been programmed to accept these actions and indifferently refused to lift a finger in the Jews' defense. The Jews were no longer seen as contributing members of German society and their fate was therefore inconsequential to the average German. The same general mindset is developing regarding Christian/traditionalists in America today.

The Jews were the main target of Nazi persecution with the confessing Christians suffering persecution, but far less. Conversely, Christians have been the main target of persecution under communism with Jews also suffering, but far less. Today, in America, fundamental, evangelical, Pentecostal and Catholic Christians and conservative traditionalists are the primary targets of the New Left and the globalists, who are contriving to push America and the whole world into the global dictatorship called the New World Order. Mikhail Gorbachev calls it the "New Civilization."

As the political left orchestrates the Gramsci strategy of undermining the culture, values, morality, and spiritual life of America, the primary opposition to their plans to debauch, socialize, and globalize America are Christian conservatives and traditionalists. Hence, they must be (indeed are being) trashed, vilified, isolated, and marginalized; and their practices, beliefs, organizations, and publications "legally" banned and criminalized. America is well into Stage Three and moving into Stage Four of the coming persecution. This thrust should accelerate dramatically over the next few years.

Part III
Preparing for the Coming Persecution

As the first two sections of this book have discussed, the stage has been (is being) set for the persecution of politically incorrect Christians and traditionalists in America. Such persecution is already in high gear in China, North Korea, Vietnam, the Islamic states, Sudan, and other parts of Africa. That it could come to America is unthinkable to the vast majority of Americans or to the vast majority of Christians in America—who remain rather fat, dumb, lazy, complacent, apathetic, and in a comfort zone begotten by over a half century of uninterrupted prosperity. Nowhere has that complacency been more clearly demonstrated than by the indifference of the American public, Christians, and even pastors, to the impeachment, Senate trial, and acquittal of President Bill Clinton in late 1998 and early 1999.

The concept of persecution or martyrdom is barely in the vocabulary of the average American Christian or pastor today. Hence, like most Christians in the Soviet Union, Nazi Germany, communist China, or Cuba—who were not aware of the onslaught against their faith until it came in like a flood and it was too late—most Americans, including Christians and traditionalists, will not be prepared for the pain and suffering which will accompany the coming persecution.

Only the remnant of believers, who still follow God's Word, seek righteousness, hate evil, and understand the times, are likely to be spiritually prepared for the onslaught against them, their families and their faith which this writer believes lies ahead in the not-too-distant future.

This last section of this book is written primarily to those remnant believers who grieve over what their country and the American Christian church have become and who will stand firm for their faith regardless of the consequences. It is based primarily on the observations and experiences of believers such as Richard Wurmbrand, Brother Andrew, Georgi Vins, Dimitru Duduman, Dietrich Bonhoeffer, Tom White, Corrie ten Boom, etc. who have endured great persecution and suffering in the persecuted Christian church in communist or former communist countries, Nazi-occupied Europe, or Islamic states around the world—believers who have found victory in the midst of the "fire" through Jesus Christ.

Chapter 16

Psychological Preparation for the Coming Persecution

It is when times are tough and persecution comes and the church is forced underground that faith is proved genuine. The House Church in China has learned that persecution is tilling of the soil.

— Anonymous Church of the Nazarene missionary

What obedience will not achieve, persecution will. . . . Hard times, like persecution, often produce more personnel, more prayer, more power, more open purses than easy times.

—John Piper

Blessed are ye, when men shall revile you, and persecute you, and shall say all manner of evil against you falsely, for my sake. Rejoice, and be exceeding glad: for great is your reward in heaven: for so persecuted they the prophets which were before you.

—Matthew 5:11-12

As recorded in **Acts 1:8**, it was persecution of the early church that resulted in the scattering of the apostles and the spread of the Gospel from Jerusalem to Judea and Samaria. It has been said that because the apostles had not moved, persecution came so the Gospel would spread.

John Piper wrote in *World Pulse* (8/18/95) the account told by Bill and Amy Stearns in *Catch the Vision 2000* about thousands of Koreans fleeing when the Japanese invaded. They settled in the Soviet Union only to be relocated by Stalin in areas including Tashkent, Uzbekistan, which was staunchly Muslim. After a few decades, the Koreans were bringing the Uzbeks to Christ.

Many examples can be given of the church increasing numerically as a result of persecution. In Vietnam one house church grew in one recent year by 12,000 souls, according to Johan Companjen of Open Doors. As Tertullian said, "The blood of the martyrs is the seed of the church."

As *Voice of the Martyrs* (8/96) wrote:

With oppression comes a greater determination. The house church movement in Cuba is growing in size and in a deeper understanding of the Christian life. The destruction of these churches has resulted in smaller groups meeting to avoid further suspicion. However, their voice does not go unheard, as many times when a church is closed, Christians take to the street, protesting in front of the police station. These believers seize every opportunity to share Christ, often witnessing to the police who confront them.

Brother Andrew's Open Doors Ministry has written:

Every human being must endure some suffering in his lifetime. It may be the physical suffering of sickness or injury. It may be the inner suffering caused by the death of a loved one, rejection by friends, or simply loneliness. Whatever the cause may be, we all seek to avoid it as much as possible. That may be one reason why Christians often avoid this subject, although it is clearly presented in the Bible. . . . Actually, the Scripture makes it very plain that Christians are subject to all the causes of suffering common to men, plus the added persecution that comes with taking a clear stand for Christ.

Richard Wurmbrand, who spent fourteen years in communist prisons, says in his book *Preparing for the Underground Church,* regarding preparing for persecution: "Preparation for [persecution] begins by studying sufferology, martyrology" (i.e., studying the lives and sufferings of those who have been persecuted or martyred for the cause of Christ).

According to the staff of Open Doors:

Thousands of Christians have stood in persecution, but tens of thousands have fallen. Even in the days of the great Roman persecutions, only a small fraction of those who had professed Christ stood true to the end. More Christians have suffered for their faith in the twentieth century than in any other time in church history. Why are some able to stand? They have learned how to sink their roots of faith deeply into the Rock, Jesus Christ—to "take unto you the whole armour of God, that ye may be able to withstand in the evil day, and having done all, to stand" (Ephesians 6:13).

In this section we will discuss the subject of persecution of Christians which is occurring today around the world and challenge American Christians to acknowledge that they may not be exempt from suffering for their faith. This section will discuss how to prepare for persecution **psychologically, spiritually, and physically.** It will not attempt to cover the accumulation of material possessions or personal or financial preparations for the difficult times which this writer believes lies just ahead. Those are covered in other writings by this writer (see appendix F). Nor will it present any eschatological information, such as the timing of the Rapture of the Church or whether Christians will go through the Great Tribulation. It has been stated by Pat Brooks in *A Call to War With Prayer,* however, that

> the same qualities that prepare the believer for Christ's return prepare him for standing under persecution! Repentance, humility, love, wisdom that come from abiding in Christ and His Word, forgiveness, fasting, and prayer—these are the characteristics of disciplined saints who will be overcomers, no matter what life holds.

Gary Bauer of the Family Research Council has written:

> From China to Saudi Arabia to Sudan, one's profession of faith in Jesus Christ is becoming an ever more dangerous act in the eyes of the state. . . . Incidents of intimidation, arrest, and torture are growing under various regimes around the world. The worst offenders are Is-

lamic fundamentalist governments and communist regimes. Millions of Christians worldwide are routinely subjected to this persecution, most of which goes unreported in the United States.

He refers to what is happening around the globe as a "plague of persecution."

This period of history has been referred to in negative terms. "This is an age of atrocity, a 'tyrant century,'" says Susan Bergman in *Christianity Today* (8/12/96) in an article entitled "The Shadow of the Martyr." It has also been said that this is an age of tolerance—tolerance for everything except Christianity.

The reported number of people martyred for their faith is astonishing. "Dr. Paul Carlson . . . told Congolese believers before his martyrdom that more believers have died for Christ in this twentieth century than in all the previous nineteen combined," as James and Marti Hefley wrote in *By Their Blood*. The Center for World Mission estimates 100,000 are martyred each year. David Barrett believes about 150,000 were martyred in 1993 and foresees that annual number as 200,000 by the year 2000. More Christians have been killed in the nation of Sudan than the number of Americans killed in all of the wars in the history of America, according to Tom White, of the *Voice of the Martyrs*.

As White has written:

The persecuted church, our brothers and sisters in China, Vietnam, Sudan, and the Middle East, also encourage us in the faith. Although they are beaten and tortured, their spirit empowered by the Spirit of God, is indomitable; their faith strong, and their hope and love in Christ resilient. They live a life similar to what the Apostle Paul has described "As unknown, and yet well known; as dying, and, behold, we live; as chastened, and not killed; As sorrowful, yet always rejoicing . . ." (2 Corinthians 6:9-10).

It has taken a Jewish writer, a fellow at the Hudson Institute in Washington, Michael Horowitz, to bring the plight of suffering Christians to the attention of Americans. However, after writing and talking about it to statesmen, most of them as well as the general public remain unaware of the atrocities that are taking place. Therefore, World Evangelical Fellowship declared the last Sunday in September 1996 as the International Day of Prayer for the Persecuted Church. An interesting comment was made about this by Brian O'Connell of World Evangelical Fellowship: "The reason Christians are being persecuted is because we are winning, not because we are losing."

Americans Are in Denial About the Possibility of Persecution in the United States

John Piper has written: "Americans are not given to suffering. We are comfortable." Then he states: "Comfort and ease and affluence and prosperity and safety and freedom often cause tremendous inertia in the church."

"Most American Christians have become couch potatoes, so spiritually out of shape we can be cowered by the mere threat of opposition, not to mention persecution. We bow to the gods of comfort and convenience, even demanding, in the name of faith, that our God give us health and prosperity," declared Maxine Shideler in the August 1996 Colorado Christian News.

Tom White, a former prisoner in Cuba and now the Voice of the Martyrs USA director, wrote in a January 1996 letter: "Persecution and pain and clandestine methods are not popular items on the Christian smorgasbord today." In a March 1996 letter he states: "A good friend said, 'The goal of American culture is to avoid suffering. We get blank looks from Christians who have learned only to look for cheap solutions.'"

Tom McConnell wrote in a 1995 article, "A Time to Prepare," that living in ease and prosperity makes it difficult to imagine. We base security on the way things are—law and order, finances, freedom—and think it would be impossible to happen here. Our attitude is really one of scoffing: It can't or won't happen here.

He states:

> The church simply cannot go on living in apathy, blindly confident of a never-ending "American Dream." This foolish delusion has kept us

from discerning the times that lie ahead. It appears that our incredible standard of living and ease of life have disconnected us from the realities of the cost of discipleship. Are we like the generation of hypocrites that could discern the weather but not the signs of the times? Whether or not this is the Great Tribulation, we cannot be certain. One thing is sure: this nation is rapidly heading into calamity.

Many people avoid anything frightening or negative as though it will not occur if they do not know about it, while others avoid standing against evil, saying, "It is just signs of end times." Some say it is instigating fear to talk about things like judgment or financial collapse. However, this writer agrees with Alan Keyes, who says: "The right kind of fear leads to the right kind of wisdom."

Even if Americans are aware of the danger, they do not seem to care. As this writer wrote in his July 1993 *McAlvany Intelligence Advisor:*

> There is no resistance from the churches of America which are in a very complacent comfort zone—the mainlines supporting the Establishment's goals; the fundamental evangelicals too busy "loving the brethren" and striving "to feel good about themselves" to notice the evil sweeping across America (or lift a finger to oppose it); . . . It is as if a spirit of blindness or delusion has settled over Americans in general and the Christian church in America in particular, and as the affronts, the insults, and attacks against our traditional, constitutional and biblical values in America grow every year, almost geometrically, the average Christian in America goes even more deeply to sleep.

It can be said that some people are "wilfully ignorant." Aleksandr Solzhenitsyn is quoted in *Persecution: It Will Never Happen Here?* as saying:

> Are we prepared to learn from the past? Are people living in freedom able to learn from those living in need? Can the lesson they have learned be taught to the free world? Yes it can, but who wants to learn? Our proud skyscrapers point heavenward and they say: It will never happen here. But it will happen. . . . Tragically the free West will only believe it

when it is no longer free. To quote a Russian proverb, "When it happens you will know it is true, but then it is too late."

In an editorial referring to the three-part series in *Christianity Today* which dealt with persecution, Michael G. Maudlin says:

And it is precisely this kind of story—about martyrs and about suffering—that the American church most needs to hear.

At CT we have again and again been struck by how our brothers and sisters in other countries handle persecution and suffering. They fight it, but they also accept it as part of the Christian life. For many, suffering is a mark of the true church. This insight is what we are in danger of losing in America, and why we need stories that remind us of this truth.

God Still Judges Nations

Scripture teaches us that, without exception, every nation that departs from God is turned into hell unless it fully repents (Psalm 9:17). Judging from the moral collapse of this nation as a whole, it is this writer's opinion that we, as a nation, are now moving rapidly into God's judgment.

As Tom McConnell wrote in *A Time to Prepare*:

Historically, God has worked to restore rebellious and unrepentant nations to Himself by allowing them to be humbled under the weight of their sin, even to the point of enslavement. We are now seeing the New World Order manifesting itself as a demonic blend of economics, politics, and religion which is coming into power as a consequence of God's act of judgment in lifting His hand of restraint against evil. The godless power of this New World Order may be allowed to enslave not only our nation, but the entire world. As a result, constitutional liberty may be abolished, our nation's standard of living is likely to fall drastically, and Christians will suffer persecution. The speed at which this judgment is enveloping our country demands swift action on our part.

Therefore, we must now prepare physically and, more importantly, spiritually if we are going to discern the Lord's direction through all of this. God is merciful and warns of his impending judgment, so that those who listen for His guidance will be equipped to deal with the issues that confront them. Without a doubt, the most pressing and difficult issues are spiritual, for if they are not settled our physical preparations, vital as they are, could be our undoing.

A blind preoccupation with physical and material concerns, to the exclusion of a genuine desire to be led and controlled by the Holy Spirit, inevitably leads to tragedy. "For what shall it profit a man, if he shall gain the whole world, and lose his own soul?" (**Mark 8:36**).

Jeremiah 2:29-3:5 speaks to us of Judah's sixteen sins that ultimately destroyed her. We could easily say "America" wherever Israel is written . . . Proverbs, Jeremiah, Deuteronomy, Isaiah, Ezekiel, etc. warn us of the abominations before God (homosexuality, adultery, pornography, criminals treated like victims, killing of children, a lying tongue, violence, etc.).

David Wilkerson says God's ways are absolutely unchangeable when it comes to His dealings with sinful nations. Isaiah 22 is an example. Wilkerson (writing in his Times Square Church *Pulpit Series*) has said:

When the Lord says, "I'm going to shake the earth one more time," He means it! He will literally shake our economy, our education system, our government—everything we put our trust and confidence in, everything that seems safe and secure. . . . I wonder: When the storm comes—when everything begins to spin out of control—how many Christians will be able to stand? How many will have the foundation of faith necessary to endure that time?"

In this writer's opinion, time for America is very short. The only hope for America is revival. Bill Bright writes:

Our nation has become like Sodom and Gomorrah, only worse because we, as the most powerful nation on earth, export our pornographic filth and corruption to the rest of the world. We are not only destroying ourselves but are playing a major role in helping to destroy the moral and spiritual values of the rest of the world as well.

In His mercy God always warns people and nations, so they can be ready for judgment. **Amos 3:7** states: "Surely the Lord God will do nothing, but he revealeth his secret unto his servants the prophets." Whether it be national calamities, judgments, or persecutions, the Lord warns his people ahead of time so they may hear and take action, lest they perish in their own ignorance—wilfully or otherwise. "For I have no pleasure in the death of one who dies, says the Lord God." There are many scriptural examples which speak to this: Noah and the building of the ark; Joseph and the famine; Samuel and the dethroning of Saul; Jeremiah and the judgments of Israel; Joseph and Mary and their flight to Egypt; Agabus and the famine.

Examples of Nations That Were Not Prepared

Isaiah 22 records an example of a society that ignored God's impending judgment and partied while the Assyrian army was gathering to attack it. David Wilkerson comments: "I am sure Isaiah's voice was drowned out by the partying crowds: 'Oh, it's only that old preacher. Don't pay any attention to him.' And so it is today: Prophetic warnings are ridiculed and ignored!"

The July 1996 NAE Washington *Insight* reported this haunting example of religious leaders oblivious to the Russian revolution that was about to take place:

Almost a quarter century ago, a remarkable story was reported. On the eve of the Bolshevik Revolution in 1917, conferences were being held in two hotels on the same Moscow street. At the consultation sponsored by the Orthodox Church, clergy vestments were the principle agenda item. In the other meeting, Vladimir Lenin and friends were finalizing plans to overthrow the existing regime.

As Robert Dugan wrote: "Today our American culture is in similar jeopardy. Many evangelical churches are going about business as usual, oblivious to the threat of virulent secularism, abetted by a moral relativism that recognizes no absolutes."

Corrie ten Boom related this:

There are some among us teaching that the Christians will be able to escape all this. Could these be the false teachers Jesus was warning us to expect in the latter days? Most of them have little knowledge of [the persecution] that is already going on across the world.

I have been in countries where the saints are already suffering terrible persecution. In China the Christians were told, "Don't worry, before the tribulation comes, you will be translated—raptured." Then came a terrible persecution. Millions of Christians were tortured to death. Later I heard a Bishop from China say, sadly, "We have failed. We should have made the people strong for persecution rather than telling them Jesus would come first."

Turning to me, he said, "You still have time. Tell the people how to be strong in times of persecution, how to stand when [persecution] comes—to stand and not faint."

[Note: This writer knows a number of American Christians who believe that Christians in America will never face persecution—that they will be raptured out before they ever have to break a sweat. The Chinese Christians fifty years ago believed the same, but their timing was off. Regardless of a believer's position (i.e, pre, post or pro, etc.) persecution could very well come to American Christians *before* Jesus returns. It seems prudent to this writer to be mentally, psychologically, and spiritually prepared for same.]

In the book *Persecution: It Will Never Happen Here,* Jan Pit relates:

During the appalling Vietnam War, church leaders from a certain Christian group held their annual conference. The southern Vietnamese city they were in resembled a fortress. There were soldiers everywhere, barricades, and a terrifying collection of weaponry. Daily attacks were being made on the city by the communist Viet Cong, yet the pastors continued to discuss the various activities which they would embark upon in the ensuing years. They even adopted a ten-year plan. Despite all the evidence, no one there thought it possible for South Vietnam to be overthrown. All were convinced the country would remain open to mission work. The church remained—unprepared.

Tom White, in a February 1995 letter to supporters of Voice of the Martyrs, wrote: "North Korean Christians today pray for Americans that we don't let our Christianity die inch by inch."

Urgency for Preparation Before, Not When, Persecution Begins

Richard Wurmbrand says: "It is not possible to give a course on the church underground, in a short time. I would urge you to put this question before your synod, before your denomination, and to ask absolutely that courses on the underground church be introduced." John Piper quotes Wurmbrand as saying: "We have to make the preparations now, before we are imprisoned. In prison you lose everything. . . . Nobody resists who has not renounced the pleasures of life beforehand."

In another publication by Wurmbrand, *We Must Prepare Now,* the preface states:

> If what some Christian leaders are saying is true, sooner or later the church must face two alternatives—socio-political compromise with anti-Christian forces or incur the wrath of a controlled political–religious hierarchy by refusing such—then Wurmbrand is right. Since these alternatives have already been posed in many parts of the world, there is no reason to believe that the area where we live will continue to escape their realities. Let us then, as Christians, prepare ourselves now and be sure that our children have a clear example before them if their turn comes.

Dr. James McKeever, writing in his January 1992 issue of *End Times News Digest,* said:

> Preparation for persecution is a bit like road flares for your automobile: when you need one it is difficult to acquire one. . . . Similarly, our armed forces today give training as to what to do if captured by the enemy and subjected to brainwashing. For soldiers to try to learn this after they are captured would be a bit too late. As we apply this to the spiritual realm and spiritual warfare, we in no way want to underestimate the power of the Holy Spirit. He can, does, and will, under cer-

tain circumstances, provide miraculous help and abilities. However, as good soldiers of Jesus Christ, there are certain things of which we should all be aware.

Although **1 Thessalonians 5:4–6** referS to Christ's return, this scripture is applicable to being prepared for whatever may lie ahead: "But ye, brethren, are not in darkness, that that day should overtake you as a thief. . . . Therefore let us not sleep, as do others; but let us watch and be sober."

Recognize That Persecution of U.S. Believers Is Possible

Hebrews 11 tells that some in the hall of faith were tortured, sawed in two, persecuted, mistreated, wore sheep or goatskins, and lived in caves and holes in the ground. If these things happened to people who lived back then, what can be expected in the time surrounding the greatest distress of all times, as described in **Matthew 24**? Christians should be prepared for the very worst of times. Then if they live in times that are better than the worst, they can praise the Lord. They need to come to an understanding now that the Lord can get them through the very worst of times and that they can be obedient to Him and victorious in these times.

Jesus warned that the world would hate believers (**John 15:17–21**). He said:

Behold, I send you forth as sheep in the midst of wolves: be ye therefore wise as serpents, and harmless as doves. But beware of men: for they will deliver you up to the councils, and they will scourge you in their synagogues; And ye shall be brought before governors and kings for my sake, for a testimony against them and the Gentiles. . . . But when they persecute you in this city, flee ye into another. . . . And fear not them which kill the body, but are not able to kill the soul. . . .

—**Matthew 10:16–18, 23, 28**

Several reports have come that Christians in China are praying for persecution to come to wake up the American church.

Sources of Persecution and Betrayal

From Non-Believers. Persecution of Christians is most likely to come from non-believers, but not necessarily because of a believer's faith in Christ. Francis Schaeffer says:

> The early Christians died because they would not obey the state in a civil matter. . . . Why were the Christians in the Roman Empire thrown to the lions? From the Christian's viewpoint it was for a religious reason. But from the viewpoint of the Roman state they were in civil disobedience, they were civil rebels. The Roman state did not care what anybody believed religiously; you could believe anything, or you could be an atheist. But you had to worship Caesar as a sign of your loyalty to the state. The Christians said they would not worship Caesar, anybody, or anything, but the living God. Thus to the Roman Empire they were rebels, and it was civil disobedience. That is why they were thrown to the lions.

In another work, *Death in the City,* Schaeffer points out that being a Christian can be costly.

> At times the price will be high in your individual family. Often there is a tremendous pressure upon young Christians as they face their non-Christian families. But the price is also high in society. You may not get the honor which you covet in the scholastic world, in the artistic world, in the medical world, or in the business world.

The price may be high indeed. In a letter to his readers in 1991, Dr. James Dobson included an example given by Soviet dissident Irina Ratushinskaya, in which the son of another dissident was paralyzed as a result of lack of medical attention because his parents were dissidents.

From Religous Individuals and Groups. Most people who acknowledge that persecution is possible expect it to come from unbelievers. However, often it comes from religious individuals or groups. Today the Russian Orthodox Church is strongly attacking missionary attempts in the former U.S.S.R. Paul said in **Acts 20:30**: "Also of your own selves shall men arise, speaking perverse things, to draw away disciples after them." **Matthew 24** indicates that they will "betray one another, and shall hate one another" and that the "love [for the Lord] of many shall wax cold."

Even Jesus was attacked by the religious crowd of His day—the pious Jews, Pharisees, chief priests, and scribes. The apostles were condemned by religious Jews. It was a devout Jew Saul who assented to the stoning of the first martyr, Stephen.

David Wilkerson writes in his *Times Square Church Pulpit Series,* "The Persecution of the Righteous" (4/13/87):

> In His going-away message to the disciples, Jesus warned them of the certainty of persecution. He said, "If they have persecuted me, they will also persecute you" (John 15:20). Who are they? Who is it who will persecute the most intimate followers of Christ?
>
> It is the religious crowd! Those with outward forms of godliness without the power of the total heart surrender—these will persecute those who glory only in the Cross of Christ. The godless, humanistic Romans were not the real persecutors of the Master. His greatest abuse was at the hands of those most steeped in the Law, the hierarchy of the church, and the masses who boasted that God was their Father.

We need to remind ourselves that infiltration of churches by communists, atheists, occultists, even Satanists, or other anti-God forces is a ploy of Satan. Just because we assume someone is a believer with pure motives does not mean that he is.

From Believers. It is estimated that eighty-five percent of the Christians turned in fellow believers during the revolution in China. Money, relief from suffering, and desire to save themselves are three motives for betraying others. Karen N. Feaver, who went with a delegation to Beijing, says in *Christianity Today:* "I have seen more than a few believers trade in their Christian birthright for a mess of earthly pottage."

Christians who talk about the possibility of persecution may be ostracized by other believers who think that they will be taken from this world before any trouble begins. In fact, some Christians feel only a cultist or non-Christian would even suggest the possibility of believers facing any physical discomfort for their faith. A firm knowledge of Scripture will help a believer face such ostracism.

The late Dumitru Duduman, a Romanian pastor and Bible smuggler who functioned in the underground church in Romania was arrested, imprisoned, beaten, and tortured by the communists on at least a dozen occasions. He once told this writer that in at least half of those cases, he was betrayed and turned in to the secret police by fellow Christians or pastors.

Many verses of Scripture indicate that believers should expect suffering. Some of the most powerful are these:

a. "Yea, and all that will live godly in Christ Jesus shall suffer persecution" (**2 Timothy 3:12**), Therefore, the question is, if we aren't being persecuted, why not?

b. "Beloved, think it not strange concerning the fiery trial which is to try you, as though some strange thing happened unto you" (**1 Peter 4:12**).

c. ". . . If any man will come after me, let him deny himself, and take up his cross daily, and follow me" (**Luke 9:23**).

d. Paul said: "That I may know him, and the power of his resurrection, and the fellowship of his sufferings, being made comformable unto his death" (**Philippians 3:10**).

Be Aware That Persecution May Be Psychological as Well as Physical

Frequently people associate physical pain with the word "persecution." However, it may also be psychological. Watching others suffer; experiencing the loss of family, friends, church leaders, church buildings; and having possessions confiscated will inflict mental pain. Of course, brainwashing is a common mistreatment. Corrie ten Boom saw her entire family taken to the Nazi death camps. She was the only one to survive. That is painful!

Painful decisions may also have to be made. Parents may have to stand before a judge and decide whether to deny Christ or have their children taken from them. Spouses may have to watch or hear spouses tormented. Only the strength of the Lord can help a person endure these trials.

Realize That Loss of Freedom May Be Gradual or Sudden

Richard Wurmbrand wrote:

> What happens in a country when oppressive powers take over? In some countries the terror starts at once, as in Mozambique and Cambodia. . . . Some regimes come to power without having real power. . . . The initial situation does not last long. During that time they infiltrate the churches, putting their men in leadership. They find out the weaknesses of pastors. . . . They explain that they would make those weaknesses known and thus put their men in leadership. Then, at a certain moment the great persecution begins. In Romania such a clamp-down happened in one day. All the Catholic bishops went to prison, along with innumerable priests, monks and nuns. Then many Protestant pastors of all denominations were arrested. Many died in prison.

Adopt These Attitudes Regarding Persecution

View It As Normal. Because most Americans previously have known little about persecution, they view it as something unusual or abnormal. However, it should be viewed as normal, something to be expected. David Neff in an April 29, 1996, *Christianity Today* editorial, "Our Extended, Persecuted Family," said: "Although persecution and martyrdom are not to be sought, Jesus, Paul, and Peter all taught they were to be expected. A Christian's duty is simply to be faithful and live the kind of godly life that would render the inevitable persecution inexcusable." It has been said that what the apostles suffered was normal Christianity.

Dietrich Bonhoeffer wrote in *The Cost of Discipleship:*

> The cross is not the terrible end to an otherwise God-fearing and happy life, but it meets us at the beginning of our communion with Christ. When Christ calls a man, he bids him come and die.
>
> To take up a cross and follow Jesus means to join Jesus on the Calvary road with a resolve to suffer and die with him. The cross is not a burden to bear, it is an instrument of pain and execution. It would be like saying, "Pick up your electric chair and follow me to the execution room." . . . Following Jesus means that wherever obedience requires it, we will accept betrayal and rejection and beating and mockery and

crucifixion and death. Jesus gives us the assurance that if we will follow Him to Golgotha during all the Good Fridays of this life, we will also rise with Him on the last Easter day of the resurrection. ". . . Whosoever shall lose his life for my sake and the gospel's, the same shall save it" (Mark 8:35).

Peter said that the death of Christ is a pattern to be followed. ". . . But if, when ye do well, and suffer for it, ye take it patiently, this is acceptable with God. For even hereunto were ye called: because Christ also suffered for us, leaving us an example, that ye should follow his steps" (**1 Peter 2:20–21**).

Susan Bergman asks herself and others: "No one is demanding that I deny what I believe; but have I denied myself—living with conditions of privilege and safety much of the world has never known—and taken up my cross, daily, in order to follow Christ?"

Rejoice. Scripture abounds with references to rejoicing in the midst of suffering. Paul and Silas set an example by singing in prison. Paul rejoices that he had the privilege of making up in his body what was lacking in afflictions for Christ's body, the church (**Colossians 1:24**). Not only did they rejoice but also they continued sharing the story of salvation through Jesus Christ while in prison and immediately upon release. This author has known missionaries like Peter Hammond, head of Frontline Fellowship (in South Africa) who have been locked up in communist jails, who have led praise and worship, singing of hymns, and evangelistic services in those prisons, ministering to fellow prisoners and guards alike.

Another poignant Scripture is **Matthew 5:11**: "Blessed are ye, when men shall revile you, and persecute you, and shall say all manner of evil against you falsely, for my sake." Luke paints a word picture of the same scripture when he writes, "Blessed are ye, when men shall hate you, and when they shall separate you from their company, and shall reproach you, and cast out your name as evil, for the Son of man's sake. Rejoice ye in that day, and leap for joy: for, behold, your reward is great in heaven . . ." (**Luke 6:22–23**). Rewards on earth are fleeting but in heaven they are eternal.

More Than Conquerors, by Brother Andrew of Open Doors Ministries, provides this insight: "Mature Christians living under persecution have frequently urged us to turn our hearts to praise, because in this way we are acknowledging the sovereignty of God, bringing glory to His name and strengthening ourselves."

In fact, the early church felt it was an honor, not punishment. **Acts 5:41** says "And they departed from the presence of the council, rejoicing that they were counted worthy to suffer shame for his name." Later it is recorded that they joyfully accepted the confiscation of their property. Writing from prison in Rome, the apostle Paul wrote to the Philippians, "For unto you it is given in the behalf of Christ, not only to believe on him, but also to suffer for his sake" (**Philippians 1:29**).

Tom White, head of Voice of the Martyrs, was in prison in Cuba for seventeen months (although sentenced for twenty-four years) for dropping Christian literature into the country from an airplane. When his teenage daughter was asked how she would feel if her father was sentenced to prison again, she replied, "I would see it as an honor from the Lord."

Do Not Fear. Samuel Lamb, who has led a large house church in China and was in prison over twenty years, says in the video *China . . . More Persecution, More Growing:* "There is no need to be afraid of suffering. Perhaps suffering by and by will come to Western countries. Then I hope all Christians in Western countries have the mind to suffer for God." The Bible says, "Take therefore no thought for the morrow . . ." (**Matthew 6:34**).

"And fear not them which kill the body, but are not able to kill the soul: but rather fear him which is able to destroy both soul and body in hell" (**Matthew 10:28**).

These attitudes are given by Jan Pit in *Persecution: It Will Never Happen Here?*

1. Fear not.
2. Persecution is a mark of true discipleship.
3. Persecution is directed at Jesus and not at the Christian.
4. Rejoice despite persecution.

5. Pray for boldness in times of persecution.

6. Do not be surprised when persecution comes.

7. Persecution is a privilege.

It is better to die for a worthy cause than an unworthy one. Peter says, "And who is he that will harm you, if ye be followers of that which is good? [He must not have known what was going to happen in the twentieth century!] But and if ye suffer for righteousness' sake, happy are ye: and be not afraid of their terror, neither be troubled" (**1 Peter 3:13–14**).

"And when they bring you unto the synagogues, and unto the magistrates, and powers, take ye no thought how or what thing ye shall answer, or what ye shall say: for the Holy Ghost shall teach you in the same hour what ye ought to say" (**Luke 12:11–12**).

[*Note:* This author once asked the late Dimitru Duduman how he handled the fear when he knew he was going to be arrested or beaten by the Romanian secret police. He acknowledged that he had some fear prior to an arrest, but that when the event actually happened, that the Holy Spirit took his fear from him, gave him a supernatural peace, and also gave him the words to say.]

This example from *The Hiding Place,* the classic story of Corrie ten Boom, emphasizes that there is no need to fear death before it comes:

Father sat down on the edge of the narrow bed. "Corrie," he began gently, "when you and I go to Amsterdam—when do I give you your ticket?"

"Why, just before we get on the train."

"Exactly. And our wise Father in heaven knows we're going to need things, too. Don't run out ahead of Him, Corrie. When the time comes that some of us will have to die, you will look into your heart and find the strength you need—just in time."

Preclude Total Mental Devastation by Expecting Persecution

It is usually the unexpected happening or accident that most easily devastates a person. Therefore, if a person is expecting that life may not continue as he knows it today and that persecution is a possibility, he is not likely to be totally devastated if it comes.

Removal of a pastor from the pulpit can easily stop the functioning of a church. In fact, a tactic of the communists when taking over a country has been to identify the pastor and all full-time workers and remove them from the areas. If one's pastor is suddenly thrown into jail, his spouse imprisoned for taking a stand against evil, or children removed from the home because God's Word is taught, it is likely to shake the most grounded person.

However, the mental shock will be much less to the individual who has acknowledged that this is likely to happen. **Realizing that Christian broadcasts and literature may no longer be available should challenge believers to hide God's Word in their hearts.** One family with whom I am acquainted stepped up Scripture memorization with their children when they realized that their children could be taken from them. Although authorities could remove the children, they could not take away the Scripture that their children knew.

It is impossible to be informed about every scenario or type of persecution that might come. This is especially true today because electronic devices are available to track individuals in ways not possible in other generations. A system is in place to track high-risk parolees by satellite which will pinpoint their location within fifty feet. Today there is even less value on human life and some groups are eager to reduce the population of the world by three billion. However, being aware of what has happened in the past might result in some very valuable psychological preparation. *More Than Conquerors* provides this list of methods previously used by communists:

Infiltration of church organizations
False accusations
Exert fear
Confiscating of church properties
Liquidation of leaders
Economic pressure
Fellowship is forbidden
Travel is restricted

Bibles become scarce (printing controlled)
Confiscation of church buildings and properties
Indoctrination
Christians are given the most menial jobs
Food rations are cut

Christians in America should ask themselves whether they could endure those types of pressures for maintaining their faith in Christ. It is encouraging and challenging to know that in spite of persecution millions of brothers and sisters in Uganda, Sudan, China, Cuba, and Albania have survived victoriously.

View the Persecution as an Opportunity to Share Christ

Richard Wurmbrand tells believers to view prison as a new place to witness for Christ. He said he had several parishes in prison and by using Morse code even shared the Gospel with people he never saw. [Morse code was used extensively by prisoners during the Vietnam War.] "So do not fear prison. Look upon it as just a new assignment given by God," Wurmbrand wrote in *Preparing for the Underground Church.*

Chapter 17

Spiritual Preparations for the Coming Persecution

Nothing is more important than knowing that a person has repented of his sins, accepted Jesus Christ as his Savior, and is living victoriously for Christ. It is the only way to be assured of spending eternity with Him and the only reason for enduring persecution. No amount of suffering will justify an individual in God's eyes and a relationship with Him will be the greatest source of encouragement and strength in troubled times.

As Richard Wurmbrand wrote in *Preparing for the Underground Church:*

> When converted I have consciously become part of a body that is a flogged body; a mocked body; a body spat upon; and one crowned with a crown of thorns, with nails driven into hands and into the feet. I accept this as my possible future fate. I will never think upon Jesus Christ as only having been crucified 2,000 years ago. The sufferings of Jesus in His mystical body must become a reality for me.

Three great weapons the Christian has been given to defeat Satan are the Holy Spirit, the Word of God, and prayer.

Rely on the Holy Spirit

As the *Bible Study Guide for Persecution: It Will Never Happen Here?* said:

> The Holy Spirit is the source of strength in times of persecution. Without Him no Christian can stand. Christians who have experienced per-

secution testify to the absolute necessity of being filled with the Holy Spirit. If we are surrendered to the Lord and experience His power while we are still free, the Holy Spirit will guide our lives now and also in the future. In times of persecution the Holy Spirit is the Comforter. He does not prevent all problems which might come our way, but gives strength despite the problems, so that we may endure.

The Holy Spirit was given to the early church in Acts 1 before persecution began. Jesus had told His disciples that He would send the Comforter and that when he came, ". . . he will guide you into all truth . . ." **(John 16:13)**. The apostle Paul says that he had been warned in every city by the Holy Spirit that prison and hardships were facing him.

The fruit of the Spirit will give encouragement and power in a time of trial: love (even for one's enemies), joy, peace, patience, kindness, goodness, faithfulness, gentleness, and self-control. Memorize the functions of the Spirit listed in appendix D in order to know what to expect of Him in times of persecution. Unity among believers will be especially important when Christians are being oppressed. Without reliance on the Holy Spirit for love and peace, it would be easy to inflict pain on another person.

The power of the Holy Spirit as promised in **Acts 1:8** will be needed to provide courage. Whoever is ashamed of the Lord in times when Christians are not threatened is more likely to deny Him in a situation that may end with loss of freedom or life. **Matthew 24:10** says: "And then shall many be offended, and shall betray one another, and shall hate one other." Jan Pit says:

> Only Christians who draw their strength from the Holy Spirit will be prepared to live and suffer for God and will remain steadfast. They will refuse to serve the world government and world religion, even though they know that their obedience to God will mean persecution, suffering, and perhaps even death.

If a person's pastor or spiritual leader is taken and that person becomes leader of a group, he will need the discernment and wisdom of the Holy

Spirit to lead others. Wisdom will also be necessary just to make decisions day by day which could have life or death implications.

Individuals should ask the Holy Spirit to reveal the gifts and strengths that they can contribute to a group of believers who are meeting without an official leader. However, spiritually grounded people, not necessarily capable, are what will be needed most.

Jan Pit says:

> In Laos we made the mistake which is so often made: We appointed capable leaders as elders instead of spiritual people. We accepted people who could read and write. (In Laos eighty percent of the nation is illiterate.) When the communists took over Laos, many "capable" leaders denied the Lord. The spiritual people were the ones who remained faithful.

Have a Knowledge of the Word of God to Avoid Being Misled
Perhaps the most effective technique of Satan to neutralize Christian outreach is to convince us that, outside of striving to be fine moral people, we are really powerless.

—Tom White, June 1995

Often when Christians depart from God's Word, it is because they do not know or understand what it teaches. As pointed out in *More Than Conquerors:* "When Christians doubt, ignore, or fail to understand the teachings of Scripture and depart from its principles, they lose their spiritual power. Many human organizations that were originally built on scriptural principles have lost their spiritual impact for this reason."

In *The Great Evangelical Disaster,* Francis Schaeffer wrote:

> Soft days for evangelical Christians are past, and only a strong view of Scripture is sufficient to withstand the pressure of an all-pervasive culture built upon relativism and relativistic thinking. . . . Without a strong commitment to God's absolutes, the early church could never have remained faithful in the face of the constant Roman harassment and persecution.

Mark 13:22 says, "For false Christs and false prophets shall rise, and shall shew signs and wonders, to seduce, if it were possible, even the elect." In fact, in Matthew 24 Jesus warns four times that in that day of great troubles, there will be many who are deceived, that many will fall away from the faith. Believers should recognize that a favorite ploy of those controlled by Satan is to misquote Scripture. Satan used this trick when tempting Jesus, who corrected Satan by saying, "It is written. . . ."

As *More Than Conquerors* warned:

> Sometimes Christians in the free world recognize the importance of the Bible, but because they have such easy access to it they take it for granted. What if it were not available to you? Do you have it "hidden in your heart?" Do you have such a clear understanding of the basic teachings of Scripture that you could stay true to the Lord if you did not have access to a Bible?
>
> Jesus is our example in our dependence on the written Word of God. He quoted Scripture repeatedly. When Satan tempted Him . . . [He] authenticated almost every book in the Old Testament by quoting from it at least once as divine authority! It is especially interesting to note how Jesus used the Scripture after His death and resurrection (such as on the road to Emmaus).
>
> Satan does not question the importance of the Bible. He has attempted to destroy it throughout history. . . . Satan has not only attempted to physically destroy the Bible, he has tried to destroy people's faith in it as well. . . . But Satan's most effective attack has been indifference. He is just as content to see the Bible remain on a bookshelf unused as he is to see it destroyed. Even if the Bible is considered a good book, or fine literature, Satan is pleased. His fear is that it will be recognized as the Word of God to men.

Memorize Scripture

During persecution, Scripture and Christian literature are banned and destroyed. Memorization of Scripture cannot start when persecution comes. It must take place while the Bible is still available. Only what has been learned in freedom will be available. God cannot bring to the memory what has not been committed to memory.

Everyone should be memorizing a minimum of a verse a week. One a day would be better. Here is a plan suggested in *More Than Conquerors:*

> Your fellowship . . . could begin a plan of memorizing whole chapters. The same chapter is assigned to two or three people. Then they can get together and write it out. With a little practice and constant review, even a small fellowship can memorize whole books like John or Philippians. . . .
>
> Passages that have been memorized should be reviewed at least once a month. When a lengthy passage has been memorized by the church, each person should write out the portion they have learned, and the whole Bible segment compiled. . . . One disadvantage of typed copies is that they look too "important" to searching policemen.

Do not assume that printed copies will always be available. In some countries possession of Scripture today may mean years of imprisonment or even death. In countries such as China where Scriptures are banned, people who have access to a copy might tear it apart so that it has wider distribution. They were also known to copy by hand what they could remember. Individuals would have to use their ingenuity to find ways to preserve Scripture. One suggestion that comes from those who work with persecuted believers is that small portions are easier to distribute than the whole Bible. Someone suggested that each family or single should create a way to preserve a portion of Scripture. Another suggestion was to carry a small copy of the Bible and U.S. Constitution.

Corrie ten Boom relates this about her family:

> When my family, my eighty-year-old father with all his children and a grandson were arrested in Holland—along with fifty of our friends—we were herded into the police station before being put in the prison. My nephew Peter came to me and said, "Auntie, what have you in your shoe?" I said, "I have **Romans 8**, what have you?" He said, "I have **Ephesians 1**, but do you know what Mom has? She has **Colossians**

3:16—"Let the Word of Christ dwell in you richly in all wisdom. . . ." You see, we were going to a place where we would have no Bibles. Thus we had hidden single pages of the Bible in our shoes, even rolled up and stuck in our hair. We had been living like this for months, ready at any time to be arrested and taken away to a place where there was only darkness. How necessary it was for us to take the light with us.

They took away my Romans, but they could not take the Word which I had hidden in my heart. I had prepared myself for the tribulation by hiding the Word in my heart—a light unto my feet, a lamp unto my path. . . .

Since I have gone already through prison for Jesus' sake, and since I met that bishop from China, now every time I read a good Bible text I think, "Hey, I can use that in the time of tribulation." Then I write it down and learn it by heart.

As Open Doors has written:

The reproduction and distribution of Scripture in a restricted society have risks involved. But as in the case of memorization, it also has spiritual rewards. . . . Even today, as you live in a free society, you can be involved in getting the Scriptures to Christians inside restrictive societies. You will realize that a high regard for the reaching and spreading of the Word can be your key to surviving victoriously!

The writer of **Proverbs** points out in chapter two, verses one through eleven the moral benefits of having His Word. "For the LORD giveth wisdom: out of his mouth cometh knowledge and understanding. He layeth up sound wisdom for the righteous: he is a buckler to them that walk uprightly" (verses 6–7).

Some who have undergone physical mistreatment for their faith have told about being unable to recall Scripture which they had memorized. Richard Wurmbrand said that there were times when he could only remember "Our Father" when he tried to recite the Lord's Prayer. However, the Lord sustained him in other ways and he remained faithful to the Lord during many years of imprisonment.

Develop a Life of Intercessory Prayer

The most powerful attack of Satan on us is to interfere with our prayer life. Although prayer is mentioned in churches, it is not practiced corporately except in a pastoral prayer once a week. The private prayer lives of believers are often weak. Developing a passion for prayer now may help to sustain a believer during trials. In *More Than Conquerors* it stated:

> Whether or not an individual has learned to have real communication (prayer) with God may be the single most important factor in his surviving victoriously as a Christian. The same would apply to the victorious survival of any group of believers in hostile circumstances.
>
> How can a group of Christians develop this kind of effective prayer communication with God? First, they must study what the Bible teaches about prayer. Review the examples given in the Scripture of those who moved the power of God through prayer. You must know the teaching of Scripture before it can affect your life. Sound biblical teaching about prayer should be continuously presented and practiced in the group.
>
> Instead of a church having one time a week designated as a prayer meeting, it would be better if each group that meets would have a time of intercessory prayer. Decentralizing prayer such as in cell groups encourages lay leadership and stimulates personal involvement. [Daily prayer in such groups is optimal.]
>
> If open persecution comes to a local assembly that has learned to pray in these various ways, the prayer life of the church will continue. Even if Christians are scattered, they can continue to share prayer requests and answers to prayer with one another, by mail . . . [however], the prayer and devotional life of the Christian family remains the basic unit of spiritual power. When Satan has won the temporary victory of completely scattering a local body of believers, the prayer fellowship of the family remains.
>
> In many cases individual Christians have found prayer their only source of strength when they have been unjustly imprisoned or exiled. . . . Learning to pray effectively is undoubtedly one of the greatest lessons a Christian can learn.

When the early church was threatened by authorities, they prayed. In

310 - Storm Warning

More Than Conquerors it says that the prayer in **Acts 4:23–31** is a model for those facing persecution. In this prayer the church:

1. Recognized the sovereign power of God;
2. Recalled the scriptural prophecies that persecution would come and accepted this fact;
3. Did not pray for deliverance from persecution; and
4. Asked for boldness and power.

God was pleased with their prayer and answered by giving them bold-ness.

As *More Than Conquerors* continued:

> The early church's dependence on prayer is evident throughout the book of Acts. Whether faced with persecution from without (**Acts 7:59–60**), strife within the fellowship (**Acts 6:1–4**), or the need to empower new believers (**Acts 8:14–17**), they turned to prayer. When the Lord desired to make changes in the course of the church, He did it through their prayers. He sent Peter to the first Gentile believers as Peter prayed (**Acts 10:9**), and set apart Paul and Barnabas as the first missionaries as the church in Antioch prayed (**Acts 13:2–3**).

The Apostle Paul thought prayer was so important that he mentioned it in every one of his letters. He said to "devote yourselves to prayer" and to "pray continually." His response to his many persecutions was to pray. The great passage in **2 Corinthians 1** (which is a good one to memo-rize) includes these words:

> For we would not, brethren, have you ignorant of our trouble which came to us in Asia, that we were pressed out of measure, above strength, insomuch that we despaired even of life: But we had the sentence of death in ourselves, that we should not trust in ourselves, but in God which raiseth the dead: Who delivered us from so great a death, and doth deliver: in whom we trust that he will yet deliver us; Ye also help-ing together by prayer for us, that for the gift bestowed upon us by the means of many persons thanks may be given by many on our behalf.
>
> **—2 Corinthians 1:8–11**

Answered prayer strengthens our faith. An example is shared in *More Than Conquerors*:

> In 1972, one area of the northern part of South Vietnam was under rocket attack and the communists were expected to take over any day. Everyone realized it could happen any day. However, a young man prayed that it would not happen so that the Gospel could be spread. The Lord assured him it would be spared. For two years the communists moved around and left that area untouched as the Gospel was shared. This was an answer to a specific prayer.

Intercede for Self and Others. Now is the time for believers to ask the Lord for wisdom and strength for themselves and others to face whatever the future holds. They should begin praying today that they and their Christian friends will not deny the Lord. As a person prays for others, a bond is developed and discernment may be more keen. They could even begin praying for those who may misuse them in the future. As admonished in the Sermon on the Mount, ". . . Love your enemies, bless them that curse you, do good to them that hate you, and pray for them which despitefully use you, and persecute you" (**Matthew 5:44**).

    Pray for Discernment (Titus 2:11–12). Unfortunately, Christians easily fall for ideas if couched in religious terms. Many make the mistake of assuming a person is a Christian if he says "God bless you," talks about spirituality, sings "Amazing Grace," or uses religious jargon. **Knowing in whom a person can confide and whether that person truly knows Jesus Christ may mean the difference between life and death.**

    Two main points of Satan's character according to *More Than Conquerors* are deceit and fear.

> He tries to misinform, confuse, and deceive believers in every way possible. But the Holy Spirit, who is the Spirit of Truth, can expose all Satan's lies, if we seek His guidance.
>
>   Satan also relies heavily on fear. It is natural for finite man to fear. . . . Satan knows this and plays on our fear, especially the fear of the unknown. Christ advised us to get our priorities straight when He said,

"And fear not them which kill the body, but are not able to kill the soul: but rather fear him which is able to destroy both soul and body in hell" (**Matthew 10:28**).

The Christian should take courage from the fact that with God's wisdom, "Discretion shall preserve thee, understanding shall keep thee" (**Proverbs 2:11**).

Christians who understand the times need to develop discernment about people; seek the counsel of others they trust; find like-minded people who can be part of a mutual support group and who they can cooperate with; and develop an instinct for what doesn't feel right. No matter how good something looks or sounds on the surface, go with your gut feeling, with your instinct, with your intuition, with that green light or check in your spirit which the Holy Spirit gives you.

Resolve Any Issue That Might Cause Denial of Christ or Betrayal of Others

Tom McConnell writes:

Pray and ask God to expose and deal with the sin and corruption of the old nature so that He may establish you for the day of adversity. Then, when persecution and judgment come, we will have settled all issues that could cause us to deny Jesus, betray our brothers, sell our eternal birthright for a bowl of security and comfort, or shrink back to destruction. Prayerfully consider **Matthew 10:32–39, Hebrews 10:35–39, and 12:15–17** and **Jeremiah 45**.

Pat Brooks writes in *A Call to War with Prayer Power:*

Jesus warns us that our love and faith must endure to the end. For this to be so, relationships must be made right with Him and with one another. We must walk in the light. Then, like Noah, we shall preach righteousness (not easy-believism) and prepare for the survival of His household until He comes (**Matthew 24:45–46**).

No quarreling can be permitted among believers who meet together. Quarrels always bring up names and bring out facts. Informants use quarrels to betray church members.

Jim Reapsome in *Pulse* has written:

> Jesus did ask God to protect his disciples, but not the kind of protection we usually think of. He had warned them they would be dragged out of synagogues and killed, so he did not pray for their safety and protection from persecution, or, as we might say, terrorists. Jesus simply asked his Father to protect the disciples "so that they be one as we are one." **They needed protection from infighting, jealousy, and clamoring for position. Unity in Christ . . . ranked higher in Jesus' prayer than safety.**
>
> . . . Jesus also prayed that God would protect his disciples from the evil one. He said he had protected them, and all of them were safe except Judas. Safe from what? Defection. Their greatest need was the protection of their souls, not their bodies. Saving faith outranks physical safety.

Study Lives of Those Who Were Persecuted
Learn Ways People in the Bible Reacted to Oppressive Authorities. Reading about biblical figures who lived under oppressive authorities will reveal that there are many ways individuals may respond. Depending on the circumstances, the Lord will direct people in different ways. Here are a few examples as shared in *More Than Conquerors:*

> **Elijah.** On one occasion, he boldly defied the king (**1 Kings 17:1**). On another, he was led of the Lord to hide (**1 Kings 17:3**).
>
> **Daniel.** In this book, Daniel and his three friends boldly faced death to defy the king, and God protected them (**Daniel 3 & 6**).
>
> **Paul.** He was especially flexible in the face of opposition. Sometimes he fled (**Acts 9:23–31**), sometimes he went to prison (**Acts 14:19–20**), sometimes he called upon God for miracles (**Acts 13:10–11**). But in all cases he allowed the Holy Spirit to show him what to do.

Be Acquainted with the Heroes of the Faith in Scripture

A study of the lives of the heroes of the faith in Hebrews 11 as well as other individuals that God warned of impending danger reveals that sometimes God delivers and sometimes He does not. Noah, Rahab, and Daniel were delivered, but ". . . others were tortured . . . And others had trial of cruel mockings and scourgings, yea, moreover of bonds and imprisonment: They were stoned, they were sawn asunder, were tempted, were slain with the sword . . ." (**Hebrews 11:35–37**). Regardless of whether they were delivered or died, they were all walking in faith. Paul, as was stated earlier, was delivered in some situations and had to endure others such as imprisonment and beatings.

Oswald Chambers says in *My Utmost for His Highest:*

> In the history of Christian culture the tendency has been to evade being identified with the sufferings of Jesus Christ; men have sought to procure the carrying out of God's order by a short cut of their own. God's way is always the way of suffering, the way of the "long, long trail." However, Scripture is full of examples of those who did not avoid the "long, long trail."

"The heroes of the faith were not shielded. They were not always given fair trails or unbiased evaluation. They were harassed and deprived. They lost everything, including their lives. The thing that kept them going was their faith," writes Dr. John A. Knight, general superintendent for the Church of the Nazarene in Trans Africa.

As Susan Bergman wrote in *The Shadow of the Martyrs:*

> **Martyr,** whose root meaning is **witness,** was first used in reference to early Christians who were put to death for their confession of faith in the one true God. . . . The term has broadened in current usage, but in the simplest understanding of martyrdom, an individual is required to deny Christ and live or confess him and die. . . .
>
> In our century, there are clear records of Christians being put to the choice between faith and life. . . . More often, though, a martyr's determination has been complicated by the layering of political or racial differences over the issue of direct spiritual opposition, and the

choice is whether to continue to follow a spiritual call and remain in known danger or to cease; whether to stay in the path of jeopardy or to find another place to serve. . . .

"The essential element in martyrdom," the contemporary Orthodox theologian Gerald Bonner writes, "is not the physical act of dying but rather a disposition of the will to live for Christ, with the necessary corollary that, by a strange but wholly Christian paradox, living for Christ may involve the necessity to lay down one's life for him."

Although martyr is frequently applied to people who have died for various reasons, Augustine said, "The cause, not the suffering, makes genuine martyrs." To the Christian, martyr should only be used to refer to those who have given their lives for their faith in Jesus Christ. He must remember that there should be no fear of doing so. "Now if we be dead with Christ, we believe that we shall also live with him" (**Romans 6:8**).

Know Why the Early Church Was Persecuted

If asked why the early church was thrown to the lions or persecuted in other ways, most people would say it was because they worshipped Jesus Christ. Although this is partially true, the real reason, as stated above by Francis Schaeffer, was that they refused to submit to Caesar; in other words, they were rebels.

Also, according to Schaeffer, there is a second reason why the early Christians faced death and why those of the twentieth century may be victims.

No totalitarian authority nor authoritarian state can tolerate those who have an absolute by which to judge that state and its actions.

. . . Because the Christians had an absolute, universal standard by which to judge not only personal morals but the state, they were counted as enemies of totalitarian Rome and were thrown to the beasts.

As an aside, this frightening thought is offered:

The danger in regard to the rise of authoritarian government in America is that Christians will be still as long as their own religious activities, evangelism and lifestyles are not disturbed. . . .

But let us be realistic in another way, too. If we as Christians do not speak out as authoritarian governments grow from within or come from outside, eventually we or our children will be the enemy of society and the state. No truly authoritarian government can tolerate those who have a real absolute by which to judge its arbitrary absolutes and who speak out and act upon that absolute.

Learn About Those Currently Being Persecuted

Reading about and praying for those who are currently being persecuted provides a way to experience persecution vicariously and is a type of psychological and spiritual preparation. The motto of Open Doors, founded by Brother Andrew forty years ago to encourage those behind the Iron Curtain, is "Remember them that are in bonds, as bound with them; and them which suffer adversity, as being yourselves also in the body" **(Hebrews 13:3)**.

As Pat Brooks wrote in *A Call to War with Prayer Power:*

If we forget them now, will God strengthen us then? Our "then" may be the day our Bibles are wrenched from us, or our time in the concentration camp. It may be before a firing squad, or something worse. It may be as we face an employer who tells us our job will end unless we deny our Lord and Savior Jesus Christ. It may be when our church is padlocked and the government says we must join the new ecumenical religion—Commu-Islam-Humanis-guru-Christianity!

Richard Wurmbrand says in *Preparing for the Underground Church:*

I have been told since I was a very young Christian to read every day; and so I did also with my son, Mihal, since he was 3 or 4, reading a page of the Bible and of the life of a saint or martyr. I read *Foxe's Book of Martyrs;* read it to your children. Teach them how martyrs overcame the moment of crisis.

The Soviet dissident Irina said that a prisoner must not give in to feelings of hatred for oppressors because it will destroy any individual who indulges in it. "'Hatred will burn out the mind,' she said. 'We tried hard to pray for the guards and those who tortured us.'"

Knowing where the greatest amount of persecution is taking place should result in Christians developing a prayer burden for individuals in those nations. Open Doors listed these nations as the ten most severe persecutors in the world in 1994: Saudi Arabia, Afghanistan, Sudan, China, Comoro Islands, North Korea, Iran, Egypt, Morocco, and Yemen. In most of these nations Islam is the dominant religion. It was encouraging to note that Albania, which had been number one, is no longer on the list and the Gospel is freely being shared. This is a result of prayers for an opening of the Gospel in that previously atheistic land.

Publications from organizations such as Open Doors and Voice of the Martyrs include names of individuals who are in prison or being persecuted. Praying for these people or writing to them, their families, or government is a concrete way to "share in their sufferings." It also might help in the release of some from prison.

Tom White wrote in *God's Missiles Over Cuba*:

> Many concerned people today have the mistaken impression that publicity concerning a prisoner . . . will cause the authorities to treat them more harshly. On the contrary, this is usually not the case. Our release is testimony to this. Vasile Rascol was released early from prison in Romania and Georgi Vins was set free and exiled from the Soviet Union because of the pressure of public opinion. . . .
>
> The backbone of the effort, the real power, [for his release] came through millions of Christians moving their lips in the most potent form of warfare—prayer.

Know Options for Churches as Oppression Intensifies

Spirit-led leadership is most important when the church is facing a hostile situation. The type of church leadership which is widely accepted in Western society today, with one man the center of all activity, cannot continue in a repressive society. It is easy for the authorities to remove the key man and stop that church's impact.

According to Richard Wurmbrand, one-third of Christians in the world operate (worship?) in secrecy with threat of extermination.

Believers may have to worship alone, in their homes, secretly, or in various ways corporately. In his November 1995 *Personal Update,* Chuck Missler wrote: "I think that real believers will increasingly meet in homes. The day may come that they don't arrive all at the same time, but drift in singly, so as not to call attention to themselves. We are locked in a very serious spiritual struggle in this country. Read **2 Chronicles 7:14** and pray. . . ."

Bishop Dzao of China said that they had neglected to teach their people how to pass the Gospel on to others. "Now all the preachers and bishops have gone . . . how few Christians were strong enough to strengthen others!"

According to the writers of *More Than Conquerors,* there are four ways churches are likely to respond as pressure comes from government or other sources:

1. The church closes;
2. They attempt to co-exist with government regulations;
3. They resist and become a protest church; or
4. They go underground.

The Holy Spirit may lead different people and churches to respond differently. There are examples from Scripture of people who reacted in diverse ways.

As Richard Wurmbrand wrote in *Tortured for Christ:* "'Underground Church' is a name given by the communists, as well as Western researchers, . . . to a secret organization which forms spontaneously in all communist lands. They call themselves Christians, believers, children of God."

The House Church movement has been the means of great growth of the Body of Christ in China. When all churches were officially closed as a result of the Cultural Revolution in 1966, people began meeting in homes. The number has varied through the years with only five or six people in some, hundreds in others, and thousands in a few. Denominational lines are gone so that the only question asked is "Do you belong to Jesus?"

Sometimes believers came together at the same time with no prior announcement. They reported, "The Lord himself told us to come."

As World Evangelism Fellowship has written: "There are more evangelicals in China than in any other country in the world, perhaps 75 million. Holding a house meeting of Christian believers is illegal. Those who are caught are often tortured. . . . Amazingly, people still come to these home fellowships."

When Idi Amin banned Christian sects and denominations in Uganda, people had to decide whether to join official churches or form house fellowships. It is reported (in *Persecution: It Will Never Happen Here?*) that "within days of the ban, thousands of secret house fellowships had sprung up across the land."

Open Doors with Brother Andrew has described what happens when a country suddenly falls to communism or some form of dictatorship. By the time communists take over a country, they have already identified the key Christian leaders on the local as well as the national level. Any one who was a full-time Christian worker before the takeover must assume he is a "marked" man. In Vietnam, even Christian businessmen who were not full-time Christian workers, but who had exercised lay leadership, were marked. These people do not have the option of going underground. They must stand for the Lord openly, and face the consequences. In the period of confusion that immediately follows a takeover, some small groups of Christians may be able to move to a different locality and become underground churches, but they must leave their "institutional" forms behind. Then through the Holy Spirit leaders will be raised up.

The early church worshipped in the temple, synagogues, lecture halls, open forums, river banks, and ships, as well as homes for worship. The New Testament specifically refers to five "house churches" (see **Romans 16:3–5, 1 Corinthians 16:19, Colossians 4:15, Philippians 1–2.**)

As *More Than Conquerors* describes:

> If the believer, because of fear, cuts himself off from all contact with other Christians, Satan will have won. [It is called "divide and conquer."] A Christian cannot survive victoriously for long if he is spiritu-

ally cut off from fellowship, worship and teaching. When physical isolation comes, the believer must turn to a deeper spiritual fellowship with Christ.

This must be coupled with an increased alertness to look for other Christians. Often a simple word, the humming of a few bars of a hymn, or the almost casual making of a Christian symbol, can be used to make contact with another secret believer. . . . It may be necessary for a believer to lead someone else to a saving knowledge of Jesus Christ to end his isolation!

While we still have freedom of worship, "Not forsaking the assembling of ourselves together, as the manner of some is; but exhorting one another: and so much the more, as ye see the day approaching" **(Hebrews 10:25)**.

Recognize That One's Security Is in Jesus Christ, Not Preparation
Although praying, fasting, and memorizing Scripture are important, a person cannot depend upon these or other preparations to help him endure. His security and strength must come from the Lord. Richard Wurmbrand has been asked which Scripture verses helped strengthen him most. His answer is:

No Bible verse was of any help. . . . When you pass through suffering you realize that it was never meant by God that **Psalm 23** should strengthen you. It is the Lord who can strengthen you, not the Psalm which speaks of Him so doing. It is not enough to have the Psalm. You must have the One about whom the Psalm speaks.

As this writer has written: "Make sure your trust is in the Lord and not your own preparedness. Pattern your preparedness according to the guidance of the Lord. Listen to what the Lord puts in your heart—don't use only your reasoning power."

Observe How Jesus Reacted to Persecution
Who did no sin, neither was guile found in his mouth: Who, when he

was reviled, reviled not again; when he suffered, he threatened not; but
committed himself to him that judgeth righteously.

—I Peter 2:22–23

One time when Jesus was about to be stoned, He slipped away and hid
(**John 8:69**).

We are told that because Christ suffered in His body, we are to ". . .
arm yourselves likewise with the same mind . . ." (**1 Peter 4:1**). John
Piper says:

> The suffering of Christ is a call for a certain mindset toward suffering,
> namely, that it is normal, and that the path of love and missions will
> often require it.
>
> Thus Peter says, "Beloved, think it not strange concerning the
> fiery trial which is to try you, as though some strange thing happened
> unto you" (**1 Peter 4:12**). Suffering with Christ is not strange; it is
> your calling, your vocation. It is ". . . knowing that the same afflictions
> are accomplished in your brethren that are in the world" (**1 Peter 5:9**).

**Why do Americans think they should be spared from what their broth-
ers and sisters in Christ in Uganda, China, the Sudan, etc. have experienced? If Americans have not been persecuted for their faith, why
not?**

In *No Little People,* Francis Schaeffer gives a great insight to those
who are preparing themselves spiritually for persecution:

> . . . Strong warriors for Jesus Christ, men and women of faith, are not
> created instantaneously; they do not come forth mechanically; they
> grow. No man has stood in a great place who has not, by the grace of
> God, stood in lesser ones before. If a person cannot stand faithful in a
> less place, how will he be able to stand in the center of his own culture
> in front of the twentieth century's own kind of fiery furnace? To be a
> man or woman of faith requires training. . . .
>
> I conclude with these key verses and charge all of us in the name
> of the Lord Jesus Christ that when confronted by a consensus which is

. our own fiery furnace in the twentieth century, and facing one of two possible outcomes, we learn to say with reality, by God's grace: ". . . O Nebuchadnezzar, we are not careful to answer thee in this matter. If it be so, our God whom we serve is able to deliver us from the burning fiery furnace, and he will deliver us out of thine hand, O king. But if not, be it known unto thee, O king, that we will not serve thy gods, nor worship the golden image which thou hast set up" **(Daniel 3:16–18)**.

Be Mentally and Spiritually Prepared to Choose Between Obeying God's Laws and Man's Laws

This is an issue which must be decided individually. Much has been discussed and written on the subject of civil disobedience and it can only be covered briefly here. One of the best books on the subject, *Is Life So Dear* by Brother Andrew, gives guidelines for those wrestling with this issue. In the preface he writes:

> Why were there believers in prison at the time the New Testament was being written? And why have Christians been imprisoned throughout the history of the church until this very day? **Because these believers decided to obey God rather than man. They decided they would obey the laws of their countries only up to the point at which those laws transgressed the expressed will of God. . . .**
>
> But most Christians suffering today really are keeping God's law! And the church itself is now living in a time in which we may all have to break the law in order to continue to worship and obey God. In fact, we may have to break the law of man and of governments in order to keep the law of God.

Francis Schaeffer gives this word picture:

> When Jesus says in **Matthew 22:21**: '. . . Render therefore unto Caesar the things which are Caesar's; and unto God the things that are God's,' it is not:

GOD and CAESAR.

It was, is, and it always will be:

GOD
and
CAESAR

The civil government, as all of life, stands under the Law of God. . . . But when any office commands that which is contrary to the Word of God, those who hold that office abrogate their authority and they are not to be obeyed. And that includes the state. . . .

God has ordained the state as a delegated authority; it is not autonomous. The state is an agent of justice, to restrain evil by punishing the wrongdoer and to protect the good in society. When it does the reverse, it has no proper authority.

A little further he states: "The bottom line is that at a certain point there is not only the right, but the duty, to disobey the state." When Corrie ten Boom and her family were faced with the Hitlerian (legal) edict to turn on their Jewish neighbors so they could be imprisoned and gassed they disobeyed the Nazis and obeyed a higher law—God's law—to "love their neighbor as themselves."

In the not-to-distant future, it will become necessary for American Christians to examine the concept of civil disobedience (from the Bible and history). At what point should the people of Egypt have said "no" to killing the male babies in Moses' day? At what point should the people of colonial America have said "no" to King George? At what point should the people of Germany have said "no" to Hitler? At what point do we say "no" to despots or tyrants in our day—when they take our money, our property, our guns, our children, our freedom?

Decide what is your choke point—when do you move to civil disobedience? For many throughout history, it was when evil leaders handed down edicts that were directly contrary to God's Word or commands. Don't set your choke point too early or too quickly, nor too late, nor never. Think through or calculate a strategy—then never look back.

There are Christians who are critical of believers who choose to resist authorities and worship secretly or carry Christian literature into countries where it has been outlawed. To this Richard Wurmbrand says:

The Underground Church is something which existed already in the time of the writing of the New Testament. We have critics who say that what we do is unlawful before God because a church should not work underground. We have to obey the authorities. . . . In the Bible it is written that he who has authority is a ruler who punishes evil and rewards good. An authority which forbids the Word of God puts itself outside of any human sphere. No Bible verse applies to it.

Be aware that if a believer determines to follow God's laws rather than man's laws then Satan will make him feel guilty for not submitting to the authority of the government. He must clearly understand the principles given in the Bible regarding his relationship to the government. Several books have been written on the subject, but some of the principles will be explored here.

As *More Than Conquerors* described:

The Apostle Paul enlarged upon this teaching in **Romans 13:1–7**. He states clearly that no governmental power exists without God's permission. This passage must be related to others, however, to avoid the error of thinking that a secular government has all authority (see **1 Peter 2:13–17, 1 Timothy 2:1–4, Titus 3:1–2**). We are taught that our responsibility to the government includes (1) being subject, (2) obeying laws, (3) doing good, (4) respecting those in authority, (5) being peaceful and friendly, (6) praying for those in authority, (7) paying taxes, (8) not speaking against them. . . .

We noticed in Jesus' response that some areas of authority belong uniquely to God. If human governments attempt to usurp this authority and infringe on these areas reserved to God, the believer must then obey God rather than men (**Acts 4:19, 5:29**). . . .

Some Christians . . . may feel led to resist the oppressive authorities for the good of their country. . . . Other Christians may seize an opportunity to flee from such a repressive country. In such cases, the Christian can expect Satan to viciously attack him with guilt feelings. This is part of the price a Christian always has to pay for any unpopular stand he may take under the leadership of the Holy Spirit. But we have learned how to deal with this whether it is true guilt, based on disobedience to God, or false guilt, based on the judgments and traditions of men.

Obviously, spiritual preparation is the most important area of preparation one can make for the coming period of turmoil and persecution which lie ahead.

Spiritual Survival Principles for the Coming Time of Persecution

1. **"Thy word have I hid in my heart."** Hide the Word in your heart—if it is, no man can take it from you (**Psalm 119:11**).
2. **Paul said, "That I may know him."** May it also be yours. In all the striving to care for self and immediate needs, let your highest ambition always remain to know Jesus (intimate knowledge) intimately—and the power of His resurrection (**Philippians 3:10**).
3. To remain in a high spiritual place instead of a more physical existence, heed Paul's word to ". . . **walk in the Spirit, and ye shall not fulfil the lust of the flesh"** (**Galatians 5:16**).
4. In times of severe testing remember that ". . . **all things work together for good to them that love God, to them who are the called according to his purpose"** (**Romans 8:28**).
5. When the love of men grow cold, remember nothing ". . . **shall be able to separate us from the love of God, which is in Christ Jesus our Lord"** (**Romans 8:38–39**).
6. In times of great deception which always lead to bondage ". . . **know the truth. . . .**" It alone can set you free. (**John 8:32**).
7. When you wonder if the testing or temptation of the time could cause you to lose your faith, remember He has promised ". . . **no man is able to pluck them out of my Father's hand"** (**John 10:29**).
8. **In every circumstance fear God, not man.** "And fear not them which kill the body, but are not able to kill the soul: but rather fear him which is able to destroy both soul and body in hell" (**Matthew 10:28**).
9. **In time of testing remember that God knows your limits better than you** and He ". . . will not suffer you to be tempted above that ye are able; but will with the temptation also make a way to escape, that

ye may be able to bear it" (**1 Corinthians 10:13**).

10. **Rejoice and don't be anxious**—the words spoken by Paul as he was in prison waiting to be beheaded—"Rejoice in the Lord alway: and again I say, Rejoice. Let your moderation be known unto all men. The Lord is at hand. Be careful for nothing; but in every thing by prayer and supplication with thanksgiving let your requests be made known unto God. And the peace of God, which passeth all understanding, shall keep your hearts and minds through Christ Jesus" (**Philippians 4:4–7**).

11. In every situation remember God can be trusted, but do not content yourself by simply believing in God but rather follow the example of Abraham, of whom it is said concerning the promises made to him, ". . . Abraham believed God, and it was counted unto him for righteousness" (**Romans 4:3**).

12. When you suffer the loss of all things—even life—nevertheless, as Paul says in **1 Corinthians 3:21–23**: ". . . For all things are yours; . . . or the world, or life, or death, or things present, or things to come; all are yours; And ye are Christ's; and Christ is God's." **Isaiah 54:10** says "For the mountains shall depart, and the hills be removed; but my kindness shall not depart from thee, neither shall the covenant of my peace be removed, saith the LORD that hath mercy on thee."

Chapter 18

Physical Preparation for Persecution

Fast for Spiritual and Physical Endurance

There are many reasons why fasting is a good discipline to develop in preparation for persecution. However, the three most obvious are (1) that it results in spiritual growth and fellowship with the Lord more than any other spiritual discipline; (2) it prepares a person to face a coming crisis; and (3) it may prepare a person for times when he will be forced to go without food.

Pat Brooks wrote in *A Call to War with Prayer Power*:

> Fasting is the golden key that unlocks the life of victory for every over-comer who is sold out to Almighty God. . . . Anyone who longs for spiritual victory will, sooner or later, learn to fast. . . . Fasting precedes or accompanies some of the greatest victories in the Bible. . . . Fasting unlocks the prison gates of bondage. It can be used of God to change hearts, circumstances, or destinies. With effective prayer, it can lift the torment of a lifetime and even the ancestral bondage of centuries or millennia in a family line. . . . Without the intervention of God's Holy Spirit, man is powerless to prevail over the spiritual wickedness in high places everywhere strutting and manifesting their satanic power on earth.

There is much in the book of Daniel that applies to preparations for difficult times. Included in this is Daniel and his three friends' partial ten-day fast which resulted in God giving them ". . . knowledge and skill in all learning and wisdom . . ." (**Daniel 1:17**). Fasting at that time in his young life may have prepared him for the future crises which resulted in his friends going into the fiery furnace and he into the lion's den.

Fasting can be a physical as well as a spiritual exercise. At the age of fourteen Hudson Taylor began the discipline of eating less food to prepare himself for the hunger he would face as a missionary in China. Eating grains which keep without refrigeration and can be sprouted for more nutrition may be helpful physically and as a preparation for times when meat is not available.

Develop Physical and Mental Endurance

Being in good physical condition prior to undergoing hardship will make it easier to endure. Having eaten correctly so that the body is not trying to deal with physical problems will be beneficial. Walking, running, and being in top physical shape will be important.

For POWs as well as prisoners for their faith, Tom White and Rev. Harry Lee talk about how they exercised even in the smallest cells. In fact, Rev. Lee was the talk of the prison guards because he could do so many push-ups in spite of the meager amount of food he was given.

Richard Wurmbrand has a Ph.D. in persecution, suffering, and beatings. He was in solitary confinement for most of his fourteen years in prison. He was beaten, tortured, and physically/psychologically abused for fourteen years by his communist tormentors, but he did not break! Why?

Although taking a daily beating is not recommended, Wurmbrand advised a woman to have her husband take a stick and beat her after she told Wurmbrand that she could not endure suffering and was considering turning in her friends. In his book, *Preparing for the Underground Church (in America)*, Wurmbrand wrote:

> . . . You will not be a member of the Underground Church unless you know how to suffer. You might have the mightiest faith in the world, but if you are not prepared to suffer, then you will be taken by the police. You will get two slaps and you will declare anything. So the preparation for suffering is one of the essentials of the preparation of underground work. . . .
>
> But what about the terrible tortures which are inflicted on prisoners? What will we do about these tortures? Will we be able to bear

them? If I do not bear them, I put in prison another fifty or sixty men whom I know because that is what the oppressor wishes from me, to betray those around me. Hence comes the great need for preparation for suffering, which must start now. It is too difficult to prepare yourself for it when you are already in prison.

Wurmbrand went on to relate the story of a pastor who had committed adultery. It was said:

His sin has not been what he has done on that evening; the circumstances were such that he could not resist the temptation. Rather that twenty years before, when not thus tempted, he had **not** said to himself, "During my pastoral life different things will happen to me. Among other things it will happen that I will be tempted to sexual sin. I will not commit it then." You have to prepare yourself beforehand for all eventualities. We have to prepare for suffering.

A suggestion made by Wurmbrand is to visualize (no, he is not a New Ager!) types of mistreatment.

We can read in **Hebrews 11** the long list of those who were sawn asunder, burned on stakes, and devoured by lions, but we must also visualize these things. Now I am before lions, I am beaten, I am in danger of being burned, etc. How do I behave in this matter?

Wurmbrand then tells about taking a children's Sunday school class to the zoo in Romania.

Before the cage of lions I told them, "Your forefathers in faith were thrown before such wild beasts for their faith. Know that you also will have to suffer. You will not be thrown before lions, but you will have to suffer at the hands of men who would be much worse than lions. Decide here and now if you wish to pledge allegiance to Christ." They had tears in their eyes when they said, "Yes."

He also says that torture can work two ways: it can make a person give up or it can harden and strengthen his resolve not to divulge information. Consider bearing pain one hour at a time.

As Wurmbrand writes:

> Torture has a moment of explosion, and the torturer waits for this critical moment. Learn how to conquer doubt and to think thoroughly. There is always one moment of crisis when you are ready to write or pronounce the name of your accomplice in the underground work, or to say where the secret printing shop is. . . . You have been tortured so much nothing counts any more. . . . Draw this last conclusion at the stage at which you have arrived and you will see that you will overcome this one moment of crisis; it gives you an intense inner joy. You feel that Christ has been with you in that decisive moment.

Simplify Your Lifestyle

> Nobody resists who has not renounced the pleasures of life beforehand. . . . There exists a Christian mortification, not a "giving up" of the joys of the earth. The Christian who prepares himself for this now will not suffer the loss of them when he is in prison. You have to use the things of the world without allowing an emotional attachment.
> —Richard Wurmbrand, *Preparing for the Underground Church*

He then suggested this exercise to be done in a supermarket.

> I look at everything and say to myself, "I can go without this thing and that thing; this thing is very nice, but I can go without; this third thing I can go without, too." I visited the whole supermarket and did not spend one dollar. I had the joy of seeing many beautiful things and the second joy to know that I can go without.

Know That Material Possessions May Be Confiscated

In the early stages of persecution, the homes of Christians may be raided to see whether there are any materials that do not comply with the laws of the land. If religious materials are banned, people may still have them, and searches may be conducted to see whether any remain.

Memorizing **Hebrews 10:34** would be valuable for that time. "For ye had compassion of me in my bonds, and took joyfully the spoiling of your goods, knowing in yourselves that ye have in heaven a better and an enduring substance." Remember that Peter says "we have left everything to follow you," and Paul talks about ". . . having nothing, and yet possessing all things" (**2 Corinthians 6:10**).

Practice Times of Isolation

Richard Wurmbrand wrote in *Preparing for the Underground Church:*

> Being placed in isolation was a technique of the communists. One of the greatest problems for an underground fighter is to know how to fill up his solitude. We had absolutely no books. Not only no Bible, but no books, no scrap of paper, and no pencil. We never heard a noise, and there was absolutely nothing to distract our attention. You looked at the walls, that was all. Now normally a mind under such circumstances becomes mad. Read great books about prison life (such as Papillon) just to catch the atmosphere. . . . I can tell you from my own experience how I avoided becoming mad, but this again has to be prepared by a life of spiritual exercise beforehand. How much can you be alone without the Bible? How much can you bear to be with yourself without switching on the radio? . . .
>
> I, and many other prisoners, did it like this. We never slept during the night. We slept during the day. The whole night we were awake. . . . In solitary confinement we awoke when the other prisoners went to bed. We filled our time with a program which was so heavy, we could not fulfill it. We started with a prayer, a prayer in which we traveled through the whole world. We prayed for each country, for where we knew the names of towns and men, and we prayed for great preachers. . . .

Wurmbrand composed over 350 sermons in rhymes so he could remember them. Fifty of these are in his books *With God in Solitary Confinement* and *If Prison Walls Could Speak.* "Your mind must be continually exercised. It must be alert, it must think. It must . . . compose different things, etc."

Practicing times of isolation is a very productive exercise. Learn to spend time alone with yourself in total silence—think, reflect, reminisce, and plan (or strategize in silence). Store up memories for times of isolation or separation from your loved ones.

Relinquish Your Need To Be Entertained

Many people cannot exist without being entertained. The thought of being in a room with no one else or without a radio or television blaring is totally foreign. Eliminate nonessentials from your life. Eliminate all time wasters and money wasters, and things you don't need—i.e., clothes, furniture, junk, etc. Eliminate television from your life. There are several reasons for doing this. First it will provide more time for the important areas of life: Bible study, prayer, conversation with family and friends, reading, etc. Second, it will allow for time to reflect on the future and how to prepare for it. Third, it will make it easier to adjust when the time comes that a person may be alone or when he has to provide his own entertainment.

Use Deep Breathing Techniques

Wurmbrand also suggested practicing physical pain so to preclude betraying one's brothers and sisters when put to the test. As he writes:

> I am a professor in torturology. At first, torture is a terrible shock and a terrible pain. It does not continue to be so. . . . [You reach a point at which] you become absolutely indifferent to everything. This is the critical moment when the need to breathe rightly is a reality. Practice breathing right.
>
> The art of breathing means much in the Hindu and Buddhist religions. . . . Read now about different kinds of breathing in the Bible. Jesus "breathed" upon the apostles. It is said that Jesus breathed upon them the Holy Spirit. So there is a certain manner of breathing which conveys the Holy Spirit. . . .
>
> Right breathing is one of the means of resisting torture. Betrayal

means rupture with the whole Church. You are a Christian in whom God and so many men trust. You have been entrusted with the secrets of the Underground Church. . . . You cannot quarrel with somebody and shout at them while you breathe rhythmically and deeply. Neither can you pass through the deep emotion of betraying if breathing so. Under torture, breathe as a traitor cannot breathe. Breathe rhythmically, quietly—very deep to the heel. The oxygenation gives a resistance to the whole body which balances your reactions and gives you a poised attitude.

Many women who have gone through natural childbirth have learned the Lamaze breathing technique to mitigate the pain of labor. Once this writer was in the hospital for five days with a very large and agonizing kidney stone. With none of the pain shots working, the only way to mitigate the pain was via Lamaze breathing. It worked—in fact it was the only thing which reduced the pain. Wurmbrand's use of breathing techniques to reduce pain therefore makes a lot of sense to this writer.

Prepare for Physical and Mental Mistreatment

It would be impossible to prepare for every type of physical mistreatment that might take place. However, these are examples of what some prisoners have endured: deprivation of sleep or food; poor or nonexistent bathroom facilities; inadequate clothing (who could prepare for the minus forty degree temperatures in North Korea?); inevitable illness; immorality; smells; lack of cleanliness; hard work in a labor camp; beatings; no daylight; no darkness for sleeping; constant dripping of water; etc. Mental tortures include brainwashing, separation from family, mental breakdown from solitary confinement, noise from many people in one area, etc.

It is likely that if persecution of believers continues for a long time that one or more family members will be taken from the home. A father or mother may have to go to prison or detention camp. Children may be taken for reeducation. Parents may have to stand before a judge and decide whether to deny Christ or have their children taken from them. Making that decision humanly would be unbearable, but they must determine not to deny the Lord.

In Cuba and China pastors frequently are taken to prison. Then wives must be strong for their husbands, children, and parishioners.

Become Accustomed to Divulging
Little Information and Keeping Silent

This is an area that is very difficult for Americans. It is the American way to be helpful, to talk freely, and believe the best of people. However, as freedom is lessened, it will become more important to divulge little information about people and activities. Even today it is suggested that telephone conversations are monitored—certain words trigger "bugging." Answering machines and portable as well as cellular telephones are suggested as possible tools for monitoring.

Every unnecessary word spoken can endanger someone. Useless talking in some countries means prison and death for one's brother. "You cannot learn to be silent the very moment the country is taken over. You have to learn to be silent from the moment of your conversation," writes Wurmbrand.

> Solzhenitsyn [relates] that the one who had been his greatest persecutor, the one who denounced him, was his own former wife. It is written in the book of Ecclesiastes not to tell the secrets of your heart, even to your wife. . . . The secretary to Solzhenitsyn was put under such pressure by the communists . . . that she finished by hanging herself. If Solzhenitsyn had kept silent, this would not have happened.

This is not suggesting lying. A person can withhold information and not divulge information without being untruthful. There is a difference between openness and being honest.

As Wurmbrand wrote in *Preparing for the Underground Church:*

> A brother had been taken to the police and was asked, "Do you still gather at meetings?" He answered, "Comrade captain, prayer meetings are forbidden now." To this the captain replied, "Well, it is good that you conform with this. Just go." The brother had not said that he conformed; he had not said that he did not go to meetings.

When Wurmbrand was asked about meetings of the underground believers, he knew he would be risking danger for them if he answered. "Where the results of resisting are beatings and tortures, you have to take them upon yourself, even if you die."

During World War II, posters around America and England warned that "Loose lips sink ships." The same applies to believers under persecution or functioning in the underground church. Be very circumspect with what you say, with information you give out. Use a "need to know" strategy, and only impart that information which is essential and only to those who are highly trusted. Even children and spouses should not be burdened with information they don't have a "real need to know."

[*Note:* This author has written prolifically on physical and financial preparation in recent years in his monthly newsletter, *The McAlvany Intelligence Advisor.* While that is not the subject of this book, sample copies of that newsletter, information on physical/financial preparations for difficult times, or on ordering another of Don McAlvany's books or videotapes can be obtained by calling 1-800-525-9556. Also, see details on same in Appendix F of this book.]

Chapter 19

Update on Persecution

The following article by Greg Nyquist, from the February 2000 *World-Net Magazine* is an excellent overview of present-day persecution around the world, and perhaps a preview of coming attractions for America:

The twentieth century will go down in history, not merely as the bloodiest and most genocidal of all centuries, but also as the century in which Western Civilization suffered its greatest setbacks since the rise of Islam in the seventh century.

At the beginning of the twentieth century, the West more or less controlled the entire world. By the 1960s, most of Asia, Africa and Eastern Europe had fallen out of the orbit of the West, devoured in large part by the two most formidable anti-Western creeds, Communism and Islam. One of the least appreciated consequences of this transformation is the resumption of a type of persecution that would have been unthinkable a hundred years ago: namely, the persecutions of Christians.

At no time in the history of the world have more Christians been subjected to persecution and murder than at the present time. According to the *International Bulletin of Missionary Research,* 605 million Christians live "under political restrictions on religious liberty" and 225 million endure "severe state intereference in religion, obstruction, or harassment"—in other words, outright persecution.

Words like "interference," "obstruction," and "harassment" don't adequately convey the sufferings of millions of Christians worldwide. Every day Christians are beaten, tortured, maimed, raped, sold into slavery or executed. Take, as one example, Mary, a young Egyptian girl who grew up as a Coptic Christian. When she was 18 years old, a group of radicals from the "Gamat Islamiya" kidnapped and raped Mary, forcing her to convert to Islam. Her captors poured sulfuric acid on her wrist in order to remove a tattooed cross, and threatened to throw the acid in her face if she didn't consent to wear the traditional Islamic veil. When Mary's father went to the Cairo police, he was told to forget his daughter and was ordered to sign a document pledging that he would cease all efforts to recover her.

Mary eventually escaped her captors and received assistance from the clandestine group "Servants of the Cross," which facilitated Mary's reconversion to Christianity. According to one of the representatives of the organization, there have been in recent years anywhere between 7,000 and 10,000 forced conversions to Islam in Egypt.

China is another country where Christians have been persecuted mercilessly. In March 1993, five Protestants from Shaanxi were rounded up by the authorities and three of them were so savagely beaten with bamboo rods that they were covered with blood. Later, they were hung off the ground and hit with rods until they were unconscious and hardly breathing.

In the Sudan, Christians are being sold into slavery. Many of the victims are female children. A typical case is Auk Ding, a Christian girl in her early teens. She was enslaved by a Muslim named Mohammed, who raped and beat her. According to the girl's own testimony, "Mohammed . . . wanted me to be a Muslim woman, so they forced me to have my genitals cut. A man did it. I don't know who he was. He tied my hands and legs down very tightly. You can still see the marks (scars on wrists visible). It was so painful. I cried and cried. that was the worst thing they did to me."

The two most important forces behind the persecution of Christians are militant Islam and Communism. Christians are seen as a threat to the state and to the religious or ideological purity of the people. As such, Christians are subjected to discrimination, harassment, threats, violence, and terror.

A. PERSECUTION UNDER ISLAM

1. Genocide in Sudan—No place in the world are Christians more brutally persecuted than in Sudan, Africa's largest country. Since gaining independence from Britain in 1956, Sudan has become increasingly torn by political instability and religious strife. In 1989, militant Islamic military officers seized power over the democratically elected government and declared a virtual *jihad* against southern Sudanese "infidels"—which is to say, against Christians and animists. A scorched-earth policy was adopted in southern Sudan and the Nuba Mountains, scene of some of the most horrifying religious persecution since the Holocaust. Whole villages have been bombed, burned and looted. Many inhabitants have been relocated into concentration camps where they have been starved until they agreed to convert to Islam. Christians have been subject to torture, imprisonment and assassination. Enslavement, rape, deprivation of water and systematic starvation are also commonplace.

As a result of these policies, more people in Sudan have been murdered than in Bosnia, Kosovo and Rwanda combined. According to the testimony of Mark T. Ajo, a church worker, before the House Committee on International Relations, "*1.9 million southern Sudanese and Nubans have already died, 4.5 million are displaced and 2.5 million are starving to death. Most of the displaced and starving are children and women.*" And most of these children and women are Christians.

Although in most other Islamic nations Christians are not being subjected to this sort of genocidal barbarity, their position in these nations is extremely unfavorable. In countries like Iran, Saudi Arabia, Pakistan and Egypt, Christians are facing increasingly hostile conditions.

2. Persecution in Iran—In Iran, Christians live under what amounts to a religious apartheid. They are not allowed to work for the government or for any state owned companies, they cannot receive promotion in the military, nor can they prepare food eaten by Muslims. Islamic radicals have in recent years assassinated several Christians ministers.

3. Persecution in Saudi Arabia—In Saudi Arabia, Christianity is expressly prohibited. Bibles, Christian artifacts, literature and churches are banned. Nevertheless, there are an estimated 580,000 Christians living in Saudi Arabia, 98 percent of whom are foreigners working in the country. Persecution of these foreign nationals has intensified in recent years. Thousands are said to be in prison and some have been beheaded. Others have been beaten, flogged and deported.

4. Persecution in Pakistan—The 2 to 3 million Christians living in Pakistan find themselves increasingly at the mercy of Islamic terrorists which the government is either unable or unwilling to control. Many Christians in Pakistan fear that a policy of "communal cleansing" is taking place. In 1986, a blasphemy law was passed which states that anyone who says, implies or insinuates anything about the Prophet Muhammad or the Koran can be punished by death, imprisonment or fine.

David F. Forte, a professor of law, testified before the U.S. Senate Committee on Foreign Relations that "the main effect of the blasphemy law is to unleash a reign of private terror against Christians and other religious minorities, frequently without the perpetrators being brought to justice."

Christians have been beaten, they have had their villages raided and their homes plundered and destroyed. Their daughters have been kidnapped, raped and forced to convert to Islam. Discrimination is pervasive. Ninety percent of Christians are either unemployed or are forced to take the most menial jobs society has to offer, such as removing human excrement from the streets.

5. Persecution in Egypt—In Egypt, especially in southern Egypt, militant Islamic groups are allowed to assault and murder Christians with impunity. In May 1992, 13 Christians in Daryut were massacred. Nine Christians were murdered in 1993, 12 in 1994. In 1996, many Christian villages were completely destroyed and their populations forced to convert to Islam by militant Muslim youths. In February 1998, gunmen killed nine Christians attending a church youth meeting in Abu Qurqas. A month later, Islamic militants wearing masks and military fatigues and armed with assault rifles killed 13 people in the predominantly Christian village of Ezbet Dawoud.

The position of Christians in other Islamic nations is not much better. In Morocco, Kuwait, Qatar, Oman and Tunisia it is illegal to proselytize on behalf of Christianity. Throughout the Islamic world, leaving Islam for another religion is regarded as apostasy and is forbidden. Apostates can be disinherited, forced to divorce their spouses and prevented from ever seeing their children again. In some Islamic countries, they can be killed.

B. CHRISTIAN PERSECUTION UNDER COMMUNISM

The other great ideological motivator of persecution against Christians is Communism. What is most extraordinary is that, despite the systematic persecution that generally prevails against Christians in Communist nations, Christianity is nonetheless flourishing in some Marxist countries.

1. Persecution in China—This is especially true in China, which in recent years has experienced one of the most phenomenal explosions of religious belief in the history of the world. According to figures compiled by Tony Lambert, a former diplomat who worked in China, Protestantism in China has, since 1979, expanded by at least a factor of 20 and possibly as much as 30. Estimates now place the Christian population of China somewhere between 60 million and 100 million.

This astonishing rate of growth has raised concerns among China's Marxist-Leninist bosses. In an effort to control religious activities, China, like many other Communist nations, requires believers to worship in so-called "patriotic" churches that are strictly regulated by the state. Since most believers suspect these government churches of being compromised by their association with the Communist (and hence atheist) government, they prefer to worship in illegal "house" churches.

In recent years, the Chinese government has made a special effort to crack down on house churches. According to the *Far Eastern Economic Review,* between February and June 1996, "police have destroyed at least 15,000 unregistered temples, churches and tombs."

Believers can be arrested and tortured merely for holding unauthorized prayer meetings or distributing Bibles without state approval.

Reports have surfaced of Chinese women being hung by their thumbs with wires and beaten with heavy rods, denied food and water and shocked with electric probes. Religious leaders are fined, thrown into prison, tortured and sent to concentration camps.

Throughout this ordeal, Chinese Christians have tried to remain upbeat and philosophical about their plight. "It's good for the church, like growing pains with children," said one church leader, 84-year-old Allen Yuan, who spent 21 years and eight months in a labor camp. Other Christian leaders are fond of referring to prison as "our seminary."

2. Persecution in North Korea—Conditions in other Communist countries like Cuba, Vietnam, Laos and North Korea are no better. In fact, conditions are probably worse in North Korea, where Christianity is completely outlawed by the state. Since North Korea is one of the most restricted and closed regimes on the planet, reliable information about what goes on inside is hard to come by. Nonetheless, it is believed that the number of Christians in North Korea is growing, and some analysts project that there may be as many as 400,000 Christians living under Kim Jong-II's Marxist tyranny. They are forced to meet secretly in small groups, rarely numbering over six, in order to avoid attracting attention.

3. The Return of Persecution to Russia and the Former Soviet Bloc States—The persecution of Christians still persists in some post-Communist nations, especially in those where the Orthodox Church seeks complete religious hegemony. This is true in Rumania, the Ukraine and especially Russia. In Russia it appears that the persecution of non-Orthodox Christians may soon begin to parallel the persecution of Christians under the Soviet regime.

On September 26, 1996, President Yeltsin signed a new anti-religoius law which, in effect, outlaws every religious organization that has appeared in Russia during the last 15 years and subjects them to surveillance by the secret police. The bill was sponsored by nationalists and Communists within the Russian parliament and by the Russian Orthodox Church. It affects nearly all of the non-Orthodox faiths in Russia, including the Assemblies of God, the Armenian Apostolic

Church, the Jehovah's Witnesses, the Mormons, the Anglican Church, Lutherans, Evangelicals and most other Protestant faiths.

The bill was passed under a false pretext. The Yeltsin administration, supported by the Orthodox Church, pretended it was submitting a "compromise" law, in response to the Dumás version, which Yeltsin had vetoed. But, except for deleting a misleading preamble in which the right to religious freedom is reasserted, the bill Yeltsin signed into law is identical to the bill he vetoed.

Since the preamble has no affect on the law itself, the whole matter was nothing more than *an elaborate charade to conceal what the Russian oligarchy was really up to: giving the state the legal right to shut down all religious activity that does not meet with the approval of all the former Communist Party hard-liners who now control the Russian Federation.*

Within weeks after Yeltsin signed the anti-religion law, police began breaking up Catholic and Protestant gatherings. Russia is lapsing back into its old totalitarian ways under an alliance of Communists on the left and fascists like Vladimiar Zhirinovsky on the right. It seems that independent religious activity is destined to come under increasing scrutiny and persecution by the Russian government.

"Inquiries, interrogations, police raids and groundless church closures will likely once again become commonplace in Russia," warned Rev. Steven L. Snyder, president of International Christian Concern.

Last August, police and security agents raided the Word of Life Church in Magadan, a city in eastern Russia, near Siberia. Church members were taken away for interrogation in the middle of the night. They were stripped of their jewelry, their fingernails and pockets were slit and they were threatened with the loss of their homes and possessions.

"This persecution is no different from that which was done under the Communist regime," stated Nickolay Voskobeynikov, the church's pastor.

Appeals have been made to the U.S. government for political protection against this persecution. It does not appear that anything will be done.

C. APATHY IN THE WEST TOWARD GLOBAL PERSECUTION

What is most disturbing about the persecution of Christians around the world is the relative apathy in America and the West. The establishment media has said very little about the plight of Christians in the Third World. And when they have run stories about the persecution of Christians, they have often adopted a skeptical attitude toward it. Consider the headline of an article run in the *New York Times* a year ago last November: "A move to fight 'persecution' facing Christians" reads the headline, with the word persecution placed in quotes!

Many political leaders in the West have reacted with even more disdain to claims of persecuted Christians. Typical in this respect is Andrew Young, the former civil rights protegé of Martin Luther King. In 1998, Young traveled to China with a small delegation of the National Council of Churches to see how Christians were getting along under Chinese Communism. His conclusions have an eerie resemblance to those of Western liberals who visited the Soviet Union in the twenties and thirties and came back chanting, "We have seen the future, and it works!"

"We found no signs of religious repression," Young declared unequivocally. "The Chinese government has recognized the role of religion in stabilizing and encouraging people to live moral and responsible lives."

The National Council of Churches proved willing to be the sycophantic mouthpiece of China's bigoted anti-religious oligarchs.

"Christians in China," declared the NCC's general secretary, Joan Brown Campbell, "are terribly offended at the . . . rumor that there's widespread, terrible persecution and asked us to advocate for a more accurate portrayal of their situation."

Those familiar with the ultra-liberal NCC should hardly be surprised that they should adopt this sort of approach to the problem of persecuted Christians. They have dismissed the efforts of evangelicals to draw attention to the plight of Christians under Islam and Communism as merely an attempt to create a new enemy.

"It's the new anti-Communism for them," charges Rev. Albert M.

Penny, the NCC's associate general secretary. This sort of dismissive attitude toward the persecution of Christians can only serve to encourage the crimes that are being committed against people of faith.

David Barret calculates that the average rate of martyrdom in the late 1990s was about 159,000 a year. If this figure is correct, it would mean that more Christians are being martyred in one week than were martyred by the pagans during the Roman persecutions in the first three centuries of the church's existence.

Michael Horowitz, an activist on behalf of persecuted Christians around the world, has warned that *unless a serious effort is made to confront the horrors of the persecution of Christians and put a stop to them, Christians are likely to become "the Jews of the twenty-first century, the scapegoats of choice of the world's thug regimes."*

[Bibliography: Marshall, Paul. *Their Blood Cries Out* (Dallas, Texas: Word Publishing, 1997); *Wall Street Journal* (July 31, 1998); *The Oregonian* (October 25, 1998); *The Washington Times* (October 3, 1997); www.persecution.org; www.family.org; www.Chihuahuas.org; www.trupath.com; www.bechristiannews.org; www.Rcagan.com; www.worldmissions.com; www.crosswalk.com]

—reprinted with permission of the Internet
newspaper *WorldNetDaily.com*

Conclusion

The United States of America, the greatest nation in the history of the world up until a few decades ago, is in decline in every way that a nation can be—economic, financial, social, political, moral, spiritual. We lead the world in divorce, violent crime, drug usage, pornography, promiscuity, illegitimate births, homosexuality, abortion, teenage pregnancies, teenage suicide, alcoholism, child abuse, and per capita prison population.

We have the most corrupt government in our history, but the great majority of Americans (including Christians) don't really care, because they feel prosperous, and because the morals of our leaders simply reflect the morals of our people. The Gramsci strategy is being intensively applied by the political left to undermine our culture.

Antonio Gramsci (founder of the Italian Communist Party) concluded in the 1920s and 1930s that the way to soften a targeted country for revolution and communism is to undermine its culture, its morals, ethics, sense of right versus wrong, its spiritual life, etc. until that country is so weakened from within that it can be easily pushed into the hands of an all-powerful dictatorship.

History has proven that a country in moral, cultural, spiritual collapse (as America is today, as the Roman Empire was in its eleventh hour, or as Germany was in the 1920s and early 1930s) is about to lose its freedom. It no longer has the will or internal strength to resist tyranny.

Alexandr Solzhenitsyn has said that the Russian people lost their freedom in 1917 because "they forgot God." The same could be said of the American people at the dawn of the new millennium. After fifty-five years of uninterrupted prosperity since the end of World War II, we have as a people forgotten God and our dependence upon Him. We have become fat, dumb, lazy, complacent, and apathetic, and have lost our ability to even tell the difference between good and evil—nor do most Americans (including Christians) take an active stand against that evil.

Francis Schaeffer said that Americans in the 1990s would be motivated only by the quest for "personal peace and affluence." Americans today (including the Christian church in America) worship the gods of materialism, affluence, pleasure, entertainment, and sensuality—in spite of the fact that the God of the Bible has said: "Thou shall have no other gods before me."

Throughout history, when countries have come to our present state of decline, they have collapsed, and either been swept away by foreign invaders, or sunk into totalitarian dictatorships—as Russia did in 1917 and Germany did in 1933. In many instances (as with Israel in the day of Isaiah, Jeremiah, and in A.D. 70, when the Roman legions under Titus destroyed Jerusalem) the Lord has judged nations. As the Lord said in His handwriting on the wall, the night that Belshazzar and his Babylonian kingdom fell to the Medes: "MENE; God hath numbered thy kingdom, and finished it. TEKEL; Thou art weighed in the balances, and art found wanting. PERES; Thy kingdom is divided, and given to the Medes and Persians." (Daniel 5:26–28). God has removed His hand of protection from such countries, turned them over to a spirit of delusion or blindness, and allowed their greatness to be destroyed. This can be seen in ancient Greece, Egypt, Assyria, Babylon, Persia, Israel, Rome, and in modern-day Russia, Germany, China, South Africa and, this writer believes in the not-too-distant future, in America.

The Bible talks about how when a people finally become corrupt and decadent enough, that God turns them over to a spirit of delusion or blindness. As 2 Thessalonians 2:10–12 says: ". . . because they received not the love of the truth, that they might be saved. And for this cause God shall send them strong delusion, that they should believe a lie: That they all might be damned who believed not the truth, but had pleasure in unrighteousness."

David Wilkerson and other Christians leaders (a tiny minority in the American Christian church) believe that the Lord is presently turning

America (including the Christian church and many of its pastors) over to a spirit of blindness and delusion. This writer agrees. Jesus warned in **Matthew 24** that there would come a day of great deception and a great falling away by supposedly strong believers. He warned of betrayals of believers by believers and a time of great persecution.

This spirit of blindness and delusion was very evident in the German church in the 1930s as the Nazi Third Reich ascended to power. As the book *A Legacy of Hatred—Why Christians Must Not Forget the Holocaust* by David Rauch chronicled, the German church was completely co-oped by Hitler and the Nazi Third Reich and became a willing participant in the entire Nazi movement—all in the name of God, Jesus Christ, and the Bible. Even anti-Semitism became rampant in the German church, who tried to justify it through Scriptures.

There were notable exceptions in the so-called confessing church such as Martin Neimöller, Karl Barth, and Dietrich Bonhoeffer—but these were exceptions and only a small minority among German Christians. The remnant of German Christians who did not bow their knee to Hitler (i.e., the confessing church) were severely persecuted by the Nazis; Bonhoeffer was executed (in 1945); and eventually even mainline Christians, who had early-on supported the Nazis, came under pressure from the Third Reich—whose ultimate goal was to completely stamp out Christianity and replace it with a pagan religion.

Can the same thing happen to Christians in America? This writer believes that it will. First to feel the brunt of persecution from what could be an emerging "Fourth Reich" in America is likely to be the remnant (the U.S. equivalent to the confessing church in Germany in the 1930s and 1940s). As Peter said: ". . . judgment must begin at the house of God. . ." (**I Peter 4:17**) (i.e., with the Christian church).

Every declining nation and civilization has its remnant—those believers who live and follow the Lord Jesus Christ with all their heart, mind, and soul; who do not bend their knee to the gods of their day; and who take an active stand against the evil in their own generation.

This remnant, whether in Israel in the Old or New Testament times; in Russia, China, or Cuba as the communists were coming to power; in Germany during the rise, rule, and decline of the Nazis; or in America today, is always a tiny minority. It is distinguished by quality, not quantity. It usually bears the early brunt of the persecution as it tries to "stand in the gap" for the country, for the Christian faith, and for the traditional values which are being discarded by the great majority—even the great majority of Christians.

In America today the remnant is made up of many in the so-called religious right (including pro-life Christians) and a small minority of believers who understand the times; who hate and oppose the evils of our day; and who are trying to take an active stand for righteousness and Jesus Christ as the foundations of our country crumble all around them. **It is to that remnant that this writer has written this book.**

This writer firmly believes that the God of the Bible is presently removing His hand of protection from America; that He is turning America (and much of the Christian church in America) over to a spirit of blindness, delusion and deception—as has clearly been demonstrated by the great non-response by Americans, Christians, and most pastors to the criminal behavior of the president of the United States; and is beginning to judge America as he did Israel in the Old and New Testaments.

That judgment is likely to take several possible forms: economic/financial collapse and the end of our prosperity and affluence; severe weather/climatic/geophysical activity including droughts, storms, earthquakes, floods, etc.; plagues, epidemics, and pandemics of viruses and new diseases such as AIDS, Ebola, Hanta virus, and a host of lethal biologicals; a tyrannical government which will take our freedoms—including wicked leaders who reject our traditional values and the God of the Bible; attacks by hostile powers—including Russia, China, North Korea, radical Islam, and/or a host of terrorist groups; and persecution of Christians and traditionalists in America.

This writer believes that America is moving into a time of great trouble and that Christians in America (especially remnant-type Christians) will shortly begin to feel the pressure of persecution. The parallels between the onset of persecution of the Jewish people in Germany and Nazi-occupied Europe in the 1930s and 1940s (analyzed above) and the onset of persecution of the Christian/religious right in America are ominous. Out of the approaching period of upheaval (e.g., economic, political), this persecution is likely to erupt.

Quo Vadis (Whither Goest) America?

Out of this period of upheaval, this writer sees three most likely scenarios (or some combination thereof): 1) America loses its freedom, sinks into a dictatorship and ceases to be a great world superpower; 2) the Christian Church in America, after a period of severe pressure and persecution, finally awakens, a national revival and turning back to God occurs, as in England in the 1700s, in America's two Great Awakenings, and as in Ninevah in the Old Testament book of Jonah; or 3) the stage could be being set for the rise of the kingdom of the Antichrist, the Great Tribulation, and the Second Coming of Jesus Christ—in which case America as a great world power could very well become irrelevant.

In **all** of these scenarios, it seems very likely to this writer that believers in the Lord Jesus Christ and in traditional values will come under severe repression and persecution—as is presently occurring in communist China, the Sudan, and in many Moslem countries. This book is an attempt to sound a storm warning, a wake-up call to believers—indeed a very unpopular and politically incorrect wake-up call—to be prepared.

Richard Wurmbrand, Dimitru Duduman, Brother Andrew, Georgi Vins, Harry Wu, Corrie ten Boom, and many others who have suffered persecution under communism, Naziism, Islam, etc. have been warning that they see all the signs of a similar great persecution approaching in America. They have warned American Christians to be prepared with God; to learn and memorize Scripture; and to develop a deep, intimate relationship with God against which the gates of hell cannot prevail. These survivors from communist, Nazi, and Islamic persecution have warned that there will be Americans, in America, martyred for the cause of Christ. Perhaps out of this persecution will come a great revival and underground church—such as we see in China today.

In any case, the Lord will look after and take care of His remnant. As David wrote in **Psalm 32:7:** "Thou art my hiding place; thou shalt preserve me from trouble; thou shalt compass me about with songs of deliverance." And in **Psalm 37:28:** "For the LORD loveth judgment, and forsaketh not his saints; they are preserved for ever: but the seed of the wicked shall be cut off."

And in **Psalm 46:1–3:** "God is our refuge and strength, a very present help in trouble. Therefore will not we fear, though the earth be removed, and though the mountains be carried into the midst of the sea; Though the waters thereof roar and be troubled, though the mountains shake with the swelling thereof."

And as Moses said on the shore of the Red Sea, with Pharaoh's chariots approaching in **Exodus 14:13–14:** ". . . Fear ye not, stand still, and see the salvation of the Lord, which he will shew to you to-day. . . . The Lord shall fight for you, and ye shall hold your peace."

The Lord is still in control—of history, of nations, of our individual lives. As the foundations crumble, He is looking for a few good men and women who will "stand in the gap." It is this writer's prayer that that will include many readers of this book. **And that is the bottom line!**

Bibliography

Andrew, Brother, *Is Life So Dear?*, Nashville: Thomas Nelson Publishers, 1985.

Bauer, Gary L., Family Research Council, letter to constituents, April 15, 1996.

Bergman, Susan, *Christianity Today*, "The Shadow of the Martyrs," August 12, 1996.

Bignall, Jeanne, *Colorado Christian News*, "Faith, Family, and Finances," August 1996.

Bonhoeffer, Dietrich, *The Cost of Discipleship*, New York: The Macmillan Publishing Company, 1963.

Bright, Bill, *The Coming Revival*, Orlando: NewLife Publications, 1995.

Brooks, Pat, *A Call to War with Prayer Power*, Fletcher: New Puritan Library, 1985.

Brooks, Pat, *Christian, Wake Up!*, Fletcher: New Puritan Library, 1980.

Buffington, Sally, *How to Memorize Scripture*, presentation at Denver First Church of the Nazarene, April 1990.

Chambers, Oswald, *My Utmost for His Highest*, Toronto: McClelland and Stewart Ltd., 1935.

Dobson, James C., Focus on the Family, letter to constituents, September 1991.

Duduman, Dimitru, *Through the Fire Without Burning*, Fullerton, Hand of Help, Inc., 1991.

Dugan, Robert P. Jr., *NAE Washington Insight*, July 1996.

Feaver, Karen M., *Christianity Today*, "Chinese Lessons," May 16, 1994.

Hefley, James and Marti, *By Their Blood*, Milford: Mott Media, 1979.

Hunt, Carroll Ferguson, *From the Claws of the Dragon*, Grand Rapids; The Francis Asbury Press, 1988.

Kennedy, D. James, *The Gates of Hell Shall Not Prevail: The Attack on Christianity and What You Need to Know to Combat It*, Nashville: Thomas Nelson Publishers, 1996.

Keyes, Alan, speech at "Steeling of the Mind" conference, 1996.

Knight, John A., *Trans African*, "Accepting Our Leadership," n.a.

Maudlin, Michael G., *Christianity Today*, "God's Smuggler Confesses," December 11, 1995.

McConnell, Thomas C., *FAMC*, "A Time To Prepare," interview on Southwest Radio Church broadcast, April 7, 1995.

McKeever, James, *End-Times News Digest*, "The Coming Tribulation," January 1992.

McKeever, James, *End-Times News Digest*, "Preparing for Persecution," September 1979.

Missler, Chuck, *Personal Update*, "Questions from Our Readers," November 1995.

Neff, David, *Christianity Today*, "Our Extended, Persecuted Family," April 19, 1996.

O'Connell, Brian, *World Pulse*, "We Quote . . . ," August 16, 1996.

Open Doors with Brother Andrew Staff, *More than Conquerors*, Baruk, 1988.

Piper, John, *World Pulse*, "We Asked . . . ," August 18, 1995.

Piper, John, *Let the Nations Be Glad*, "The Supremacy of God in Missions Through Suffering,"* Grand Rapids: Baker Book House Co., pp. 71-112.

Pit, Jan, *Persecution: It Will Never Happen Here?*, Orange: Open Doors with Brother Andrew, 1981.

Pit, Jan, *Bible Study Guide for Persecution: It Will Never happen Here?*, Orange: Open Doors with Brother Andrew, 1981.

Poland, Larry, *How to Prepare for the Coming Persecution*, San Bernardino: Here's Life Publishers, 1990.

Power, Richard, speech to Colorado District NWMS Convention, Church of the Nazarene, July 17, 1996.

Reapsome, Jim, *Pulse*, "Protection from What?," January 19, 1996

Schaeffer, Francis, *The Complete Works of Francis A. Schaeffer: A Christian Worldview, Volume Three: A Christian View of Spirituality*, Westchester: Crossways Books, 1982.

Schaeffer, Francis, *Volume Four: A Christian View of the Church*, Westchester: Crossways Books, 1982.

Schaeffer, Francis, *Volume Five: A Christian View of the West*, Westchester: Crossways Books, 1982.

Schneck, Paul and Robert, *The Extermination of Christianity: A Tyranny of the*

Consensus, Lafayette: Huntington House, 1993.

Shideler, Maxine, *Colorado Christian News,* "Is Your Child's Faith Strong Enough to Survive When Faced with Persecution?," August 1996.

Stachura, Mike, "Advancing Churches in Missions Commitment," letter to constituents, July 1996.

ten Boom, Corrie, *The Hiding Place,* Minneapolis: A Chosen Book, 1971.

Turley, Terry, *Concerned Women for America Colorado News Digest,* "The Battle Over Who Will Control America Is Just Beginning," August 1996.

White, Tom, *God's Missiles Over Cuba,* Bartlesville: Living Sacrifice Book Co., 1981.

White, Tom, *The Voice of the Martyrs,* letter to constituents, December 1994.

White, Tom, *The Voice of the Martyrs,* letter to constituents, July 1995.

White, Tom, *The Voice of the Martyrs,* letter to constituents, November 1995.

White, Tom, *The Voice of the Martyrs,* letter to constituents, December 1995.

White, Tom, *The Voice of the Martyrs,* letter to constituents, January 1996.

Wilkerson, David, *Times Square Church Pulpit Series,* "The Persecution of the Righteous," April 13, 1987.

Wilkerson, David, *Times Square Church Pulpit Series,* "Are You Ready for the Coming Storm?," March 4, 1996.

Wilkerson, David, *Times Square Church Pulpit Series,* "It's Time to Weep for America!," July 29, 1996.

World Evangelical Fellowship, letter for publicity for International Day of Prayer for the Persecuted Church.

Wurmbrand, Richard, *Preparing for the Underground Church,* Bartlesville: The Voice of the Martyrs, Inc., n.a.

Wurmbrand, Richard, *Tortured for Christ,* Bartlesville: Living Sacrifice Book Co., 1967.

Appendix A

Additional Books

Andrew, Brother, *Battle for Africa,* Old Tappan: Fleming H. Revell Company, 1977.

Andrew, Brother, *A Time for Heroes,* Ann Arbor: Servant Publications, 1988.

David, Brother, *God's Smuggler to China,* Wheaton: Living Books, 1981.

Dobschiner, Johanna-Ruth, *Chosen to Live,* Palm Springs: Ronald N. Haynes Publishers, Inc., 1969.

Doll, Armand, *The Toothpaste Express,* Kansas City: Beacon Hill Press, 1976.

Dowdy, Homer, *The Bamboo Cross,* New York: Harper & Row, Publishes, 1964.

Frank, Anne, *The Diary of Anne Frank,* London: Pan Books, 1947.

Hirschmann, Maria Anne, *Hansi,* Wheaton: Tyndale House Publishers, 1973.

Kerstand, Reinhold, *Blood and Honor,* Elgin: David C. Cook Publishers, 1980.

Miller, Jesse, *Prisoner of Hope,* Kokomo: Scott Lithography, 1988.

Paulson, Hand, *Beyond the Wall,* Ventura: Regal Books, 1982.

Lam, Nora, *China Cry,* Nashville: Thomas Nelson Publishers, 1991.

Lanham, Megan Gabriel, *Snatched from the Dragon,* Nashville: Thomas Nelson Publishers, 1990.

Lawrence, Carl, *The Church in China,* Minneapolis: Bethany House Publishers, 1985.

Lindsell, Harold, *The Gathering Storm,* Wheaton: Tyndale House Publishers, 1980.

Rose, Darlene Deibler, *Evidence Not Seen,* San Francisco: Harper & Row, 1988.

Sung Ming Dr. & Min Tsu, *Never Alone,* Kansas City: Beacon Hill Publishers, 1983.

Puebla Program on Religious Freedom of Freedom House, *In the Lion's Den,* Anderson: Bristol House, 1996.

Solzhenitsyn, Aleksandr I., *The Gulag Archipelago,* New York: Harper & Row, 1973.

ten Boom, Corrie, *A Prisoner and Yet . . .*, Fort Washington: Christian Literature Crusade, 1954.

Weigand, Edith S., *Out of the Fury,* Denver: Zhera Publications, 1987.

Wooding, Dan, *Twenty-Six Lead Soldiers,* Westchester: Crossway Books, 1987.

Videos

A.D.—experiences of the early church after Jesus' ascension—GF

After the Revolution—story of Romanian Christians—VOM

Against Great Odds—small group saving African Christians—GF

Amish, The—example of self-sufficiency lifestyle—GF

Assisi Underground—Saving Jews from German occupation in Italy—GF

Bamboo in Winter—Chinese woman following Christ today—GF

Becket—uncompromising devotion to God—GF

Breaking the Silence—reports of worldwide persecution of Christians—WEF

China Challenge—Church growth under persecution—WMP

China Cry—story of Nora Lam who escaped from China—MC & GF

Comenius—driven from home for his beliefs in seventeenth century—GF

Diary of Anne Frank, The—two families in hiding from Nazis—GF

Dietrich Bonhoeffer—his faith demanded he oppose Hitler—GF

Early Warning—story of end-times—GF

Eleni—woman enduring persecution for her children—MC

Empire Conquered, An—persecution in Roman Empire—GF

Faces of Vietnam, The—persecution of believers in Southeast Asia—VOM

Freedom from Fear—Nigerian Christians under persecution—VOM

From Christ to Christianity—See *The Trial and Testimony of the Early Church*

God's Outlaw, John Tyndale—GF

Hiding Place, The—family in concentration camp for hiding Jew—GF

How Should We Then Live?—The rise and fall of Western culture—GF

Hutterites, The: To Care or Not To Care—living a simple lifestyle—GF

I, Paul—Story of Paul in 2 Timothy—GF

If I Perish—Korean Christians defying Japanese capture

In Prison with Psalm 107—testimonies of women in Romanian prisons—VOM

Inn of 6th Happiness—missionary leads children across enemy terrain—GF

John Wycliffe—risks life to give Bible to common men—GF

John Hus—a martyr—GF

Leaping China's Great Wall—Christians in China today—VOM

Man from Aldersgate—story of John Wesley—GF

Miracle at Moreaux—Jewish children hidden by Catholics—MC & GF

More Love to Thee—North Korean underground church—VOM

More Persecution . . . More Growing—Pastor Lam in China—VOM

More Than Conquerors—story of Pakistani Christians—VOM

Nikolai—Soviet young man is harassed for his faith—GF & OD

One Way Door—Corrie ten Boom ministers to prisoners—MC

Orphans of Ayacucho, The—terror in Peru—VOM

Peter and Paul—drama of lives of two apostles—GF

Question 7—15-year-old in East Germany must decide what is correct—GF

Quo Vadis—struggle between early Christians and Nero—GF

Radicals, The—story of Anabaptists—GF

Reformation Overview—six-set series covering Wycliffe, Hus, Luther, Zwingli, Calvin, the Anabaptists, and Tyndale—GF

Right to Kill, The—euthanasia—GF

Saint John in Exile—story of last living disciple—MC

Scarlett/Black, The—priest organizes underground to hide Jews—GF

Schindler's List—life in Germany during World War II

Story Keepers, The—five-set series, children's version of early church in persecution—FOF

Trial and Testimony of the Early Church—six-set series covering foundation, spread, accusation, persecution testimony, transition—GF

Truce in the Forest—woman ministering to American and German soldiers—MC

Years of the Beast—witness the years of the Tribulation—GF

Zwingli and Calvin—story of the Swiss Reformation—GF

Key to sources:

FOF—Focus on the Family

MC—Mount Carmel, Inc.

VOM—Voice of the Martyrs

WMP—World Missionary Press

GF—Gospel Films

OD—Open Doors

WEF—World Evangelical Fellowship

Principles of Scripture Memoriaztion

by Sally Buffington

Why Learn Bible Verses?
1. It is a command (**Deuteronomy 6:6, Colossians 3:16**).
2. It gives confidence in witnessing.
3. It enhances ministry.
4. It is food for the soul.
5. It helps overcome sin and worry (**Psalm 119**); it is the Sword of the Spirit.

Points to Remember When Memorizing
1. Learn the reference and say it before and after the verse.
2. Find the best time of day for you for memorizing—be consistent. It might be part of a person's quiet time.
3. Keep a steady pace—don't do too much and don't slack off.
4. Do a thorough job—learn it word perfect. Mistakes are hard to correct.
5. When reviewing, don't glance back.
6. Visualize the verse.
7. Meditate on the verse—focus on the subject. Think about circumstances: who, why, where, how.
8. Paraphrase—restate.
9. Review immediately, frequently.
10. Set reasonable goals.

Ways to Memorize and Teach Bible Memory
1. Repetition—get comfortable with the flow. One person suggested reading it fifty times.

2. Divide the verse into segments.

3. Look for voice fluctuations.

4. Emphasize key words.

5. Sing Scripture.

6. Write the verse.

7. Use the buddy system (**Proverbs 27:17**).

8. Develop an attitude of confidence.

Guidelines for Future

1. Keep lists of verses for memory.

2. Mark memorized verses.

3. Pray the verses learned.

4. Keep verses with you to work on at odd moments such as waiting in traffic or in line at the grocery store.

Resources on Scripture Memory

It Starts In Your Mind, by Chuck Swindoll, Cassette LLm1-A & B

Scripture to Study

Daniel, Acts, First Corinthians 1, First Peter (memorize), verses mentioning *tribulation* or *persecution.*

Appendix D

Functions of the Holy Spirit

1. Comforting—**John 14:16**
2. Convicting—**John 16:7–11**
3. Teaching—**John 14:26**
4. Reminding—**John 14:26**
5. Testifying of Christ—**John 15:26**
6. Guiding (leading)—**John 16:13**
7. Revealing—**John 16:14**
8. Glorifying Christ—**John 16:14**
9. Supplying power—**Acts 1:8**
10. Speaking through us—**Mark 13:9–11**
11. Bearing witness with us—**Romans 8:16**
12. Helping—**Romans 8:26–27**
13. Interceding—**Romans 8:26–27**
14. Giving spiritual gifts—**1 Corinthians 12:4,11**
15. Regenerating—**1 Corinthians 12:3**
16. Confirming our salvation—**Ephesians 1:13**
17. Assuring us—**Ephesians 1:14**
18. Producing His fruit in us—**Galatians 5:22**

—Source: *More than Conquerors*

Attacks Upon the Institutional Churches

1. Infiltration of churches.
2. Government takes control of church buildings, hospitals, schools.
3. Activities held during church times [Sports!—MW].
4. Buildings too small to accommodate number of worshippers.
5. Believers scattered to reduce their influence.
6. Winning away loyalty of children.
7. Refusing educational opportunities for children of believers.
8. "Liquidation" of anyone opposing government plans.

—Source: *More Than Conquerors* (19–20)

Simple Acrostic for Preparation

T Take time to study God's Word, memorize verses, pray, and get informed every day.

R Recycle information: send copies on to others.

U Use time and money to get out truth.

T Trim down lifestyle to maximum simplicity, cutting out all activities which hinder the items above.

H Heed the signs of the times: act on the truth you know.

—Source: Brooks

Getting Out of Harm's Way

Acquiring Gold for Insurance

"Those entrapped by the herd instinct are drowned in the deluges of history. But there are always the few who observer, reason, and take precautions, and thus escape the flood. For those few, gold has become the asset of last report for inflation and monetary turmoil."

—Anthony Sutton
The War on Gold

Gold has protected wealth against a variety of dangers at different times in our history. Sometimes gold has protected against the dollar, at other times against rising oil prices, also at times of war, and times when we have seen gold used as political flight capital.

Gold knows no borders—ask the Vietnamese boat people, or the White Russians of the pre-Revolutionary Soviet Union, or the Jews who escaped from Nazi Germany, who bought their way to freedom and a new life with gold. Gold is the most liquid financial asset in the world. It is also the most portable, most hideable, and is the most widely recognizable and accepted form of money in the world.

Of course, these are worst-cast scenarios. However, some people anticipate the worst possible case. Gold acts as a barometer of instability resulting from political, social, moral, and economic dislocations, and offers the ultimate in liquidity and therefore makes it the best wealth insurance policy you can acquire.

Proverbs 27:12 says, *"A prudent man foreseeth the evil, and hideth himself; but the simple pass on, and are punished."*

For more information on precious metals, how to acquire them, and use them to protect your family, contact our firm.

1-800-525-9556

INTERNATIONAL COLLECTOR'S ASSOCIATES
Since 1972

 DON McALVANY is the highly respected editor of the McAlvany Intelligence Advisor. His monthly intelligence newsletter analyzes global, economic, political, and financial developments and their effect on our families and personal finances. With a background in intelligence work, McAlvany is sought by high level political and business leaders throughout the world for consultation on global financial trends. Don is a well respected speaker at Christian, political, monetary, and investment conferences worldwide.